When Christians Disagree
Series Editor: Oliver R. Barclay

Pacifism and War
Editor: Oliver R. Barclay

Pacifism and War

Edited by Oliver R. Barclay

WHEN CHRISTIANS DISAGREE

Jerram Barrs
Sir Frederick Catherwood
Robert E. D. Clark
Arthur F. Holmes
Alan Kreider
John Peck
Neil Summerton
Willard Swartley

Inter-Varsity Press

INTER-VARSITY PRESS
38 De Montfort Street, Leicester LE1 7GP, England

First published 1984

British Library Cataloguing in Publication Data

Pacifism and war.—(When Christians disagree)
1. War Religious aspects—Christianity
I. Barclay, Oliver R.   II. Series
261.8'73   BT736.2

ISBN 0–85110–727–3

Set in Linotron Sabon
Phototypeset in Great Britain by
Input Typesetting Ltd, London SW19 8DR
Printed in Great Britain by
Oxford University Press

*Inter-Varsity Press is the publishing division of the
Universities and Colleges Christian Fellowship (formerly the
Inter-Varsity Fellowship), a student movement linking
Christian Unions in universities and colleges throughout the
United Kingdom and the Republic of Ireland, and a member
movement of the International Fellowship of Evangelical
Students. For information about local and national activities
write to UCCF, 38 De Montfort Street, Leicester LE1 7GP.*

When Christians Disagree

Introducing the series

There are many subjects on which the teaching of the Bible is quite clear. There is a substantial core of Christian theology and ethics that we can confidently proclaim as 'biblical teaching', and those rejecting as well as those accepting the authority of that teaching will agree that such a core exists.

As we try to work out the application of biblical teaching in detail, however, we find areas in which there is no such clear consensus. Christians who are trying equally to be obedient to the teaching of Christ and his carefully instructed apostles come to different conclusions about such subjects as baptism and church government. Some of their differences have been resolved after debate. In Protestant circles, for instance, few would now wish, as some once did, to excommunicate people for advocating birth control. Further discussion has brought substantial agreement. Some questions, however, are not so easily resolved at present; and there is a need for healthy discussion among Christians so that we may arrive, if possible, at an agreed view. If that is not possible, then all of us need to re-examine our view in the light of Scripture and to exchange views, so that we may ensure that our position is not the product of wishful thinking, but is really faithful to the Bible. All of us are influenced in our thinking by our traditions, our education and the general climate of thought of our age. These forces tend to mould our ideas more than we realize, and to make us conform to the fashion of our time, or the traditions in which we were brought up, rather than to revealed truth.

This series of books under the title of *When Christians Disagree* attempts to tackle some of these current debates. Each book has the same fundamental structures. A series of starting 'theses', or a statement of a position (usually excluding the more extreme views on either side), has been sent to the writers. They have been asked to agree or disagree with the 'theses' and to set out a Christian position as they see it. They then have the opportunity to respond to one or more of the other articles written from a different point of view from their own. A short closing summary attempts to clarify the main issues in debate.

All the contributors seek to be ruled by Scripture. Since they do not agree between themselves, the crucial issue is whether one view or another is more consistent with the teaching of the Bible. Some of the problems arise out of the impact upon us of new cultural patterns. These new patterns may or may not be healthy, and that has to be judged by the application of biblical truth which is always health-giving – the good and acceptable and perfect will of God. We are not arguing whether it is easier to believe or do one thing or another in today's world. We are not even asking whether a Christian position seems stupid to the cultured man of today. We are asking whether there are revealed principles that give us at least some guidelines, and perhaps even a clear answer to our problems.

The Bible is authoritative in more than one way: in some areas explicit teaching is given; in other areas the question is left open in such a way that we know there is no universal 'right' answer. Worship provides an example. There are some broad principles; but the Bible seems authoritatively to allow, and perhaps implicitly to encourage, variety in the details of the style and ordering of worship. In such cases we will solve the problem in our own age and culture in obedience to the more basic explicit teachings that we have.

In the areas that this series explores there are some things laid down clearly in Scripture and some that are not. There is, for instance, no biblical instruction as to whether husband or wife should dig the garden; there are no explicit limits drawn to the coercive powers of the state, nor any delineation of the nature of the world before the fall – except that it was very good.

The arguments, therefore, concern first of all whether the Bible does or does not settle certain questions and secondly how far we can go in confident application of those biblical truths that we are given. The demarcation line between these here is important. If we can agree what is clearly taught then all else is in a secondary category, where we know that human opinion is fallible. Some of our discussion is above the line and is therefore most important. Some falls below it and cannot be as vital, even if in practical terms we have to adopt a policy.

OLIVER R. BARCLAY

Contents

Contents

Introduction: the debate

Oliver R. Barclay

This book is about the application of biblical teaching to a very practical area of life. It affects not only military service and nuclear disarmament; it also affects whether the Christian engineer or research scientist should do defence work with a good conscience, whether the policeman should be willing to be armed and to use arms to deal with an armed criminal, and in a lesser way whether the schoolteacher will be happy to punish wrong-doers in a school or only to try to bring moral pressure to bear on them. The Christian engineer should not do defence work unless he is resolved in his conscience that it is a proper occupation for a Christian – then he should do it with enthusiasm and not in an apologetic way. If he is not satisfied, he ought to find other employment. The policeman should be clear whether he may forcibly resist evil and carry a gun in certain circumstances. The school-master must be convinced that the forms of punishment he uses are a right and proper exercise of his duty. Whether he can do so or not depends on his answers to the three main questions that lie behind nearly all of this debate.

1. Is it part of the duty of the Christian to help the state authorities (and lesser authorities like schools) to

11

restrain and punish evil-doers by the use of force where moral persuasion is not effective? Put another way, may Christians be agents of God's 'wrath', as the state is called to be, even using 'the sword' for that purpose?

2. Is it part of the duty of the Christian to help the state to defend its citizens or its territory, to contend for international righteousness and to maintain law and order even, where necessary, by the use of violence including killing people?

3. If violence is justified in some circumstances, are there limits to the means that can be used when all else fails and evil will be expected otherwise to triumph? In particular, is it possible to justify the holding of nuclear weapons?

This book follows the pattern of the other books in the series 'When Christians Disagree'. A set of theses was sent to authors who take different views. They were each asked to comment. The authors were then paired off and each pair was invited to reply to the articles written by the other.

The length of articles and replies is not altogether even. Those who took more space on their articles had to be asked to be very short in their replies, and Professor Swartley, Dr Alan Kreider and Dr Neil Summerton each preferred this option. Since the second article was written by two authors and was relatively long, Sir Frederick Catherwood was brought in to write a short article dealing with an issue which had not otherwise been adequately discussed.

The structure of the book is as follows, with each essay followed by a short reply from someone on the other side.

The first round
Professor Holmes describes a 'just war' position, though he is a nuclear pacifist.

Professor Swartley and Dr Kreider describe a Christian

pacifist position in the Mennonite tradition.

Sir Frederick Catherwood comments on Professor Holmes's paper, arguing against a nuclear pacifist position.

The second round
Dr R. E. D. Clark describes a pacifist position typical of the 'Fellowship of Reconciliation' tradition.

John Peck describes a non pacifist position, drawing heavily on the idea of nationhood.

The third round
Dr Jerram Barrs describes a non pacifist position in the Calvinist tradition with a strong emphasis on justice.

Dr Neil Summerton describes a practical pacifist position which does not accept all the views of the other pacifists, but is very sharply critical of the 'just war' concept, which he finds totally unrealistic.

The conclusion
I have written this myself, trying to crystallize out the main points of debate.

Finally, I must thank the authors for their patience, for their willingness to shorten articles or edit them in other ways, and above all for their work in setting out the different positions which they maintain.

Some opening theses

1. The teaching of Christ in the Sermon on the Mount
must be taken as a very important part of the Christian
faith, not to be dismissed as irrelevant to the Christian
today. It was given in a situation of enemy occupation
and it gives us a fundamental programme for all Christians
at all times.

2. The Sermon on the Mount describes, amongst other
things, the character of the Christian and the characteristic
response of the Christian to evil things said and done
against him. We do not dare to water this down. Peter,
for instance, in 1 Peter 2:21–25 urges us to follow the
example of Christ in suffering rather than retaliating. We
can speak of this as the way of the cross to which Christians are called.

3. Certain teaching of Christ however (*e.g.* Matthew
23) and his example in Matthew 21:12–13 show that
Jesus did believe that we should sometimes resist evil in
the community. He told his disciples to pay taxes to the
military rulers, and he was respectful of the authority of
even so pathetic a figure as Pilate. He stated that Pilate's
power to spare him or to kill him were given to him by
God (John 19:11).

4. Paul in Romans 13, and Peter in 1 Peter 2, teach

14

explicitly that the state authorities are appointed by God to 'punish those who do wrong and to praise those who do right'.

5. Even if Christians personally should not resist evil, it is therefore not God's will that evil should be unresisted and unpunished. He has appointed powers to do just that.

6. Part of the function of the 'powers' in Romans 13 is to execute God's *'wrath'* – something that presumably the Christian should never do in a personal capacity.

7. The problems of the Christian therefore revolve round these questions:

a. Are we agreed that evil should be resisted – if necessary by force – or is force (violence) always wrong? Should evil in society be countered by society only by 'overcoming evil with good'?

b. If evil should be resisted in society, even if necessary by force, then by whom should it be resisted? Can the Christian share in this task as a minister of God's wrath? In practice, can a Christian be a policeman or a judge, traffic warden, prison officer or even a schoolteacher charged with discipline and punishment?

c. If we agree that, within the state, evil must sometimes be resisted by force and evil-doers restrained and punished, does this extend to international peace-keeping? Could it ever be right to wage war, for instance to defend the Jews from extermination by Hitler, or for a state to fight a purely defensive war against invasion?

d. Can we discover criteria for what is a justifiable, and what is not a justifiable, war?

e. If it is right for the power to have armies for defence, can a Christian be a member of the armed forces with the obligation sometimes to kill members of the opposing armed forces? Alternatively, must the Christian leave these tasks to non-Christians while they remain thankful for what armies do to restrain evil and encourage peace in God's purposes of good for society? Should a Christian at most be a member of a non-combatant corps (*e.g.* unarmed ambulance corps)?

f. Are there any limits to the use of methods of war?

Does there come a point where, although it could be right to kill members of the enemy's armed forces (usually conscripted) if they are trying to kill you, there are methods being used that are so evil in themselves, or in their effects, that a Christian must insist the state must never use them? This is even if the result of that stand would be victory of evil and the destruction of a great deal that is good. Are there, in effect, limits to the methods by which evil should be resisted? For example, is unilateral nuclear disarmament something that Christians should urge upon their government, and be glad to see implemented, even if it meant the almost immediate overrunning of the world by powers opposed to Christianity?

g. Can a Christian ever glory in military victory or in war?

1
A just war:
defining some key issues

Arthur F. Holmes

*Biblical materials · Theological issues . Implications
for a just war theory · On glorifying war and nation*

Throughout the history of Christianity, 'just war' theories
have found widespread acceptance in both Protestant and
Roman Catholic branches of the church. War, it is insisted,
is terribly evil in its causes, conduct and consequences.
Yet because violent aggression is so unjust, it must be
resisted, and God has entrusted to governments limited
uses of force in maintaining a just peace. If such a task,
however sickening and tragic, is divinely ordained, then
Christians should be willing to participate.

In presenting this kind of view, I shall start by looking
at some key biblical materials, then I shall focus on two
crucial theological issues, before developing the line of
thought into a Christian version of the just war theory
and applying it to contemporary concerns.

Biblical materials

An appropriate starting-point is the Sermon on the Mount,
where two major emphases stand out. The first relates to
the attitudes which Christ enjoined and which he himself
was to exemplify. Meekness (Matthew 5:5) implies a
readiness to suffer unjustly (5:10–12), a willingness to
turn the other cheek and go the second mile, instead of

17

resisting extortionate demands (5:38–42). Mercifulness (5:7), on the part of those who know God's mercy, means forgiving others as we have been forgiven (6:12–15). Peace-making (5:9) contrasts with the angry outbursts that lead to violence (5:21–26) and with the acquisitiveness that turns a concern for righteousness into jealous fault-finding (6:19 – 7:5). All this and more is summed up in the law of love which calls us to unselfish concern even for our enemies (5:43–48).

The second emphasis relates the Sermon on the Mount to the law and prophets of the Old Testament. The repeated formula in Matthew 5 – 'You have heard that it was said ... But I say to you' – does not replace Old Testament teaching with something altogether different, but rather corrects misunderstandings and the legalistic stress on externals that were current in the Judaism of Jesus' time. His criticism of anger and lust (5:21–30) does not replace the Old Testament law against killing and adultery, but gets at the attitudes involved and already forbidden in the tenth commandment about coveting. 'You shall love your neighbour and hate your enemy' (5:43) nowhere appears in the Old Testament, but something like it appears in the Dead Sea Scrolls of the Essene community,[1] and seems to be a superimposition on the law, rather than the Old Testament law itself. Indeed, Jesus taught that the law of love is itself the primary concern of Old Testament law (Matthew 22:34–40; *cf.* Deuteronomy 6:4–5; Leviticus 19:17–18, 33–34), and he explicitly applied it to relationships between Jews and Samaritans, traditional enemies though they were (Luke 10:30–37).

This continuity with the Old Testament extends to the attitudes we first noted. Meekness is lauded throughout the Old Testament, specifically in Moses (Numbers 12:3), and Jesus' beatitude in that regard is itself taken from Psalm 37:11, 'the meek shall possess the land.' Mercifulness likewise, for Jesus (Matthew 23:23) explicitly endorses Micah's statement that the Lord requires us to do justice, to love mercy and to walk humbly with God

A just war: defining some key issues

(Micah 6:8). Amos indicted Edom for angrily abandoning mercy in military action against Israel (Amos 1:11). Peace-making, moreover, echoes the Old Testament's lament over war and violence and its promise of a kingdom of *shālôm* (1 Chronicles 22:7–9; Psalms 46:8–11; 68:30; 120:6–7; Isaiah 2:3–4; 9:6–7).

Similarly, Jesus cites the sixth commandment, 'You shall not kill' (Matthew 5:21), not to discard it but to highlight the underlying concern that reconciliation should replace blood feuds. In Mosaic law, it should be noted, the sixth commandment was not exceptionless: capital punishment is allowed for at least ten different crimes, and instructions are given about military actions. While the sixth commandment stresses the overall sanctity of human life, therefore, its specific focus is primarily on violence by private individuals in murder and blood feuds: the Sermon on the Mount cuts the ground from anything of that sort.

Even more important for our purposes is Jesus' endorsement of retributive justice. He cites the *lex talionis* ('An eye for an eye', Matthew 5:38), detaching it from the personal vendettas to which it had illicitly been extended. Its Old Testament context was criminal punishment, and Jesus still speaks of punishment in retributivist terms (5:21–30; 7:13–23), acknowledging governmental authority in this regard (John 19:11). The *lex talionis* (Exodus 21:24; Deuteronomy 19:15–21) protected offenders from indiscriminate retaliation and dispropor-tionate punishment, for in the Ancient Near East punish-ment was notoriously severe and often arbitrary. Indeed it is not very long since pickpockets were hanged in Britain. But 'an eye for an eye' ruled out such extremes, limiting punishment to what was proportionate to the crime (not 'a life for an eye'), and then only after an investigation and fair trial. As a limiting principle it stood for what was both just and compassionate. In endorsing it, the Sermon on the Mount endorses the state's function of resisting evil and punishing evil-doers. But while upholding this retributive activity, it denies to private indi-viduals any right to take the law into their own hands. It

19

allows just retribution, but not spiteful vengeance or angry retaliation. A just society is its concern, along with genuine personal love.

This concern for a just society includes not only retributive but also distributive justice. The former has to do with civil order and criminal punishment, plainly mandated to government (Romans 13:1–5; 1 Peter 2:13–15). The latter refers to an equitable distribution of the benefits and costs of a society. It therefore opposes bribery and corruption in government, unfair business practices, perversion of legal processes. Jesus' concern for distributive justice is evident in his concern for the poor (Matthew 5:3), for those unjustly treated (5:11–12), for divorcees (5:31–32), for personal integrity (5:33–37), as well as in his reminder that God's providence is distributed to all alike (5:44–48).

This combination of justice and love runs throughout Scripture. The Old Testament law codified a system of distributive and retributive justice, whose underlying spirit is one of love: a love that seeks justice for all, even forgoing justice for oneself out of concern for others. The psalmists sing of justice and love, lauding thereby the moral character of God (Psalms 85:7–13; 89:14; 103:6–8), and the prophets hold people and nations accountable in these regards.

In Paul's letter to the Romans, government's use of just force against evil-doers (13:1–7) is recognized in the middle of an extended exposition of the law of love. Paul there condemns hatred (12:14), retaliation (12:17), a vengeful spirit (12:19) and over-reaction to evil (12:21), asking Christians to go a second mile in loving their personal foes (12:14, 20–21) and in becoming peace-makers (12:18). He calls on them to love one another rather than killing or stealing (13:8–9) and doing evil to others (13:10). All this fulfils God's law. Yet in this very context Paul asks for obedience to the authorities, because they are required to resist evil, even with the sword. Government must be given its due, taxes must be paid which go to support the use of force (*cf.* 1 Peter 2:12–15). Justice and love go together.

A just war: defining some key issues

Theological issues

The biblical materials we have discussed affect two theological issues which underlie the disagreements Christians have about war: the relation of the Old and New Testaments and the relation of Christians to government.

a. *The relation of Old and New Testaments* is crucial to the war question, in that the Old speaks much more than the New about participation by believers in military action. Theological traditions which find considerable discontinuity between the two Testaments therefore tend more to non-participation than those which find essential continuity. Such is the case with the Mennonite view, for example, which draws its pacifism primarily from certain New Testament emphases, whereas Roman Catholic and Reformed thought are traditionally non-pacifist because of their greater emphasis on the continued pertinence to believers today of Old as well as New Testament teaching.

I have tried to show that Jesus endorsed the Old Testament law and prophets while correcting Jewish misconceptions. Consider his explicit statement on the subject in Matthew 5:17–20; he came, not to abolish what the law and the prophets required, but to fulfil it, to fill it out and complete it. The apostle Paul states that the Old Testament commandments are all summed up in the law of love. His verb (*anakephalaio*, Romans 13:9) is a legal term used of summarizing the evidence presented in court. It discards nothing of what was presented earlier, but rather brings it all into focus. The law of love thus sums up what the Old Testament ethic is about: a compassionate love that works for justice and peace. The Hebrew term *shālôm* also conveys this ideal: not merely absence of conflict, but a just peace in which people's needs are so adequately and fairly met that they sing and dance for joy. And none can make them afraid.

The point is that the Bible maintains one and the same unchanging ideal throughout its pages, an ethic to which all peoples are accountable at all times and places, an ethic of justice and love. That people and nations now or in the past do not measure up to this ideal no more invalidates it than traffic violations invalidate traffic laws, or murder invalidates the criminal law. In a just society, however, criminal acts carry consequences, and evil must be resisted.

It must be stressed that this is not an ethic of love alone: such would not be fair to either Testament. Throughout the Bible justice too is stressed − God's justice, social justice, just business dealings, and the just man. Nor does justice simply reduce to love, for whereas love is a self-giving concern for the good of persons and operates inter-subjectively, justice is equitable treatment of persons in the objective structures of society, as well as in dealings between private individuals. Love indeed motivates the pursuit of justice. It goes a second mile beyond what justice alone requires. It therefore tempers justice with compassion. But love alone cannot effectively resist evils in society, nor is it God's entire way of doing so.

The admonition not to resist (Matthew 5:39) must be kept in its context, where Jesus separates the *lex talionis* (which he endorsed) from individual behaviour. A personal affront, he says, is no matter for retribution: there love will go the second mile, repaying evil with good, even suffering for righteousness' sake. And the overall biblical context stresses, as we have seen, the need to resist violence and to punish those who do evil.

The church resists evil by its preaching and teaching, by ministering to the needs of the oppressed and underprivi-leged, by protesting social injustice, by supporting just government. Individual Christians should resist it by participation in the church's activity, by legal action, political process and moral persuasion, by education, through the media and by support of arms controls and progressive disarmament. What they may not do as private individuals at their own initiative is to use violence.

In a fallen world inhabited by haughty, avaricious, violent and vengeful people grouped in nations weaned on pride and self-interest, words and deeds of love will often be ignored, distrusted, repudiated. Sin is too deeply rooted and pervasive to be controlled by loving response alone. Reinhold Niebuhr's classic essay, 'Why the Christian Church is not Pacifist', speaks to this: the good news of the gospel, he insists, is not a law of love but rather the message of divine mercy at work in our hearts.[2] The Bible sees human history not as a gradual triumph of good over evil, but as a conflict which only God himself can ultimately resolve.

Niebuhr wrote in response to the idealistic liberal theology he had once espoused, that found expression in the social gospel of the late nineteenth and early twentieth century. It was rooted, he argued, in Renaissance optimism about the creative goodness of the human spirit rather than in the biblical history of human sin and perfidy. No inevitable human progress exists to ensure the emergence of God's kingdom of love. Realism rather than unbiblical idealism must prevail.

The idealistic pacifism of the liberal theologians differed greatly from the historic pacifism of the Mennonite tradition, with its emphasis on a special calling Christians have received to bear witness to the way of love. Yet the same caution must be given: love alone cannot effectively resist evil (both biblical and secular history make that plain, as well as the doctrines of sin and punishment), nor is it God's way of doing so.

b. *The relation of Christians to government* is therefore the second theological issue, since God has entrusted the maintenance of a just peace to the civil authorities. But we must enlarge the scope of consideration to ask about the overall biblical approach to social evils.

The Old Testament not only enunciates moral law against murder, adultery and stealing, but also develops extensive case-laws to protect slaves from cruelty and abuse, even requiring the release of Israelite slaves in the year of jubilee. The evils of slavery are limited by law lest all sense of justice be violated. And the authorities were to uphold that law, with force if necessary. The prophets keep these standards before the nation, continually drawing attention to the underlying demand for justice and compassion, and to the rights of the widow, the fatherless, the poor and oppressed. Meantime God's grace is at work in human hearts, and the gospel so fully displayed by Jesus reaffirms the Old Testament law of love. Love motivates justice, and so Paul tells Philemon to receive his runaway slave as a brother. Yet the full promise of the kingdom still awaits establishment at the coming of the King. Law, prophet, gospel, kingdom: this is the biblical pattern not only regarding slavery but also regarding divorce, and, I suggest, regarding uses of violence, even war. It is not just the gospel while we await Christ's kingdom, but also the church's prophetic ministry exposing injustice and lack of compassion, plus the moral law enforced, if necessary, by the authorities. God resists evil through the institutions he has ordained.

Today most of us live in pluralistic societies rather than in the theocratic state of ancient Israel, where the entire law of God was the law of the land. Yet this difference in no way changes God's mandate to governments to resist evil and uphold justice in society. The mandate is complicated in many moral matters for a pluralistic society,[3] but not in regard to violence and injustice. There the mandate is unambiguous: resist unjust force, with force if necessary.

This mandate even grants limited power of life and death: recall capital punishment and instructions about warring in the Old Testament, and Paul's use of the term 'sword' in Romans 13. To claim that nothing has more worth than a human life would imply that nothing is worth devoting one's life to, nothing worth dying for. And that is plainly false, for then Jesus should not have given his life, nor should God have commanded lethal force, as he evidently did on occasions in the Old Testament.

It should also be noted that neither Romans 13 nor 1 Peter explicitly addresses war and soldiering, for both are directly concerned with civil order and the *lex talionis*. Within the Roman empire, however, the *pax Romana* was upheld by force, and the imperial borders were the site of all too frequent conflicts. Both Jesus and the apostles had contact with Roman soldiers, some of whom became believers, but they say nothing about that profession, as Jesus apparently did in the case of the adulteress (John 8:1–11). It is hard therefore to avoid the continuity of Romans 13 with the Old Testament's acceptance of limited international war for just ends.

But what does this say about Christians participating? May the believer properly participate in *whatever* functions God appoints to institutions he ordains: in the family, begetting, raising and disciplining children? In the state enacting just laws and maintaining civil order? If force is divinely entrusted to government for just ends, and if the Christian should support just government in its rightful functions, then should he not also be willing, however regretfully, to participate in just uses of force?

The Mennonite teaches that there are two separate kingdoms and two corresponding vocations, the earthly and the heavenly, and that these are mutually exclusive, so that while God has indeed ordained government, the Christian's vocation lies in the church and its witness to a life of love. Pacifism is then a God-given *vocation* for believers rather than an *ethical* obligation incumbent on all human beings.

On the other hand, the Bible speaks of God's kingdom as *including all* the nations of the world and calls on kings and rulers to worship and serve him. The New Testament contrast between the kingdom of light and the kingdom of darkness is rather between God and Satan, between good and evil, than between church and state. Good and evil are sadly mingled in any nation and any government, it is true, but (as the Westminster Confession points out) so too they are still mingled in the visible church. Yet both church and state are ordained by God, under his sovereignty, as agencies in the kingdom of God on earth.

Some in the early church also took a 'two vocations' position. Tertullian, for example, prays for the safety of princes and for their brave armies, thankful for their role in maintaining peace and resisting evil.[4] He advises against Christians joining the military, mainly on the grounds that pagan rites and immoral practices are part and parcel of service in Caesar's army, rather than because of the illegitimacy of force.⁵ Origen goes so far as to say that Christians fight the emperor's enemies by prayer: the weapons are different because of a different vocation, but the conflict may be just.⁶

To support government's use of force for just ends is to recognize its divine appointment and to admit the moral legitimacy of its task. Governments are called by God to use force if and when necessary. I therefore fail to see why a Christian is not called to participate. Believers in the Old Testament plainly did, and the New Testament records cases of centurions and government officials becoming believers (Acts 10; 13:7–12), but never reports that they resigned their official posts. The Old Testament records war after war in which God's people were involved, sometimes at God's explicit command. King David, a 'friend of God', was a man of war who sought God's help when he went into combat. Did Jesus change all this when he told Peter to put up his sword (Matthew 26:52)? Hardly, for Peter was not a soldier engaged in military action, but a private individual caught in an act of violent resistance to the authorities, an act of anarchy rather than of lawful government.

Some have proposed that Old Testament wars teach us the futility of taking up arms, that war breeds more war, and that this points to the non-violent way made explicit in the New Testament.⁷ A costly lesson and ghastly pedagogy, this! That war breeds more war, in both biblical and secular history, is hard to deny, for it is not war that will end all wars, unless it be a final holocaust destroying the entire race. But what warrants force even in the New Testament is the tragic necessity of defending life and justly restoring at least a temporary peace. This kind of realism comes out in Jesus' warning about 'wars and rumours of wars' (Matthew 24:6–7) and in the eschatological picture of the armies of heaven fighting to establish the Messiah's reign of peace and justice for ever (Revelation 19:11–16).

If God in the past initiated military actions that resisted evil, if God now entrusts to governments just uses of force in resisting evil, if he calls believers to governmental functions, and in the past expected believers to fight for just ends, then it follows that the Christian may continue to serve when a just cause requires it. Nor is this antithetical to the law of love, if love moves us to justice. Martin Luther, in fact, insists that even war can be a work of love, like that of a doctor who amputates to save a life.[8]

Implications for a just war theory

The essential continuity of the Old and New Testaments in regard to ethics, along with the case for Christian participation in legitimate governmental functions, has led us to conclude that Christians may therefore participate in a just war. But what sort of war is just? What would this allow? Christian just war theorists, from Augustine to Aquinas, the Spanish theologians Francisco da Vitoria and Francisco Suarez, on through Calvin and John Locke and Hugo Grotius to present writers such as Paul Ramsey, have carefully developed criteria that fall into two groups: *jus ad bellum* (justice in going to war) and *jus in bello* (justice in the conduct of war). The purpose is to keep the causes, ends and conduct of war under the constant moral scrutiny of justice and love. We start with the *ad bellum* rules.

a. *Just cause*: the only morally legitimate occasion for going to war is to resist unjust attacks, for force may be used only against evil. Note that, if this rule were universally followed, there would be no aggressors and all war would cease. The just war theory thus aims ideally at the elimination of all conflict. But failing that, justice allows defence only against aggression. It does not allow force as an instrument of national policy, nor does it allow war for ideological or religious causes, or wars of retaliation. Restitution is one thing, but a vengeful and retaliatory spirit or action is another (Romans 12). Defence, of course, is difficult to define with precision, and the literature discusses at length the legitimacy of pre-emptive strikes and preventive wars.[9] But the emphasis is on defence against hostile forces, not on defending national honour and pride. The pagan Cicero, for instance, had allowed the avenging of dishonour, something which is missing in Augustine.

b. *Just intent*: the only morally legitimate purpose in waging war is to restore a just peace for friend and foe alike – a long shot from revenge or conquest. A just peace, after all, is the purpose of government itself, and indeed is God's ultimate purpose in human history (Isaiah 2:1–4; 9:1–7; 11:1–9).

c. *Last resort*: the use of force is not the only means government has at its disposal, nor is it to be used until all else fails: moral persuasion, negotiation, even compromise. As rational beings, we should settle disputes rationally; as peace-loving beings, we should settle them peacefully. Yet when violent aggression cannot be prevented, it should be resisted with force.

d. *Official declaration*: if force is entrusted to lawful government, then it may be initiated only by the highest constitutional authority, not by private individuals or parties on their own initiative. Only government and those it authorizes for its just ends may actually use force.

These criteria lay out broad contours for the kind of war which it would be justifiable to wage, but as in much of human life, specific cases are often ambiguous. The allied conflict with barbaric Nazi aggressors was clearly justifiable. Israel's self-defence against violent invasion or terrorist attack likewise, although one wonders whether prior paths to peace have been sufficiently explored. But the jingoism that immediately avenges the least hostile act out of a nationalistic 'Macho' mentality – this is plainly wrong.

But is all fair in love and war? In a just war entered for a just cause, with just intent and as a last resort, there are still moral limitations on the use of force. The *in bello* criteria speak to this.

e. *Limited objectives*: if the purpose of war is a just peace for friend and foe alike, then destruction of an economy and totally crushing the national spirit are unjustified, and even more so is the refusal to settle for anything less than unconditional surrender. A just peace can never be unconditional.

f. *Immunity of non-combatants*: if force is entrusted to a government and put in the hands of authorized agents, then those not involved in the use of force should not be the objects of any direct attack. This rule protects not only prisoners of war, medical personnel and those they tend, but also civilians who are not involved in military action or preparations. During the Second World War, the Roman Catholic ethicist, John Ford, argued on this basis against Allied obliteration bombings of German cities like Hamburg and Dresden.[10] Directed intentionally against civilian populations, it aimed to demoralize the German forces by destroying their homes and killing their families. Ford showed that even with national mobilization for modern war, a large percentage of the population is by any imagination non-combatant: infants and mothers, schoolchildren and teachers, nursemaids and milkmen, retailers and plumbers, and on and on and on – not to mention those already wounded and out of action. Intentionally to slaughter such non-combatants for any end is blatantly immoral.

At the same time we must recognize that unintended casualties among non-combatants often accompany direct attacks on clearly military targets. Roman Catholic ethicists justify this by employing a doctrine of double effect: the effect primarily intended, and the concomitant but undesired effect. While one's primary intention may be just, the undesired but predictable consequences of an action must also be weighed.

g. *Limited means*: since force is justified only in resisting evil, it must be proportioned to what is needful, and to securing a just peace for all. To wage war justly is to consider both friends and foes. The *lex talionis*, we must remember, outlawed disproportionate punishment: it also outlaws disproportionate violence, even in a just war. Military action should seek not to annihilate the enemy totally, but only to prevent it continuing or renewing aggression. This has far-reaching implications, as we shall see, for modern weaponry.

h. *Reasonable hope of success*: if a just end cannot be achieved, then no purpose remains for conflict and for either inflicting or suffering casualties. Without a just end, it is wrong to fight. Likewise, if the just end cannot be achieved *by just means*, then it is wrong to continue the war. No end can justify any and every means whatsoever. There must be reasonable hope of success within just war criteria if a country is justifiably to engage in or to continue a conflict.

Biblical basis for allowing only limited war is readily at hand. On the eve of invading Canaan, Old Testament Israel was instructed to negotiate for peace before besieging a city, and after capturing a city to spare the women and children. Scorched earth policies were forbidden, lest they destroy future food supplies (Deuteronomy 20:10–20). Among other of the prophets, Amos condemned excessive military violence and cruelty (Amos 1:3–15) – echoes again of a *lex talionis* and the call for justice and love. But the case is not confined to biblical bases. Appeals are also made to a universal moral law binding on all peoples by virtue of common human nature. This is evident in Cicero, Augustine, Aquinas and many others: indeed the Bible itself speaks of some such general revelation in ethical matters (Romans 1). The sixteenth-century theologian, Francisco da Vitoria, condemned King Philip of Spain's wars against the American Indians, insisting that the use of force is justified only for defensive purposes, and not for political expansion, nor for economic gain, nor to convert the Indians to the Christian religion. The reason is that all human beings have God-given rights, whether or not they are civilized by European standards.

The Dutch jurist Hugo Grotius, in his celebrated treatise *On the Law of War and Peace*, published in the context of religious wars, also based limitations in the rule of natural moral laws, and so laid the foundation for later international law. The Geneva Conventions, along with army regulations of many countries, follow this lead.

As far back as Vitoria, moreover, the need is recognized for selective conscientious objection. If not every war a country enters is morally justified in terms of just cause and just end, then the morally informed person of good conscience – and most of all the Christian – should refuse to fight and otherwise to support the war effort. Vitoria spelt this out by saying that the authorities should initially be credited with moral restraint, but if it becomes clear that they are not acting justly in going to war, then the soldier should refuse to serve. Likewise it must be added that in the course of conflict one might find it morally necessary to refuse an unjust order, whether to attack non-combatants directly or to use utterly disproportionate violence or to fight when no hope remains of success.

This leads us to the terrible problem of nuclear weapons. The horrendously disastrous nature of a nuclear holocaust, spreading death and destruction across large segments of the globe, far exceeds any proportionality to just ends. Yet nuclear attacks on cities would destroy not only military capability, but also medical capability, the economy and the political system, in addition (directly or indirectly) to the majority of a nation's population. All this far exceeds any moral ends for going to war and makes sheer mockery of any notion of justice or love. Mutually assured destruction appropriately forms the popular acronym, 'Mad'.

But if anti-city nuclear war is morally unthinkable, what of anti-force nuclear weapons? At first glance it might appear that they use limited force against attacking force. But I am not satisfied. Escalation seems almost inevitable when a powerful military machine has its back to the wall, and this means imminent danger of anti-city strikes with mutually assured destruction. Complete nuclear abstinence, usually called 'nuclear pacifism', is therefore the only prudent course to follow in terms of a just war.

It becomes a matter of the greatest urgency, one for which Christians in every nation should press, to secure nuclear arms limitations as a first step towards nuclear disarmament. Nuclear warfare is no longer war but universal suicide. Nobody can win. Obviously multilateral nuclear disarmament is the most desirable route to follow. Obviously, too, a morally aware government will announce and maintain a 'no first strike' policy. Unilateral nuclear disarmament, it is said, would encourage aggression and nuclear blackmail, but this is debatable: it assumes a callous and sadistic enemy who would slaughter for no purpose. Whoever would want to take on the vast post-holocaust problems of a destroyed nation with all the economic, political and human costs to the ruthless victor? Beyond that, no moral cause and no moral ends could by any stroke of the imagination justify a morally responsible decision to launch, join or support such nuclear destruction. Nuclear pacifism, I conclude, is the course Christians and all morally responsible persons should follow. And no matter how one regards Communism, it would be morally preferable in the final analysis for us all to be red than for hundreds and hundreds of millions to be dead, while survivors struggle for existence in a fallout-saturated world devoid of any effective economic or political order or medical resources.

Nor should we stop with nuclear disarmament. Chemical and bacteriological weapons must also be banned because of their almost uncontrollable effects on non-combatants as well as combatants for an extended time after all conflict has ceased. And in regard even to conventional weapons, the Christian will seek ever-increasing limitations if he is heartily committed to a just peace for all humankind.

The nuclear pacifist, however, should learn from total pacifists, such as those in the Mennonite tradition, that to work for peace is not just to protest against war. It is to alleviate the injustices that stir conflict, to bring healing and relief to those who suffer from the fighting, to bring love and hope to humankind, and so to bear witness to a way of life which warring nations have so obviously missed.

A just war: defining some key issues

On glorifying war and nation

Finally, let no-one glory in his strength. Scripture calls
believers to trust in God, even when they go to war.
Humble and joyful thankfulness is certainly proper when
a just cause achieves a just end by just means, but always
it should be muted with a deep and lasting sorrow for
friend and foe alike who have suffered and still suffer from
the process.

Nineteenth-century nationalism encouraged the tendency to glorify war. The German philosopher Hegel
thought it built national spirit and embodied the sovereign
emergence of Absolute Spirit in history. Tennyson's *The
Charge of the Light Brigade* immortalized the pointless
sacrifice of human life to a stupid military blunder. War
can perhaps bring out the best in people, but it can also
bring out the worst: callous disregard of life and property,
a cruel and vengeful spirit, utter disregard for the dignity
of persons created in God's image and an almost idolatrous pride in nationality and might. But nations as we
know them today are historical accidents, a product of
migration and conflicts and cultural developments over
thousands of years. Where once families and tribes lived
in contact with each other and sometimes fought, city
states gradually emerged, then principalities, and only
quite recently the nations we know today. The unification
of Great Britain came earlier than the unification of Italy
or Germany, but all of us – the United States and the
Soviet Union included – are composites of different ethnic
and cultural groups that have merged along the way for
a vast variety of reasons. Nations and empires are largely
arbitrary things, nothing to invoke undue pride when we
recall the violence and suffering they cost.

Undue pride of nation and undue pride at power and
success are what underlie the tendency to glory in victory
or in war. But the Christian is first a creature of God along
with every other human being. Loyalty to God means
global concern, internationalism rather than an exclusive
nationalistic spirit. Peace on earth requires goodwill,

33

justice and love for all. The Vatican II Conference in 1966 rightly called for community among nations, declaring that even limited defensive war is justified only as long as no competent and powerful international authority exists.

Rather than glorying in war and what it secures, we should always regret it. Augustine advised soldiers going to war to repent in advance, because of the attitudes and actions that would likely erupt. In medieval times, soldiers returning from battle were supposed to do penance for weeks. This is a more appropriate attitude than the glorification of war. God forgive us, we must say again and again, in the moral dilemmas that life in a fallen world holds, but what else could we do than what we have done?

If glorying is appropriate at all, we should rather glory in peace, in a just peace for friend and foe alike, and in the God of peace who will beat guns and missiles into instruments for human good. In this regard a Christian just war theory stands much closer in its driving concerns to Christian pacifism than to any kind of militarist spirit. War, at very best, is a tragic necessity in the pursuit of *shālôm* amidst a fallen race.

Response to Arthur Holmes

Willard Swartley

I fully affirm Arthur Holmes' appeal to Jesus as the final
authority and his categorical refusal of nuclear war, but I
must also register disagreements:

1. Arthur's assumption – and thesis – that 'if government is divinely ordained, then Christians should be
willing to participate' lacks biblical support. The if-clause
is used to argue only for Christian submission (Romans
13:1–7), and this is to be distinguished from obedience
(see my article).

2. In his appeal to the Old Testament for a theological
warrant for retributive justice, Arthur fails to distinguish
between intra- and international categories. This inadequacy leads to another false premise that the Old Testament accepted 'limited international war for just ends'.
Old Testament scholarship understands Israel's warfare
within the 'holy war' species, which in Israel consisted
essentially of God's victory by miracle. Attempts at 'international war for just ends' in the time of Israel's kingship
were condemned by the Old Testament as Israel's apostasy
– seeking to be like the nations. Since Arthur's argument
for Christian participation in war is based largely upon
the principle of the continuity of the Old and New Testaments, his misunderstanding of Old Testament warfare

leaves his position without biblical foundation. The just war concept and criteria are not to be found in Old Testament holy warfare; further, no convening trajectory from Old Testament holy war to the just war theory has been or can be demonstrated – and certainly not through the New Testament. The just war theory has its roots in the Greco-Roman world, not in Yahweh's holy war of the Old Testament.

3. Arthur's discussion of the *lex talionis* fails to follow the thought-sequence of the text which he cites (Matthew 5:38). The intrusion of concern for retributive justice distorts Jesus' teaching. When this teaching is later acknowledged, Arthur limits it to *individual* behaviour and thus has Jesus accepting the *lex talionis* for governmental and social morality. But Jesus said nothing of the sort: the first-century context for Jesus' teaching on non-resistance and love for the enemy was the political subjugation of the Jews to the imperialistic Romans. The notion of two levels of morality, justified by the distinction between individual (personal) and political (social) responses, has no basis in the teachings of Jesus. Nor does it have much practical basis when tested in the realities of contemporary life and decision-making. For where does the personal sphere end and the social sphere begin? And is there ever a situation where one is excused from personal responsibility?

4. Niebuhr did not regard non-resistant-pacifism as 'unbiblical idealism' but as a *biblical* idealism that could not address effectively political realism. Hence arises the hard choice between biblical realism (the pacifist commitment) and political realism (Niebuhr's war-as-necessity theory). And Niebuhr cannot be cited even as a just war theorist; he held war itself to be sin, but necessary in the cause of justice (as he defined it!). Justice was the goal, not the means; Niebuhr thus accepted the evil reality of war and did not camouflage it by the adjective '*just*'.

5. Arthur's description of Mennonite teaching on two kingdoms and two vocations comes from Lutheran/Reformed theological glasses. If used by Mennonite theo-

logians, the concept of vocation is single, the call (*vocatio*) to follow Christ (Ephesians 4:1). And it is not heavenly, but earthly, – touched often with suffering and also joy.

6. Arthur's comments about something having 'more worth than human life' are misleading. Indeed, we are called as Christians to be willing to die for the cause of the gospel – and even for the neighbour's and enemy's welfare. But the real issue is: what cause is worth killing for? To infer, as Arthur does, that one might kill for national or family security is alien to New Testament teaching.

7. The just war criteria are a mental cipher and moral delusion. They falsely assume that wars are declared on the basis of rational and theologically moral considerations. Which war in human history was so declared and waged? Arthur is to be commended for his honest and conscientious effort to apply these criteria, thus providing both moral legitimation and negation of certain wars and moral negation of nuclear war categorically. But in this effort his contribution is not representative of the actual function that the doctrine has had in the history of Christian moral thought. If applied seriously today, the just war theory would mean support of 'just revolutions' in developing countries; the concept of 'legitimate government' becomes farcical in many of these cases.

8. The pacifism of the early church had deeper roots than avoidance of idolatry. Its basis was the new law of Christ,[1] love for the enemy, and membership in the household of God international, a new humanity as sign and hope of God's new cosmic creation.

2
Pacifist Christianity: the kingdom way

Willard Swartley and Alan Kreider

The teaching of Jesus and the apostles · Biblical
perspectives on government and war · The church ·
Christian response to government and evil · Conclusion.

Threatened by nuclear genocide/cosmocide, we can at last
see clearly that Jesus' word about 'those who take the
sword' could become humanity's epitaph: 'they perished
in nuclear holocaust'. Within the context of this ominous
threat the biblical teaching on war and peace has become
an imperative of prophetic urgency: 'Return from your
evil ways', or the 'sudden end' will come upon you, and
there will be none who survive to deliver (Zechariah 1:4;
cf. Jeremiah 21:4–14; Hosea 10:13–14; Zephaniah 1:18).

This new threat of cosmic tragedy, which Einstein
foresaw in saying that 'the unleashed power of the atom
has changed everything but our way of thinking',[1] has put
old issues in sharper perspective. Now, more clearly than
ever before, war's true nature as 'an act of force which
theoretically can have no limits' is evident.[2] The radical
position of early Christianity and, we believe, of Scripture
is therefore of highest relevance to believers in our thermo-
nuclear age.

We write from within the tradition of the historic peace
churches (Mennonites, Quakers, Church of the Brethren)
which for over four centuries has held that all war is sin.[3]
But we are also part of a much wider Christian pacifist
tradition that goes back to the earliest history of the

church and that has had representatives in every generation. In the three centuries closest to Christ, every Christian theologian who pronounced on the subject declared that believers must refuse to participate in war.[4] The early church's disciplinary regulations also maintained this position. Any Christian who after conversion joined the army was to be excommunicated; likewise, any Christian was to be excommunicated who, having been converted while in the army, took life.[5] The Jesus-centred love of enemy and respect for life of the early Christians resulted in persecution and suffering.

In the fourth century, after the conversion of the Emperor Constantine to a semblance of Christianity, many aspects of Christian life and teaching began to change. Among these was the church's position on Christian participation in warfare.[6] Although the theologians continued to honour pacifism for those (especially clerics) who would be perfect, for ordinary believers they devised a theory which would justify and, they hoped, would limit military violence.[7] In this they drew heavily from pagan moralists.[8] It thus took Christian theologians over 400 years to discover the just war theory, which ever since has been the official position of the major Christian traditions.[9] In each generation, as military technology has become increasingly lethal, non-pacifist Christian ethicists have continued to justify warfare; a very few, swimming against the stream with increasing desperation, have sought to limit it.[10]

The result is our current position of agony and peril under the mushroom cloud. We affirm, however, that it is not too late for Christians to adopt for our day the church's original teaching on warfare, and we rejoice that a growing number of believers who are doing precisely that are finding a distinctive prophetic relevance.

The teaching of Jesus and the apostles

Jesus' teachings in the Sermon on the Mount are foundational to discussion of this issue because, as is widely agreed, they represent Jesus' response to the violence of his first-century world.[11] Jesus not only forbade retaliation against those who do evil (Matthew 5:38–42; Luke 6:27–36), but he commanded his disciples to love the enemy and pray for persecutors, because in this response they reflect God's own nature (Matthew 5:43–48). This teaching matches Jesus' later injunction forbidding the use of the sword (Matthew 26:52; *cf.* John 18:36; 2 Corinthians 10:4; Revelation 13:10).[12]

New response to enemies

This response to enemies, Jesus makes clear, distinguishes his disciples from sinners who love only those who love them (Luke 6:27–36).[13] It could be, of course, that the enemies to whom Jesus was referring were solely personal, individual enemies. As ethicist Paul Ramsey, echoing the dominant post-Constantinian tradition, has argued, 'Jesus here deals only with the simplest moral situation in which blows may be struck, the case of one person in relation to but one other'.[14] Who were the enemies – individuals who wished the disciples ill, or the national, collective enemy?

The word for enemy (*echthros*) is often used in the singular for the Satanic enemy and occasionally in the plural for individual foes (*e.g.* Matthew 10:36). But in the plural its dominant meaning in the Synoptic Gospels is for the Jews' corporate, military enemy.[15] Zechariah, in his song (Luke 1:71,74), exulted in the liberation that the Messiah would bring 'from our *enemies*, from the hand of all who hate us'. Similarly Jesus, weeping over Jerusalem because it had been blind to the things that would make for its peace (Luke 19:41–44), forecast the imminent day when 'your enemies' will act in a markedly military way: they will erect siege-works around the city, demolish its buildings and 'dash you to the ground, you and your children'.

Certainly Zechariah and Jesus had in mind the Romans.[16] As the occupying power ruling Palestine by force since 63 BC, they had offended Jewish religious sensibilities.[17] Pontius Pilate had not only 'mingled the blood of the Galileans with their sacrifices' (Luke 13:1), but he had caused outrage by diverting the sacred treasure (*corban*) to build an aqueduct and by erecting Caesar's images in Jerusalem.[18] The Romans had also imposed a heavy financial burden upon the Jews, impoverishing the Jewish people through tax-collecting collaborators. Thus Jesus' teaching abounds with references to debtors, absentee landlords and tax-farmers. And the Romans were willing to use their imposing military force. Their brutality was keenly felt by the people of Sepphoris, a town located only three miles north of Jesus' home town Nazareth. There, after a major revolt headed by Judas the Galilean when Jesus was around ten years old (in AD 6), the Romans retaliated by crucifying two thousand people.[19] Quite aptly, Martin Hengel has described Palestine in the time of Jesus as 'a politico-religious tinderbox'.[20]

Crushed by oppression and sustained by hope, the Jewish people expected God to intervene by sending a Messiah. Inspired by Davidic precedents and revenging emphases in both apocalyptic and intertestamental writings, they expected the coming Messiah/king to be God's instrument of judgment and liberation.[21] 'Send thy terror upon all nations,' they prayed. 'Lift up thy hand against the foreigners . . . Rouse thy anger and pour out thy wrath; destroy the adversary and wipe out the enemy' (Ecclesiasticus 36:2–3,7).

Jesus' proclamation of the coming of God's kingdom, from the outset of his ministry in deed and word (Mark 1:14–15), was therefore politically provocative to Jews subjected by Roman rule. All the religious parties of the time, the Essenes, the Pharisees, the Sadducees and the Zealots, had their own hopes and strategies for hastening the coming of the kingdom. But Jesus judged all of these to be inadequate: the Essenes' withdrawal to preserve purity; the Pharisees' focus upon interior piety through careful observance of the law; the collaborationist manoeuvrings of the Sadducees and Herodians; and the violence of the Zealots.[22] Jesus' disciples probably

41

expected Jesus to be a Zealot liberator (Luke 24:21); so did the Jewish people (John 6:15), who in calling for the release of Barabbas (an insurrectionist and murderer, probably a Zealot, Luke 23:19) demonstrated their disappointed rejection of an enemy-loving Messiah. Yet Jesus persisted steadfastly, in the face of these pressures, in proclaiming a kingdom in which the sons and daughters of the Father would manifest social behaviour markedly different from that of the world around them.

'Love your enemies!' This command, 'the heart of the proclamation of Jesus',[23] was shockingly radical and relevant in this setting of expectancy and endemic insurrection. Its location in the Gospel accounts shows its importance in Jesus' ministry. In Luke 'love your enemies' stands as Jesus' very first ethical teaching (Luke 6:27). In Matthew, in the Sermon on the Mount in which Jesus established a 'pattern of life in the kingdom of God',[24] three of the six antitheses deal with the problem of violence; and the command of the culminating antithesis, 'love your enemies', reveals what it means to be children of the Father.

The disciples were to love their enemies because God, who sends the rain on the just and the unjust, loves all people, regardless of their good or evil deeds. If the disciples behave similarly, they will be like the Father and will enter into the divine character; it is 'peacemakers' and enemy-lovers who, according to Jesus, are the children of God (Matthew 5:9,45). If the disciples behave like the Father, they also will be unlike those whom they most resented —the oppressive, God-denying Romans and their publican toadies (Matthew 5:46–47). In contrast, the Zealots, who wanted to expel the Romans by force ('Whoever spills the blood of one of the godless is like one who offers sacrifice'[25]), would still be living by the enemy's values, and thus would not be children of the Father.

Within the framework of this child-father relationship Jesus called his disciples to go beyond retaliation. Jesus' negative command, 'Do not resist one who is evil' (Matthew 5:39), should be understood as congruent with and standing in the service of his positive command to love the enemy;[26] it thus accords with the standard apostolic teaching, 'Do not be overcome by evil, but overcome evil with good' (Romans 12:21; *cf.* 1 Thessalonians 5:15; 1 Peter 3:9).[27] This radical challenge to reconcile ourselves with our enemies through loving them, and doing good instead of evil, accords with God's own response to us (Romans 5:8–10). As Ronald Sider puts it, 'One fundamental aspect of the holiness and perfection of God is that He loves His enemies. Those who by His grace seek to reflect His holiness will likewise love their enemies – even when it involves a cross.'[28] Pacifism is thus not passivism. It is rather the enlistment of every response in the positive ministry of reconciliation (2 Corinthians 5:18–20).

Jesus' life, death and our response
Jesus not only taught a new response to enemies, but he also lived it. Numerous writers have shown how Jesus' temptations were the 'old party' strategies (Pharisee, Sadducee and Zealot) to bring in the kingdom.[29] But Jesus refused them all, committing himself to a servant interpretation of divine power and Sonship. The sharp interchange between Peter and Jesus, following Peter's confession of Jesus as Messiah, dramatically focused the issue. Peter rebuked Jesus because Jesus' view of Messiahship clashed with Peter's political Messianic hopes (Mark 8:31–33). Then Jesus sharply rebuked Peter: 'Get out of my way, Satan!' thus echoing Jesus' own reply to the devil in the third temptation (Matthew 4:10; 16:23).[30] In the temptations, and in this clash of wills over Jesus' Messiahship, the method of conquering evil emerged again, like it did in Jesus' teachings, as a central issue for Jesus and his followers.

Nor can it be said that this non-violent way of responding to evil and enemies is to be confined to Jesus and his unique mission. For Jesus' teaching about his own passion is linked firmly to his call to discipleship, both in Mark 8:34 and 10:42–45. Those who would follow Jesus are asked to deny self and take up the cross (8:34–35). They are to refuse the way of the earthly rulers, who use power to lord it over others (Mark 10:42; Luke 22:25); instead, they are to adopt the ethics and life-style of the servant who gave himself for others (Mark 10:45).[31]

In his teaching, life and death, Jesus thus refused to use violent power to 'handle the enemy' and thereby 'control evil'. From start to finish he demonstrated a unique response to the problem of evil, refusing to accept 'realistic', 'lesser evil' solutions to enemy threats, whether these be masked politically, socially or economically. Indeed, he exposed the moral inadequacy of 'the good intentions' of the rulers who used force and violence to keep peace. In his crucifixion he made a public example of them (Colossians 2:15), for they failed to recognize God manifested in the flesh. They crucified him (1 Corinthians 2:8)!

In this event, a master key unlocking the meaning of history, we encounter both the pretentiousness of political power and the unpretentious power of the atonement. Jesus' death exposed the fallen nature of the powers and at the same time liberated humanity from their tyranny. Hence the New Testament and the early church understood one of the major benefits of the atonement to be freedom from the powers (Romans 8:38; 1 Corinthians 15:24; Ephesians 1:21; 3:10; 6:12; Colossians 2:15; 1 Peter 3:22).[32]

Freedom from the powers and freedom from the law were two correlative benefits of Jesus' victory. Both had built walls and created hostilities between peoples – as they do today. Jesus means freedom from all these bondages. The power of the atoning gospel brought – and brings – former enemies together into one new community – a new creation, a new humanity (2 Corinthians 5:17; Ephesians 2:15). What the victorious Romans only pretended to do in their vaunted *pax Romana*, the dying Messiah achieved: the uniting of Jews and Gentiles,[33] former collective enemies, into one body of peace, the *pax Christi*. Indeed, what neither the empire nor the law could do, God accomplished through the *cross* of Jesus Christ: the creation of a new humanity through loving forgiveness, reconciling peace, and faith that does justice (justification).[34]

When traditional doctrines of the atonement, therefore, fail to relate Jesus' crucifixion to the social reality of peace, they are incomplete. 'The work of Christ', writes theologian Marlin Miller, 'inherently means the making of peace between human enemies . . . . Peacemaking between enemies . . . belongs fundamentally to the death and resurrection of Christ.'[35] Similarly, Ronald Sider, quoting Romans 5:8,10, says 'Jesus' vicarious cross for sinners is the foundation and deepest expression of Jesus' command to love one's enemies'.[36]

Jesus: King and Warrior
Though the New Testament abounds with teaching on love for all people, including enemies, and calls disciples to suffer rather than avenge themselves against evil, the New Testament account of God and Jesus stands also in fundamental continuity with the Old Testament images of king and divine warrior. Jesus was born king of the Jews (Matthew 2). In his baptism Jesus was acclaimed king, God's royal Son (Mark 1:11 quotes Psalm 2:7), and affirmed to be servant (Mark 1:11 also quotes Isaiah 42:1). Further, Luke 4:16–19 declares Jesus as God's anointed (king), who takes up the servant mission of proclaiming the *shālôm*-gospel of jubilee (Isaiah 52:7; 61:2)!

Luke's nativity hymns echo the warrior motifs of the Old Testament (1:32–33, 46–55, 68–79). Especially in Mark, Jesus came to combat the forces of evil, attacking the demons and crushing the power of evil (1:21–28); 3:22–27; 5:7–13; 9:14–29). In all the Gospels Jesus attacked and condemned the unbelief and hypocrisy of the Pharisees (Matthew 12:33–45; 23:1–39; Mark 7:1–14; Luke 11:37–54; 16:14–15; John 8:12–59). Similarly, in all the Gospels Jesus launched a campaign against both personal and social evils, especially injustice to the crippled and outsiders (Mark 2:1–12; 3:1–6; 7:24–37; Luke 4:18–30; 14:1–4; 15:1–2, 11–32; John 5:1–18). In this warfare, however, Jesus stood firmly in the holy war prophetic tradition: his weapons were not military and his concern was not his own defence; he combated evil solely through the power of his prophetic word and action, thus doing the work of God (John 5:17).

This prophetic work of Jesus reached its climax in Jesus' cleansing of the temple. The cleansing, as many writers indicate,[37] must be seen as a bold prophetic act in which Jesus showed his authority over Israel's most holy place. Jesus directed this prophetic act against two injustices: the economic exploitation (overcharging) in the selling of sacrificial animals (note that pigeons, the sacrifice of the poor, are especially mentioned), and the injustice of infringing on the worship of the Gentiles (note that 'he would not allow any one to carry anything through the temple [court]'). Of this misuse of the temple, Jesus said, 'This house which is to be a house of prayer *for all nations* you have made a den (hang-out) for robbers' (see Mark 11:17). If you want to see Jesus go into action, just cheat the poor and squeeze out the Gentiles!

Jesus' cleansing of the temple is often used as a biblical argument to support the Christian's use of violence in war. This is a misuse of this incident and of Scripture. For Jesus' action was thoroughly prophetic, depending on the power of the word. Even though some translations of John 2:15 portray Jesus using the whip of cords against people, an alternative exegesis (reflected in NIV, NEB, GNB) takes the phrase 'with the sheep and oxen' to be explanatory of the 'all' (*pantas*) that Jesus drove out with a whip. Verse 16 supports this interpretation in saying that Jesus, after driving 'all' out, spoke to those who had been selling the pigeons.[38]

We must give due attention to Jesus' role as Warrior fighting against evil, and we must also note that the Gospels fully integrate this emphasis with another theme, Jesus the Servant. Jesus won the battle through his courageous stand for justice, his meekness in forgoing self-defence, and finally his humiliation in self-sacrificial suffering (Philippians 2:5–11). The Holy Warrior, in accord with Isaiah 52:13 – 53:12, won the battle as Faithful Martyr (Revelation 1:5), obedient unto death. The Lion was a Lamb (a description of Jesus used 28 times in Revelation); the Warrior won by his death and by the sword of his mouth (5:9–10; 19:11–16; 1:16).

Jesus' life and death as Holy Warrior against evil serves as a model for *our* Christian battle against evil. We are called to stand for justice and fight against evil (Ephesians 6:10–18). But our weapons must not be carnal (2 Corinthians 10:4); we must rely solely upon the power of the prophetic word and suffering love. And so-called political obligations may not excuse us from this Christian way. Faithfulness to this way will bring hardships, sometimes persecution, and perhaps even death. But as William Farmer has cogently argued, the New Testament is a martyrs' canon![39] For just as the Lamb Jesus conquered the beast (Revelation 17:14) and our faithful foreparents conquered (Revelation 12:11; 15:2), so we as faithful disciples of Jesus are also called to conquer through 'patient endurance', even unto death (Revelation 2:7, 11, 17, 26; 3:5, 12, 21; 21:7).[40] The call is hard and pointed: will we *own* this biblical tradition and live it out?

Biblical perspectives on government and war

For this topic we habitually turn to Romans 13 and often stop there. This is unfortunate. A much wider biblical perspective must be considered.

Yahweh: King and Warrior

In the Old Testament Israel initially had no human king; Yahweh was their king. In the exodus Yahweh defeated the military might of the Egyptian empire by a nature miracle; Israel, whom God was liberating, had only to 'be still' and to 'see the salvation of the Lord' (Exodus 14:9–14). In later battles under the judges, Israel's foot-soldiers did participate in mopping-up operations, some of which were genocidal in nature;[41] but their participation was incidental to the decisive military thrust, which was

Willard Swartley and Alan Kreider

Yahweh's miracle – by means of crumbling walls (Joshua 6:20), a hornet (Joshua 24:12), thunder (1 Samuel 7:10), and a suddenly swollen stream (Judges 5:21). From a military point of view Israel's actions were equally bizarre. As Yahweh's instruments the Israelites wielded such 'weapons' as trumpets (Joshua 6), empty jars and torches (Judges 7 – 8), a tent peg (Judges 4 – 5), and brook pebbles in a slingshot (1 Samuel 17:48–49). Significantly, Yahweh also commanded them to be inferior to their enemies in more conventional weaponry – in numbers of soldiers (Deuteronomy 20:1–8; 1 Samuel 24) and in military technology (Joshua 11:6, 9). Yahweh did this for a good reason. A sizeable infantry and a chariot force might make Israel independent, boasting that 'My own hand has delivered me' (Judges 7:2). Yahweh wanted the victories to be by miracle, wholly of grace and not of human works. The land was a promise and gift to Israel. It was not, Joshua reminded them, conquered 'by your sword or by your bow' (Joshua 24:12).

Israel's role in this drama to accomplish God's purpose, however, was not passive. God called Israel to learn rather the power of another weapon: *Yahweh's word*. Moses' call to Israel from Egyptian bondage focused upon his willingness to be Yahweh's prophet, to speak Yahweh's *word* to Pharaoh (Exodus 3 – 11; Hosea 12:13). God established Israel as a nation at Sinai by giving the torah; only by living the *word* of the torah would Israel continue to be God's people. Further, God's *shālôm* for the whole earth, indeed Yahweh's justice, was (is) established by the *word* (torah) of the Lord going out of Jerusalem to the nations of the earth (Isaiah 2:1–4; 11:1–9; 32:1, 16–17; 52:7–9; Ezekiel 34:23–29). Luke-Acts shows the fulfilment of this vision (Luke 1:79; 2:14; 10:5–6; Acts 1:8; 8:12; 9:31; 10:36; also Ephesians 2:13–18). Clearly, God's *shālôm* never was merely the absence of war; but truly, truly, the military violence of the nations never was, is, nor will be the way to achieve God's justice and *shālôm* upon earth.

After Israel adopted human kingship, Yahweh, who had

fought for their defence (Deuteronomy 33:26–29; Psalms 68:17–18,33; 136:10–22), was soon fighting against them (Isaiah 3:1–3, 25–26; 10:5–7; 13:3–5; Jeremiah 21:4–6). Indeed, from the beginning it was clear that Yahweh was not simply *for* or *against* Israel: when Joshua asked, 'Are you for us, or against us?' Yahweh's army commander answered, 'No' (Joshua 5:13–14)! When Israel, 'like all the nations', chose a king to 'go out before us and fight our battles' (1 Samuel 8:5, 19–20), they rejected Yahweh's defence and grace for their protection; indeed, they rejected Yahweh as king (1 Samuel 8:7; Hosea 13:10–11). [42] Thereafter Israel began to amass military power – numerically imposing footsoldiers (1 Chronicles 12:14, 21–22) and technologically sophisticated chariots (2 Samuel 8:4; 1 Kings 10:26). Through the prophets Yahweh denounced the covenant people for their militarism and alliances with pagan states (Isaiah 2:7–10; 31:1–3; Nahum 2:13). When they repented and trusted Yahweh for protection, Yahweh again defended them by miracle (2 Kings 6:8–23; 2 Chronicles 20; Isaiah 37). But their customary lack of repentance led them to defeat and exile (Hosea 10:13–15). Only when a future Messiah/king would come to triumph in meekness and 'cut off the chariot and the war horse' (Zechariah 9:9–10) would Israel return to true fidelity to Yahweh.

A most important lesson from Israel's experience is that the prophets never pointed back to Israel's national history to legitimate an arms build-up; on the contrary, they appealed to past victories to argue against military alliances, political designs and the recourse to military power (Isaiah 7:1–14; 31:1–3). Their history assured them that Yahweh faithfully cared for Israel's defence. [43] While this lesson cannot be transferred simplistically to a nation today, it does apply to the church. Christian believers, who corporately are God's people, should not depend upon military power for their security; and Christian truth cannot be defended by military power. Nor should pacifist Christians play the game out of two pockets: it's wrong for me personally to fight, but it's right to vote for a strong military government because it's the job of government to defend its citizens. Pacifist Christians must be willing to trust God all the way, even if that means suffering and death.

New Testament views of government

The New Testament reflects different views of government. These might be classified into negative, somewhat positive, and more normative views. Texts which view government negatively, in coalition with evil, are Matthew 4:8–10 and Luke 4:6–8 (Satan is over the kingdoms of the world); Ephesians 6:11–12; Revelation 13 (the beast wars against God's people); 1 Corinthians 2:6–8 (and indirectly 1 Corinthians 6:1–6); and most explicit of all, Mark 10:42. Further, numerous historically descriptive texts either implicitly or explicitly criticize political power, among which are Jesus' description of Herod as a fox (Luke 13:31–33); Jesus' reference to Pilate's massacre of the Galileans (Luke 13:1–3); Jesus' refusal to defer to the authorities;[44] Jesus' crucifixion and the frequent mention of Christian persecution at the hands of kings and political leaders.[45]

New Testament texts which view government somewhat positively, with a degree of theological assessment, are Romans 13:1–7; 1 Timothy 2:1–4; Titus 3:1 and 1 Peter 2:13–17. Numerous historically descriptive texts also show favourable attitudes, especially towards the Roman government: John the Baptist did not criticize the political-military vocation as such (Luke 3:19); the first Gentile convert to Christianity was a Roman centurion (Acts 10; cf. Luke 7:1–10); Roman law appeared as a friend and saviour to Paul (Acts 18:12–17; 22:22–29; 25:23–27) and Paul appealed directly to Caesar (Acts 26:32).[46]

Only as one looks beyond this double dimension of government does one find a theological basis for the Christians' and the church's relationship to government. It is fallen from God's purposes in its alliance with evil, but nevertheless commissioned in creation (Colossians 1:16) to be an agent of God's *wrath* to promote good and restrain evil (Romans 13:3). This theological foundation, which provides a normative view of the rulers, derives from Christ's victory over the powers. Having disarmed the powers, exposing their actual nature and allegiance (1 Corinthians 2:6–8; Colossians 2:15), Christ has authority and rule over all powers (Ephesians 1:19–23; Colossians 2:10; 1 Peter 3:22). The powers, therefore, which can never separate believers from God's love (Romans 8:35–39), must never receive ultimate allegiance from Christians. Jesus Christ, not state authority, is Lord.

Further, some of the above texts suggest criteria by which Christians are to discern the limits of obedience to government: political leaders are to promote the good and punish evil (Romans 13:3); they are ministers of God's wrath *when* they attend to this very thing (the participle in 13:6 may be taken temporally); believers must distinguish between what is due to Caesar and what is due to God (Romans 13:7);[47] and Jesus' reply to the tax question (Mark 12:17) indicates that the claims of God transcend the claims of Caesar.[48] Believers are not urged to be especially deferential to the authorities. Whereas they are to 'love' the brotherhood and 'fear' God, they are admonished merely to 'honour' the emperor as they 'honour' all people. In other words, they are to treat the emperor as they would treat anyone else – with respect (1 Peter 2:17; *cf.* 1 Timothy 2:1–2). Believers are not told to obey (*hypakouō*)government, but to submit (*hypotassō*) to it.[49] Where a word for obedience is used (*peitharchein* in Titus 3:1), it is qualified by readiness to do every *good* (RSV honest) work. Finally, Romans 13:1–7 is framed by both an ethic of love which seeks to overcome evil with good and a clear call to be unconformed to the world (12:2). The Christian is to be always Christian, fully and joyfully. To say yes to government's call to war jeopardizes the Christian's basic confession of faith and baptismal vow (Acts 2:36; Romans 10:9–10; Philippians 2:11).

Willard Swartley and Alan Kreider

The church: its nature and witness

Notably absent from the theses proposed for this forum of essays is any reference to the central role of the church in God's purposes to witness to Christ's defeat of the old order and the victory of his kingdom. This is unfortunate, because the New Testament's emphasis falls not upon the Christians' responsibilites to government but to the household of God.

The nature of the church
Only as believers take seriously what it means to be the 'body of Christ' can the social significance of Christ's atonement have resurrection efficacy so that the pretensions of the powers can be unmasked. Most Protestant discussion of the Christians' obligations to government falls short precisely at this point.[50]

Paul's great concern, in contrast, was that he would be running in vain if the *corporate* vision of Christian strategy, uniting Jews and Gentiles in the cross, were undermined by works-righteousness or party discord (Acts 15; 1 Corinthians 1:10–25; Galatians 2:1–10). For to Paul, to whom God had given this mystery by revelation (Ephesians 3:2–8), the church was God's demonstration in history, to the powers, that irreconcilable enemies can be and are being reconciled, living together in one commonwealth as holy citizens and children of one divine family (Ephesians 2:19; 3:8–10).

As members of the one body of peace with Christ as Head, Christians are called to identify fully with Christ's life, death and resurrection victory. We are called to live lives of servanthood (Matthew 25:31–46; Mark 10:42–44; John 13:1–13), to suffer with Christ (2 Corinthians 4:10; Philippians 3:10f.; Colossians 1:24; 1 Thessalonians 1:6), to suffer hostility from the world for faithfulness to Jesus' way (Mark 8:34–37; 2 Timothy 2:3; Hebrews 11:1 – 12:5; 1 Peter 2:20f.; 3:14–18; 4:12–16; 5:10) and to share in Christ's victory over death (Romans 6:1–14; 1 Corinthians 15:22–24; Colossians 1:12–14;

52

Revelation 2 – 3; 12:10ff.; 17:14). As John H. Yoder notes, the New Testament writers do not call us to copy Jesus by being celibate or wearing sandals. They call us to imitate him solely 'at the point of the concrete social meaning of the cross in relation to enmity and power', in which 'servanthood replaces dominion [and] forgiveness absorbs hostility. Thus – and only thus – are we bound by New Testament thought to "be like Jesus" '.[51] Further, only as we walk 'in the Spirit', in the power of Jesus' cross and resurrection, can we live non-violently.[52]

When we fully grasp the significance of Christ's life, death and resurrection for the church, our relationship as Christians to governments comes clearly into focus. Christ is Head over the church; government powers are under his feet (1 Corinthians 15:24–26; Ephesians 1:19–23; Colossians 2:10). Participation in Christ's body is therefore our primary calling. Consequently, when we Christians take up arms in war, are we not severing the bond of Christ's peace, mocking his death and resurrection? As evangelist and theologian Myron Augsburger writes, 'To affirm that one is a member of the Kingdom of Christ means that loyalty to Christ and his Kingdom transcends every other loyalty. This stance transcends nationalism, and calls us to identify first of all with our fellow disciples, of whatever nation, as we serve Christ together.'[53]

The witness of the church
Christian participation in war also cripples the mission of the church. 'We cannot kill [one] for whom Christ died . . . We cannot take the life of a person God purposes to redeem.'[54] Killing the enemy deprives him of the opportunity to repent. 'From an evangelical perspective,' Augsburger argues further, 'it may be said that whenever a Christian participates in war he has abdicated his responsibility to the greater calling of missions and evangelism . . . The way for Christians to change the world is to share the . . . good news of the Gospel rather than to think we can stop the anti-God movements by force.'[55]

When Christians take up the sword, for whatever

national cause, and thereby turn their backs on God's call
to the church to demonstrate the peace of God's new
humanity, the missionary cause around the world is not
only set back by at least a generation; often it is rendered
permanently incredible.[56]

When the church, by refusing war, treasures its unity in
the body of Christ and demonstrates reconciliation and
servanthood (Mark 10:42–45; 2 Corinthians 5:17–21), it
bears witness to the powers that a new order of life has
come. Reconciliation of enemies, peace-making, *has
already happened*, through Jesus Christ!

Christian response to government and evil

Theses 5 and 7 raise the question: since God has commissioned the government to restrain evil, is it not therefore
appropriate for Christians to assist them in that restraint?
Can we as believers not serve God's 'servant' in good
conscience (Romans 13:4)?

The logic of biblical thought, however, goes in a
different direction. Since governments often function as
the perpetrators of evil as well as restrainers of evil, *and
since Christ has provided the final answer to evil*, we
Christians are called *to bear witness* to Christ's answer,
even to governments (Ephesians 3:8–10). The most
important responsibility of the church towards governments and to evil in society is to live as a new society
experiencing and demonstrating the reconciling reality of
the gospel. Then we can with integrity point to the cross
and proclaim, 'Christ has conquered, is conquering, and
will conquer evil. He is the way!'

this thinking guides Paul's thought in Romans 13:1–7.
Having been expelled from Rome together with Jews in AD
49 by Claudius' edict (Acts 18:1–2),[57] Jewish Christians
returned to Rome during the years AD 54–56; at this time
also a tax revolt was brewing against Neron Caesar.[58] The
likely issue behind Romans 12 – 13, written at this time,
was how the Christians should respond to the government
and the evil manifest in the tax problem, the evil of injus-

tice and the evil of revolt. The *major* theme of Romans
12:9 – 13:10 is how to respond to *evil* (recurring eight
times, 12:9, 17(2), 21(2); 13:3, 4, 10). Christians should
not repay evil for evil (12:17), but always seek to overcome evil with *good* (12:21; *cf.* 12:9; 13:3). Doing the
good, making peace (12:18) and loving the neighbour
(13:7–10) are the Christian responses to evil;[59] avenging
evil is forbidden to Christians, for vengeance (12:17, 19;
13:4) belongs to God and the servant of wrath (12:19;
13:4–5).

The significance of this for thesis 7 is that Christians
are called to a distinctive Christian ethic; they do not need
to be burdened with policing society. Specifically, they do
not need to resist evil by evil means; Christ has shown
them a new and better means of resistance. Christians are
not ministers of God's wrath (let the authorities be this),
but the ministers of God's reconciling love (2 Corinthians
5:17–20). Nor did Paul tell the Christians to withdraw
from a difficult situation of societal evil; they are to stay
in it (in Rome, to which Paul himself wants to come
[Romans 15:22–29]), and there demonstrate Christ's new
response to evil. By so doing, they will also be a witness
to the authorities (Ephesians 3:8–10), that it is *God* who
really reigns. Not Caesar but *Christ* is Lord. His victory
over evil guides the Christians' response.

From this point of view, the answers to the specific
questions in thesis 7 are clear in principle, but more
difficult in application. In principle, we Christians are
called to be in society, in the thick of the fray, resisting
evil and working for good. To describe the methods we
are called to use, we may point to a theoretical continuum
of response ranging from utter inactivity (ignoring the
evil), on the one extreme, to lethal violence (killing people
who do evil), on the other extreme.[60] Neither extreme is
acceptable for disciples of Jesus, for neither is consistent
with love. The abdicationist extreme does not take evil
seriously; the extreme of lethal violence does not take the
possibility of one's own evil seriously. Neither extreme
genuinely considers the possibility of converting the

enemy; the latter extreme, in fact, makes his repentance and reconciliation definitively impossible. In other words, we cannot resist evil either by wishing it away or by using (from our point of view) a lesser evil. We cannot combat a big lie by a little lie. We must resist evil by good, and falsehood by truth.

Our calling

We Christians, therefore, may participate in all aspects of our society which are consistent with our calling; conversely, we may not accept positions of responsibility which exclude love as the answer to evil. The extent of participation in societal structures will and should raise difficult questions for Christian believers. And in our attempts to answer them, we must maintain a genuine flexibility in decision-making. The individual Christian's conscience and the discernment of our communities of faith are essential guiding resources. In no case, however, may we Christians take positions that lead us, either personally or by the logical extension of our actions, to take the life of the enemy or evil one. This is incompatible with the way of Christ. To serve therefore in regular or revolutionary armed forces, in the military branches of the civil service, or in industries manufacturing armaments violates the Christian ethic of peace-making, doing good and loving the neighbour; indeed, God may be calling those who have jobs in these areas to take the risky step of resigning and seeking other employment.[61]

There are indeed many avenues of service and witness that are open to Christians.[62] Clearly, we will engage in the ministry and struggle of prayer for governments, our enemies and our persecutors.[63] Non-violent Christians have discovered that through prayer God, in impossibly fraught situations, has worked miracles of deliverance.[64] Christians may also, as a rule, teach in schools, hold public health positions, and serve as traffic wardens (while psychological force, and, on occasion, physical force for restraint, will be used in these occupations, we Christians should refrain from using any type of force which is not an expression of care for the well-being of the persons to whom the force is applied).[65] We may engage in trade union activities, in non-violent demonstrations and even in civil disobedience for prophetic witness. In many societies, we will not be able to serve as judges or policemen, because these occupations have been ruled out by the obligations which they have been given either to take life or to sanction the taking of life. However, in those societies (such as the UK) which have rejected the death penalty and have a largely unarmed police force, these may be appropriate avenues of Christian involvement. Significantly, the early church allowed believers to carry out police duties; but if they took life, it excommunicated them.[66]

Christians .in positions of public responsibility must recognize, however, that the laws and institutions of most societies often function to protect the self-interest of certain privileged groups of citizens. For this reason, when we Christians seek to advocate policies which express the biblical mandates for justice, peace and respect for life, we may well lose our jobs.[67] Even so, we support the efforts of fellow believers deliberately to take such positions in order to witness to the gospel; we advocate such effort not because we think that we can thereby Christianize the system, but because we seek to demonstrate Jesus' kingdom way in the structures of society.

The primary challenge to the Christian, then, is not to avoid sinful involvement; it is rather to select involvement that gives positive expression to Jesus' teachings. The challenge before us as Christians is not to be agents of *state-government* law and justice, but to be ambassadors of *God's* way of setting things right (justification) through Jesus Christ. Our vocational employment, therefore, should seek to express our Christian vocation of bearing witness to *God's* justice and *shālôm*.

Christians in today's world are a minority in virtually every society. In the UK, for example, a recent survey indicates that only 11 per cent of its populace attends church at least once a week.[68] Our Christian calling, as a significant minority, therefore, is less to preserve any society as it is, than it is to change that society so that it increasingly reflects the values of the kingdom. The most significant areas of Christian involvement will often thus not be in customary jobs in society. They will rather be in ill-defined and struggling ventures that are attempting to change it. This is not easy. The forces of the status quo are established, respectable and well-funded. In the UK, for example, Defence Sales Organization, the government agency which promotes the export of UK-manufactured weapons, has a well-paid staff of 350;[69] the Campaign Against the Arms Trade, which publicizes data concerning the export of British weaponry to countries such as Argentina, has a poorly-paid staff of two which works in constant fear of being bombed by the National Front. Similarly, there are innumerable research jobs in private defence industries and in the Ministry of Defence, which in 1980–81 had a research and development budget of £1.67 thousand million.[70] By way of contrast, those who are doing research into alternative and non-violent modes of defence are few and ill-funded: for example, the 18-month budget of the Alternative Defence Commission of the University of Bradford's School of Peace Studies is only £26,400.[71] Indeed, the most significant efforts for change may not have been thought of yet. What our desperate situation requires is Christians – reborn, filled with the Spirit, empowered to live the life of the kingdom – who will pray, think and struggle to do something creatively new.

Is war ever justifiable (thesis 7d)? Surely yes, by the government's standards. But why should the church in a theoretical, rational way formulate standards which justify religiously and morally what governments do in their more demonic role, even though as agents of God's wrath? To do this in the age of nuclear war, the church gives cause for unbelievers to suspect its sanity. Nor need we Christians say 'it is right for the power to have armies for defence' (thesis 7c). Why should we Christians need or want to *justify* the violence of the state? We have more important, and more specifically Christian, things to do. God has given us a Sword, the weapon of his Word. Using it, let us insistently call on governments to adopt policies which as much as possible will be in keeping with their assigned task of promoting good and restraining evil. Let us encourage them, for their own welfare and that of the citizens, to be a bit more non-violent and militarily modest than they think is prudent.[72] Let us point out to governments that lethal violence never achieves what its proponents maintain.[73] Let us warn them urgently of the certain consequences of their reliance upon nuclear and other weapons of indiscriminate destruction.[74] And, above all, let us individually and corporately as the church be present in the midst of society, witnessing to the newness that is in Christ and his kingdom.

Conclusion: the beginning and the end

We began this essay, of necessity, by placing our reflections in a doomsday setting. We suggested that human history may well end with God's epitaph, 'They perished in nuclear holocaust.' We conclude this essay, however, with the certain hope that God's purpose to reconcile all things in Christ will be fulfilled. The gross disparity between these two emphases raises basic questions of coherence. How could human history end in catastrophic self-destruction and yet fulfil God's purposes of reconciliation?

The only possible coherence in such disparate emphases is suggested by the biblical prophetic tradition. The Old Testament prophets as well as the book of Revelation regularly employed the imagery of cosmic judgment in which the present order of life ends and a totally new order begins.

Despite its apparent lack of coherence according to ordinary logic, the apocalyptic genre is the only one that can do justice to today's realities. There is simply no way to get from the present course of human history to the reconciliation of all things in Christ and the new heavens and the new earth, except through the purgation of judgment, described by the most potent doomsday imagery in the biblical record (Joel 3:11–16; Amos 8; Zephaniah 1:14–18; 2 Peter 3:8–13; Revelation 18; 19; 21). We do not employ this imagery and cite these texts to forecast a programme of end-time events. The imagery rather serves the purpose, as it always has in the biblical tradition, of describing a radical discontinuity in history, between the present and the future. We must therefore not press the imagery here or at the beginning of this essay in a literalistic way; nor must we ignore the reality towards which it points.

From this image of prophetic apocalypticism we make three concluding observations:

1. The present course of geo-political events, with the increasingly incomprehensible swelling of military budgets and the staggering obliterative potential of the more than 50,000 nuclear weapons in the world, is heading towards humanity's self-immolation.

2. Only a radical conversion of men and women to Christ and his kingdom values of 'justice, peace and joy in the Holy Spirit' (Romans 14:17) can avert cataclysmic destruction, unprecedented suffering for humanity, and the veritable discreation of the part of the cosmos of which we are stewards.

3. God alone knows the way through the future to the fulfilment of his purposes, a path through judgment to the reconciliation of all things in Christ.

Response to Willard Swartley and Alan Kreider

Arthur F. Holmes

The reader who has carefully examined both my essay and that of Willard Swartley and Alan Kreider may well have been surprised to find such large areas of agreement between us. In my judgment the just war tradition and the so-called 'peace Churches' share common concerns and should make common cause. We agree in resisting the evils of war and violence. We agree in protesting that nuclear war is utterly unthinkable. We agree in rejecting the idolatrous tendency in excesses of nationalism. We agree that our primary task is reconciliation and peace-making. We agree in rejecting hate, retaliation and a vengeful spirit. We agree that the final solution lies in the power of Christ's gospel and the coming of his Kingdom on earth. In all this we agree, and our disagreements must never detract from that fact.

Yet brotherly disagreements do exist, and it would be neither honest nor loving to gloss them over. They are disagreements, by and large, which run the length of church history and represent the theological divide between the Anabaptist heritage on the one hand, and that of Reformed theology on the other.

To begin with, however, I find the rhetoric exaggerated and misleading. Instead of speaking of the uses of 'force',

a more neutral term, Willard and Alan speak of 'violence'.
'All war', we are told, 'is sin' – yet their argument shows
it to be alien only to the vocation of Christians. ('Sin' is
surely not relative, but universally the same whether one
be a Christian or not.) Political and economic approaches
'mask' evil, as if they find no positive mandate today in
God's creation. Jesus stands in the prophetic 'holy war'
tradition but uses spiritual weapons only – regardless,
surely, of the allegorizing involved, regardless of Revelation 19: 11–21, and regardless of whether the Old Testament prophets ever advocate 'holy war' at all! The authors
in fact seem to confuse 'holy war' with 'just war' concepts.
They cite von Clausewitz that war is 'an act of force which
theoretically can have no limits', despite the fact that von
Clausewitz was a Hegelian militarist, not a just war ethicist, and they talk as if just war ethicists appeal to 'the
government's standards'.

Failure to make careful distinctions invites confusion.
Just war theory rejects both militarism and holy wars. It
subjects governmental standards to constant ethical scrutiny. The prophets were critics of war and violence, not
preachers of bloody crusades. War is a horrible evil to be
sure, but it does not follow that all war is 'sin', unless all
evil is sin. And to label all military action 'violence' rather
than 'force' loads the question about whether it is morally
legitimate or not. As crucial issues as these require more
careful logic.

More significant is their handling of the historical and
biblical evidence for their position. The first centuries, it
is implied, unanimously refuse Christian participation in
war. Willard and Alan cite a 1946 article by Roland
Bainton. Yet in a 1960 book he wrote: 'The position of
the Church was not absolutist, however. There were some
Christians in the army and they were not on that account
excluded from communion.'[1] He sums up the picture:

> ...until the decade A.D. 170–180 we are devoid of
> evidence; from then on the references to Christian
> soldiers increase. The numbers cannot be computed.

The greatest objection to military service appears to have been in the Hellenistic East. The Christians in northern Africa were divided. The Roman church in the late second and third centuries did not forbid epitaphs recording the military profession. The eastern frontier reveals the most extensive Christian participation in warfare, though concurrently we find there a protest against it among groups tending to ascetic and monastic ideals.

The attitude of Ecclesiastical writers toward military service on the part of Christians during the same period shows a correlation with the data on actual practice.[2]

As I pointed out in my essay, even writers who rejected the idea of Christians soldiering prayed supportively for the Emperor's army in their peace-keeping task.

The use of biblical material likewise appears too selective. God used supernatural means in Israel's battles, we are told, so that the soldiers' participation was 'incidental' to the decisive military thrust. It should be kept in mind, however, that crumbling walls (Joshua 6:20) crush people to death, and that the Red Sea drowned an army. That too is violence. Yahweh also commanded military action at times (Numbers 31; Joshua 8; 11; *etc.*), and gave instructions about recruiting soldiers and preventing needless violence (Deuteronomy 20). To say that God gave them victory in unconventional ways by no means denies participation by believers in military service. The evidence simply does not support that conclusion. Nor of course does the evidence allow us to condone all that Israel did in her wars. The conclusion must be more discriminating than either of these generalizations.

New Testament materials too are not always well interpreted. Peter's use of the sword had nothing at all to do with war: he was not a soldier, and his was not a governmental exercise of power. He was rather resisting the arrest of Jesus, potentially an act of anarchy. Jesus' rebuke to him is therefore irrelevant to the legitimacy of participating in governmental military action. Similarly, appealing to the Gospel account of non-violence towards the Roman authorities misses the point. The Romans were not only an army of occupation (one of several in the intertestamental history of Palestine), but also a peace-keeping force which stabilized the Middle East and kept it from pillage and bloodshed. A Zealot revolt would not in any case have been a defensive action by a duly consti-tuted government in the exercise of its proper powers. That question in fact is not explicitly addressed in the New Testament, unless it be by implication: neither Jesus nor the apostles, for instance, ever told soldiers to quit the military.

The most important text, however, is Romans 13: 1–7, which we both interpret in its context about love and non-retaliation. What I find missing in Willard Swartley and Alan Kreider is any reckoning with the God-given role of government in regards to distributive and retributive justice. The significance of the God-given 'sword' is ignored when we are told that Jesus 'disarmed'(!) the powers. I shall return to this shortly.

Not only, in my judgment, do Willard and Alan mis-interpret the biblical and historical evidence, they also misunderstand the just war theory. As an *ethic* it brings a moral standard to bear, by which every military cause and every military action is judged. The function of this ethic is *not to justify war*, as they repeatedly assert, but to limit it and to lead to its elimination. The only just cause (defence against unjust violent aggression) is the one inherent in God's mandate to government – not defending the church or the truth, for that would be an ideological war which the ethic condemns. The only just intention is the restoration of a just peace for friend and foe alike – not retaliation or vengeance. If these rules were followed on all sides, war would be eliminated. The just war ethic is a peace-making and peace-keeping agenda and not a licence for aggression and hate. And from Augustine around AD 400 to Paul Ramsey today it has stressed the role of love, both in seeking a just peace, and in tempering the means employed in its pursuit.

War, moreover, is not accepted in just war theory because it may be the lesser evil. That kind of calculation is part of a utilitarian ethic with its cost/benefit assessment of consequences. But a Christian ethic is not utilitarian, not just consequentialist, for some moral duties are fixed in ways that benefits are not. One such duty is to respect God's mandate to government with respect to justice and peace.

King of all creation

It is here that we reach the very core of our disagreement, and I refer the reader to the treatment of the relation of Christians to government in my essay. Willard and Alan hold to the two-kingdoms or two-vocations theology, which I reject in favour of the Reformed doctrine that Christ's Kingdom embraces all of creation, hence all the kingdoms of this world. He is, even now, King of kings and Lord of lords, whether rulers acknowledge him or not. Just as the family and the economic order and the church are mandated by God as instruments for his purpose in this world, so too is government. This holds no endorsement for any one political or economic system, any more than I think it does for any one family structure or form of church government. Nor does it deny the mingled presence of good and evil, like wheat and tares, in all these parts of the Kingdom. It does, however, assert that God works his purposes in history not only through the church as we know it, but also through the other structures he has ordained and in which also we participate.

This more Reformed theology of society, however, is opposed to the two-kingdom view, which in our authors' case sees the political order as a mask for demonic powers, a mask which Christ pulled off, showing the state to be identified with Satan's kingdom rather than that of the Christ. They support their view by taking Paul's use of 'powers' in Romans 13: 1–3 to refer to demonic agency in governments.

Elsewhere in the New Testament, Paul plainly speaks of 'powers' as a hierarchy of angelic beings. The Colossian heresy took them to be intermediaries between God and humans, but Paul insisted they are created by God (Colossians 1:16) and subservient to the power of Christ. The influence of alien, demonic powers in human affairs is therefore limited. Whether the powers of Romans 13: 1–3 are demonic is a different question. Our authors think they are. But many scholars deny that the passage refers at all to angelic beings, fallen or unfallen. Others again recognize a dual reference to both angelic beings and political powers, but stop short of making the state a mask for demons.[3] It seems plain biblically that the state as such is *neither* divine nor demonic, but is God's servant, whether rulers recognize this or not, and despite the evil aspects against which we must guard.

Of course evil influences are at work in the political as in economic and other social orders within this fallen world. Admixture of good and evil is everywhere. But the close identification of governmental with demonic power leads Willard and Alan to an almost Manichean dualism of good and evil that obscures the moral ambiguity in life, in the life of the church as well as in politics. It precludes a positive view of the role of human governments in God's governance of his creation. Yet the sword is still God-given for the sake of peace and justice, even though it is abused.

The choice between our two views, then, is not a test of biblical fidelity or Christian love, but a choice between two theologies of politics. One excludes Christian participation in governmental uses of force, the other allows it selectively. The exclusivist position is explicitly such:

Jesus 'combatted evil *solely* through the power of his prophetic word and action'.

We 'must rely *solely* upon the power of the prophetic word and suffering love'.

Yahweh triumphed in battle by miracles '*wholly* of grace and not of human works'.

The New Testament calls us to imitate Jesus '*solely* at the point of the concrete social meaning of the cross in relation to enmity and power . . . *only thus* . . . are we bound . . . to be like Jesus'.

'. . . *only* as we walk in the Spirit . . . can we live nonviolently.'

'The challenge . . . is *not* to be agents of state-government law and justice, *but* to be ambassadors of God's way . . .'

'We have *more important,* and more specifically Christian, things to do.'

'*Only* a radical conversion of men and women . . . can avert cataclysmic destruction.'

But I question the basis for such exclusivist claims, because they exclude God's grace and providential power from the political realm. It is not a matter of either/or: *either* the word and love of God *or* 'secular' means like governmental uses of force. In the Old Testament record, God employed *both,* and calls his people to *both* forms of participation. There is no secular-sacred dichotomy.

I revert therefore to the line of argument in my original position:

1. God's mandate to governments includes the selective use of limited force in defence of peace and justice against violent attack.

2. Christians may properly participate in what God mandates to governments.

3. Therefore Christians may participate selectively in governmental uses of limited force in defence of peace and justice against violent attack.

While the difference between this and what Willard Swartley and Alan Kreider advocate is extremely important, it is nonetheless not a disagreement about peace-making as such, but about the means God employs to that end, and in which we might participate.

3
A case against nuclear pacifism

Sir Frederick Catherwood

*The duty of a government · Nuclear pacifism ·
Disarmament · Mutual fears · Facing the cost of nuclear
reduction · No 'first use'*

Having read Arthur Holmes' contribution on the concept of a just war, I shall comment on his somewhat apologetic defence of the duty of government to protect the citizen, and to question his acceptance of nuclear pacifism.

The duty of a government

Arthur accepts that the civil authorities have the right to command obedience to the law, and the duty to punish 'even with the sword'. It is put, however, rather as an admission of an unpalatable fact of life, an unfortunate but necessary aberration from the law of love, and the ideals of the Sermon on the Mount. He says, 'Love alone cannot effectively resist evils in society, nor is it God's entire way of doing so.'

In this defensive attitude, Arthur Holmes runs the risk of accommodating the Christian position to the flood-tide of humanism which now controls the intellectual assumptions of most Protestant countries, and is now beginning to affect Roman Catholic countries too. Humanism does not recognize the inherent power of wickedness. It sees sin as a disease curable by human treatment, humane institutions or humane therapy. Since the rise of humanism, penal laws have been 'reformed', and crime of all kinds is rising by over 10 per cent a year. Violent crime is rising faster, and such crime among the young very much faster.

The ordinary person is bewildered. He sees a little old lady battered, and sometimes killed, for the week's old age pension in her purse; and the criminal is given a suspended sentence, and walks out free. At the end of the line, the humanist does not believe that any crime justifies the death penalty. Since death is final, and there is nothing beyond, equally nothing is worth dying for. Opinion polls show that the ordinary citizen does not follow this logic. He finds himself living in an increasingly violent society and feels that he needs protection. For that he can look only to the state. The little old lady is entitled to turn the other cheek, but the state is not. On a truly biblical view, the state has an inalienable duty to protect and to punish. Furthermore, the Noachic covenant, under which God promised that he would not bring another universal catastrophe, orders murderers to be executed (Genesis 9:5–6).

The humanist view, that nothing is worth dying for, has also affected discussion of war. 'Better red than dead' is for many people so obvious as not to be worth arguing. That is not how civil liberties were won, and certainly not how the Christian church was built. But the minority tradition of pacifism, represented by Quakers and Mennonites, has been strongly reinforced by mainstream Humanism.

None of that is, of course, an argument for war, let alone for nuclear war. We do need to remind ourselves, however, that a great many of those who influence intellectual opinion cut out of the argument at a much earlier stage than the orthodox Christian. Not for them the harrowing anxiety of deciding between a just and an unjust war, let alone the even more terrifying decisions on the use of nuclear weapons. I believe in being more positive than Arthur Holmes. Both defence against evil, and punishment of evil, are duties laid upon the government. According to 1 Peter 2:14, the government is 'sent by him

[God] to punish those who do wrong and to praise those who do right'. We must not be apologetic about a duty to be a minister of God's *wrath* (Romans 13:4).

Nuclear pacifism

I can well understand those Christians who are prepared to argue for a just war, but believe that possession of nuclear weapons is immoral. This position, however, needs better justification than Arthur Holmes gives it, arriving at his position as he does after two brief paragraphs. He does it on the pragmatic grounds that 'Complete nuclear abstinence, usually called *"nuclear pacifism"*, is therefore the only *prudent* course to follow'. If the Christian is to convince the politician, however, he must do it on Christian grounds and not on the political grounds of 'prudence'.

While we must all wish to abolish nuclear arms, the present situation, in which several nations possess them, cannot be dealt with by nuclear pacifism, which is a refusal ever to use them, and so logically a commitment to destroy one's nuclear weapons while others keep theirs. We must, I believe, keep our own nuclear capacity until the weapons pointed against us are dismantled. Meanwhile we should use ours only to destroy the nuclear weapons on the other side. We should never use them in a first strike, nor to destroy cities nor deliberately to aim at populated areas. Unilateral nuclear disarmament would, in my view, be a failure in the government's duty to resist evil and to protect our own and other citizens from evil.

Although the orthodox Christian position requires the state to protect its citizens, Christian morality knows nothing of 'total war'. It enjoins the use of minimum force. It allows attacks on the armed forces which threaten the country, but not on innocent civilians. No-one believes that a war can be fought without civilian casualties, for few battlefields are completely clear of civil population – not even the Western desert in the Second World War. And frightened soldiers fighting for their lives do not always discriminate as they should. Military policy, however, more coolly calculated by governments and armed services, should make conscious and positive attempts to avoid risk to civilians.

Oliver Cromwell was a Christian, a statesman and a great general, and in calling Drogheda to surrender he followed the usual custom of guaranteeing civilians only on orderly surrender. He had, in the event, to take the city by force, but the 'usual custom' is not sufficient justification, and he has never been forgiven for the consequent slaughter of civilians.

That judgment is right; human life is sacred. God gave it, and only God can take it. The only exception in this divine law is that someone who despises the sanctity of life, and takes that of another, forfeits his own; the 'powers that be' must bear the sword. But force must be used as narrowly as is possible for the defence of the citizen. Jesus said that two swords for the self-defence of the eleven apostles was 'enough', but forbad the use of one of them against the authorities.

In military defence, that limitation puts any weapon of mass destruction, any weapon which cannot be limited to military targets, into a prohibited class.

So how have the democracies of all countries, which put the highest value on the individual, accumulated such a horrendous array of weapons of mass destruction? If we are to get out of our dilemma, we need to understand how we got into it.

Few people today defend the bombing of Hiroshima and Nagasaki. It was done to shorten the war, in the belief that the fanatical suicidal Japanese would never surrender, that thousands more lives would be lost, and that it was better that those lives should be enemy lives rather than those of allies and civilians caught in the battle. Similarly the 'fire-storm' bombing of Dresden was meant to shorten a war in which millions were butchered in the last year of a fanatical, racist dictatorship.

The effect, however, was to make the nuclear bomb a credible weapon in Anglo-American hands. And the

Americans then threatened its use to fill the gap left by the departure of their main armies from central Europe. The Soviet Union, inevitably, developed its own weapons. Instead of re-building its traditional defence in Western Europe, NATO preferred to retain the threat of a nuclear response to conventional attack. The nuclear weapon was cheaper; it gave 'more bang for the buck'. When the 'think-tanks' began to think the unthinkable, to speculate on actual nuclear war 'scenarios', and to ask whether America would really risk retaliation against Chicago in order to save Europe from conventional attack, it became clear that the doctrine of 'massive retaliation' did not really stand up to examination. Why, at that point, did both sides not call a halt?

There seem to me to have been a number of reasons for drifting on, which still exist. First and foremost, NATO still needed some means of stopping a conventional attack if it was not prepared to pay for conventional defence. General Rogers, Commander of NATO (Europe), has estimated that if we were to rely on conventional defence, spending would have to go up by a third. Politicians doubt whether the public would be prepared to stand that kind of increase. The Generals, however, regard nuclear weapons as a cheap and dangerous response to attack, and want them removed from the battlefield. Field Marshal Lord Carver is the most informed and eloquent advocate of that point of view. The Generals believe that Soviet generals facing the same problem would take the same point of view and that, as a start, battlefield nuclear weapons could be removed from Central Europe. While we refuse to spend more on conventional defence, however, we have either to rely on nuclear battlefield weapons, or to swing over to pacifism and abandon the defence of ourselves and our allies.

On the week of the Bonn peace march in the Autumn of 1981, I spoke to a group of Christian students in the University of Dusseldorf. Faced with the stationing of nuclear cruise missiles in the German Federal Republic, their inclination was to move, not to nuclear pacifism, but to complete pacifism. We spent three hours in discussion, and at the end most of them accepted that a Christian did not also have to be a pacifist.

On the other hand movements such as the Campaign for Nuclear Disarmament will understandably not persuade the majority of citizens if they appear to leave their country defenceless. It seems to me that a Christian argument which recognizes the need for self-defence and the necessity to pay for it, but which condemns reliance on weapons of mass-destruction, is not only right, but would actually gain the support of the majority of citizens if it was an option. That, however, is not an argument which is currently being put by CND.

Disarmament

Once we cease to rely on weapons of mass destruction for our defence we are left with the problem of disposing of the stockpile. That is insoluble today, not just because the Soviets are difficult and suspicious, but because we, on our side, actually need the weapons to supplement our conventional defence in Western Europe. Once we became able to conduct a conventional defence without them, then they could, as the military commanders on both sides wish, be removed from the weaponry of NATO and the Warsaw pact. Although there is an iron curtain for civilians down the centre of Europe, there has been no peace treaty. The three allied Commanders-in-Chief in Berlin all worked with their Soviet counterpart. Both sides have access to the other side as of right, not only in Berlin but beyond. My wife and I have travelled in the car of the British Commander-in-Chief through Checkpoint Charlie under strict instructions not to offer our passports for examination, since his car travelled as of right. Both sides seem to be very well informed on the dispositions and attitudes of the other side. I do not believe it is wishful thinking to accept that no military Commander-in-Chief, on either side, wants to face the alternative between the destruction of his army and a nuclear holocaust. All nuclear weapons, including battlefield nuclear weapons, are secured by coded controls to prevent unauthorized use, so that a junior commander in danger of being overrun cannot put a nuclear shell up the barrel and fire it off. But, while we rely on battlefield nuclear weapons to defend Western Europe, there would be pressure early on to grant either 'selective release' or, more dangerously, 'general release' for use in case of need.

The military men to whom I have spoken do not believe that there would then be a civilized exchange of views on the hot-line between the Kremlin and the White House. They point out that the side which gets in the first strike of intercontinental ballistic missiles will be able to 'take out' most of the land-based nuclear missile system of the other side. All of those sites will be targeted by satellites within a few years. The US fixed bases are more vulnerable to a Soviet pre-emptive strike. Although the power attacked would fire back through the attack, the temptation to pre-empt the other side would be immense.

The present safeguard against a pre-emptive strike is the threat that if the NATO land-based missiles were to be destroyed, the sea-based missiles would destroy Russian cities. Without this threat the policy of retaliation ceases to be credible; but with the threat, it ceases to be moral. For it threatens what Christians believe to be wrong, the deliberate killing of civilians, and that on a scale never before contemplated in human history.

Some argue that, even if the action is immoral, the threat is not, for it is the threat which has preserved the peace. But a threat to commit an immoral act is itself immoral. If we would not do it, it is a deceit, and while one man might successfully deceive another, it is hardly likely that a dozen governments, resting on democratic election by over 400 million people, can successfully act out a lie. It is surely more reliable to preserve the peace by a strong, and therefore credible, conventional defence force than through a scarcely credible threat by civilized countries nominally professing Christian standards to engage in a slaughter without precedent in human history.

A case against nuclear pacifism

We must, if we are to defend ourselves, have a deterrent against conventional attack in which we ourselves believe, one which we would actually use without hesitation or fear, which would be known to be capable of halting the attack. That can be only an adequate conventional force, which we should put in place as soon as possible. We have to recognize, however, that it is not an easy decision for the Germans, who are in the front line of such an attack, and who might lose considerable ground before it was halted. The present military thinking is that this problem can only be overcome either by having our forces capable of immediate counter-attack, or by at least holding guided weapons which could reach and destroy the attack's support forces.

Where does this differ from a position such as that of the Campaign for Nuclear Disarmament, and that of nuclear pacifism? For what reason would a Christian wish to hold on to weapons which cannot be used? The most important difference is that CND, for example, makes no alternative proposals on defence. Adequate conventional defence would enable us to defend ourselves, without short-range nuclear weapons, against conventional attack, and this would remove the major obstacles to multilateral disarmament. Both sides can make a start on the removal of the battlefield nuclear weapons, and then proceed to the negotiation of the stockpile. But – and this is the other difference – if we are to remove the stockpile we must be able to remove it on both sides, otherwise the threat remains. For one country to remove its own stockpile does little to remove the threat overhanging mankind. It is no part of Christian love or duty to opt out, trying to protect ourselves while leaving others vulnerable.

In the meantime, the NATO alliance retains its right to maintain and place weapons to destroy the nuclear weapons aimed at American and European targets. That is a fundamentally different position from the present twin threats that we may make 'first use' of nuclear weapons against a conventional attack, and that we may use them against civilian populations in cities. These are the two

75

threats that a Christian must find it especially hard to square with his conscience. 'No first use' and 'no deliberate use against mainly civilian populations' are the decisive positions on which Christians must stand. Once we no longer need the weapons to defend ourselves, they are relegated to the role of bargaining counter and, during bargaining, to the role of temporary deterrent against *nuclear* aggression.

Mutual fears

The late Professor Sir Herbert Butterfield compared the problem of nuclear disarmament to the dilemma of two armed criminals locked in the same cell, neither trusting the other enough to drop their gun out of the barred window. We cannot understand the dilemmas of disarmament unless we understand that the fears are mutual and merited. After all, the West invented the nuclear weapon, used it and has consistently relied on the threat to use it again. The Soviet Union did not invent it, has not used it and its threats have been responsive. It lost 20 million combatant and civilian dead in an attack from Western Europe well within the memory of the present leaders. We should at least be able to understand their suspicions and believe that their immense armaments are not entirely a product of a Communist plot to rule the world. It is therefore conceivable that they may really want to disarm and that their expressed fears of a nuclear holocaust may be genuine. We should ask ourselves also, if American military attitudes sometimes worry us in Europe, what must they do to the Russians?

The rulers of the Soviet Union, however, are not angels either. They are the last European imperial power and in Hungary, Czechoslovakia and Afghanistan they have used their power to hold and enlarge their empire; in Poland, they have threatened to do so by putting their armed forces 'on manoeuvre' in and around the nation in response to the rise of the free trade union, 'Solidarity'. They seem to have imperialist ambitions in Africa and South East Asia, and their powerful modern navies sail the seven seas, although they have little international trade to protect. An East German Ambassador, when once asked why the Soviets had such an immense navy, replied, 'I asked one of our own admirals that and he said, "I don't know, it worries us too." '

This situation explains why successive governments in Britain have favoured multilateral disarmament, and have been against the build-up of nuclear arsenals, but are not in favour of denying ourselves the ability to destroy the weaponry of the other side without corresponding and verifiable reduction on both sides.

It is, of course, arguable that *any* use of nuclear weapons causes civilian casualties; that even the destruction of a missile silo in Siberia would cause *some* fall-out. So, both the hard-liners for full nuclear response and the CND argue that no intermediate position is valid, and there is no safe route back. While that may have been true in the past, however, I don't think it is true now. New missiles are now very precise. Their warheads have lower yields and are no bigger than they need to be for the immediate task of destroying the weaponry aimed against them. It is possible to have very much bigger bombs, but it is not necessary. (One of the arguments for having the Trident submarines to succeed the present Polaris submarines is that Trident's warhead contains separately and precisely targetable bombs, while Polaris is not precise and can be used only against big targets such as inhabited cities.) But we cannot yet limit all our weapons, or their fall-out, to Soviet nuclear weapons, and we cannot target their submarines, and the converse is true for the Soviet Union; so the argument for multilateral disarmament is strong on both sides.

Meantime the Soviet Union have begun placing in the USSR the SS20 missile, which is an accurate mobile ballistic missile. This has a range of 4,000 miles and can hit a target in Western Europe from as far back as the Ural mountains on Russia's Asian border. Since the missile is easily moved, it is, like the nuclear submarine, not vulnerable, unlike silo-based ballistic missiles, to tightly-targeted counter-attack.

In response to this weapon, NATO has deployed the Cruise missile, a pilotless plane, guided by a map in the nose-cone whose computerized radar-sensing system costs as much as the rest of the weapon. In densely populated Western Europe, however, with its free and open society, it is not so easy to hide the missile. Even though dispersable in a crisis, they would have to be kept meantime in guarded areas which would become known and targeted. The proposal of NATO governments to site the Cruise missiles in Europe caused consternation, and triggered the peace movement in Germany and the revival of CND in Britain. It was meant as an assurance by the Americans that they would not leave Europe open to the SS20, which could not reach America, but they would put in their own weapons on European soil to match this new accurate and elusive Soviet weapon. But the prospective appearance of a nuclear weapon in the villages of Europe has raised questions all over again on nuclear weapons, not just on the dangers of escalation to big intercontinental weapons and retaliation against cities, but on the feasibility of fighting a war with battlefield nuclear weapons in highly-populated Germany.

Facing the cost of nuclear reduction

It is argued by most NATO governments that it is necessary to station the Cruise to have the SS20 removed. The Geneva INF talks aim to do this, either under the 'zero option' or under an alternative which, to begin with, greatly reduces the numbers on each side. It might be sensible to go on to the removal of all targetable weapons from Europe, making it a nuclear-free zone between the super powers. But that can be done only at the cost of adding a third to the defence budget for more expensive conventional weapons.

This would leave us in an alliance which possessed nuclear weapons, but did not rely on them; an alliance committed to multilateral negotiations, but with the vital addition that it would still be capable of defending itself when those negotiations were successful. We would remain in a dangerous world where there would still be 'wars and rumours of wars', but we would no longer live a hair's breadth from the holocaust.

If most people come to believe that war must inevitably mean nuclear war and, with it, the end of life for most people in Europe and North America, then many will become pacifists. The danger of relying on nuclear weapons for defence is that we shall lose the will to defend ourselves. The Christian view is that government is obliged under divine mandate to defend its citizens, and that obligation would be undermined.

More dangerous, the nuclear deterrent will not be credible if most people come to believe that, whatever governments may threaten by way of deterrence, they would not actually risk using weapons which would trigger Soviet nuclear strikes against our crowded urban society. Even if it was morally acceptable to threaten what it would be wrong to do, that policy runs the risk of all lies; in the end, no-one believes you.

If, then, the only credible deterrent against Soviet tanks coming across the Iron Curtain is enough conventional anti-tank guided missiles to stop them, we need to face up to the cost.

No 'first use'

Professor Michael Howard, who is perhaps our most distinguished military historian, wrote to *The Times* in February 1983: 'Thirty years ago, in 1953, the United States and her European allies deliberately took the decision to rely on "nuclear deterrence" for one very simple reason; it was cheap. It gave us . . . "a bigger bang for the buck" . . . Many Christians, of whom I am one, see no moral dilemma inherent in the possession and, if necessary, the use of nuclear weapons to deter their use against our own people . . . It is the *initiation* of the use of these weapons that causes so many of us such profound concern: and we have come to depend on that initiation because we have acquiesced in a decision to maintain a standard of living far higher than that of our adversaries rather than provide the resources for a convincing defence by non-nuclear means of the territories of Western Europe. This surely is a matter not of simple resource allocations but a fundamental moral choice and on which the churches have not only the right but the duty to pronounce ... and provide us with the guidance which Christians of all denominations are so anxiously seeking today.' The General Synod of the Church of England has now provided this guidance. It is against 'first use'. I have tried to show why and how I reach the same view myself, and what I believe the practical consequences of that view to be.

Response to
Sir Frederick Catherwood

Alan Kreider

In his 'case against nuclear pacifism', Sir Frederick Catherwood makes several valuable points. He well appreciates
the non-angelic nature of both super-powers, and is
correct in his observation that their 'fears are mutual and
merited'. He is equally aware of the gravity of the current
geopolitical situation; we are, he reminds us, within 'a
hair's breadth of the holocaust'. And his correct assessment that the Polaris missiles (upon which British nuclear
forces will depend throughout the 1980s) are imprecise
and 'can be used only against big targets such as inhabited
cities' places them – by his own criteria – into a 'prohibited
class' of intrinsically immoral weaponry.

Elsewhere, however, Sir Frederick is less illuminating.

1. Sir Frederick's negative assessment of Arthur
Holmes's just war-based nuclear pacifism is based on judgments which are unfair. Nowhere, for example, does
Arthur deny that governments may engage in retributive
judicial and military activity. But as a scrupulous just war
adherent, he does insist that *there must be limits* to this
violence if justice is to be maintained. Furthermore Arthur
(along with pacifist Christians like myself) would never
doubt that there are causes that are worth dying for; he
is rather stating that there are no causes worth killing for

81

on an unlimited scale. Least fair of all, surely, are Sir Frederick's criticisms of Arthur Holmes for being 'off-hand','pragmatic' and hasty ('arriving at his position . . . after two brief paragraphs'). On the contrary, Arthur simply applies with care a traditional Christian moral stance (the just war theory) to the weaponry and strategy of our day. And his repudiation of nuclear weapons comes, not as an illogical burst of insight, but as the culmination of a sustained biblical and ethical argument. One can disagree with the just war theory on biblical grounds, as I do (see Willard Swartley's and my article); but to pretend to maintain the just war theory without denouncing nuclear weapons is, in my view, to commit a *non sequitur*.

2. The standard by which Sir Frederick judges Arthur's article (argument 'on Christian grounds and not on the political grounds of "prudence" ') is also useful in evaluating Sir Frederick's own work. Unfortunately, as one does so, one finds it hard to avoid the conclusion that Sir Frederick establishes his proposed alternative policies (summarized in points 3–5 below) far more by emphatic assertion than by biblical or theological argument; and he then proceeds, on the basis of reasoning that seems manifestly prudential, to argue a lengthy political case. This is not to say that Sir Frederick's policies are unreasonable; they are in fact in keeping with an emerging consensus among Western strategic thinkers. But because they are advanced – by both Sir Frederick and others – by a mode of argument that is primarily secular, they should be scrutinized with care by Christians.

3. Sir Frederick asserts that 'we must keep our own nuclear capacity until the weapons pointed against us are dismantled'. This appears sensible, but it in fact means that Britain's weapons are being determined by the weapons of her enemy, and not by the intrinsic morality of those weapons. Furthermore, it is sensible only if deterrence is stable. This, however, is no longer the case, for the technologically-enabled precise targeting of new missiles (which pleases Sir Frederick for moral reasons) is enabling both sides to move towards a first-strike capability.

Finally, by contending that nuclear weapons are necessary for Britain's security, Sir Frederick is giving the 151 out of 157 sovereign states in the world who are still non-nuclear an impetus to acquire nuclear weapons for their security. His logic leads towards universal proliferation, and the result is an increasing insecurity for everybody. As the Alternative Defence Commission has recently argued,[1] the UK is more likely to achieve relative security through non-nuclear defence strategies. If the government, like the Campaign for Nuclear Disarmament, took these strategies seriously, we would not need to stockpile or use the weapons which Christian morality condemns.

4. Sir Frederick would limit British use to precisely targetable nuclear weapons which could 'destroy the nuclear weapons on the other side'. This sounds discriminate, even antiseptic. In fact – given the nature of even the most accurate nuclear weapons – their use would lead to immense, indiscriminate suffering. It is not simply that these weapons often go astray, or that arresting escalation short of all-out nuclear war would be a 'miracle'.[2] It is also that in the UK, as in many other countries, nuclear weapons are sited close to centres of civilian population, which would be destroyed along with the weapons by blast and fire. Furthermore, counterforce nuclear attacks (against hardened targets such as silos and bunkers) must primarily be 'ground-bursts', which produce the plumes of lethal radioactive fall-out which kill civilians hundreds of miles from the explosions.[3] If one 'intends' only to destroy weapons while anticipating that in fact one will kill millions of civilians, one is engaging in moral sophistry. It is thus hard to see any essential moral difference between the anti-city Polaris missiles which Sir Frederick condemns (he is *so* close to nuclear pacifism!) and the more precise Trident missiles which he somehow manages to find acceptable.

5. Sir Frederick opposes the first use of nuclear weapons. This means, apparently, that he favours the second use of nuclear weapons, in retaliatory or revenge strikes. I question, however, that biblical morality would

find it preferable to have two decimated populations rather than one. I also pray that it is not the historic mission of the West to destroy the Christian Church in Russia, which the Soviet state itself has not been able to eradicate.

In sum, Sir Frederick disappoints because, when faced with nuclear weapons whose monstrous evil he almost recognizes, he is unable to speak a clear 'no'. As such he is trapped in a 1,600-year-old Christian tradition which has found it difficult to place limits on warfare, and has given moral sanction to each 'improved' weapon which technology has given us.

It is hard to turn around. As Professor Sir Herbert Butterfield, who was a member of Christian CND, commented, 'When we seem caught in a relentless historical process, our machines enslaving us, and our weapons turning against us, we must certainly not expect to escape save by an unusual assertion of the human spirit.'[4] Thousands of Christians – just war adherents as well as pacifists, theologians as well as lay persons – are now making such an assertion. In response to nuclear weapons, the two great traditions of Christian thinking about warfare are thus, at long last, working together.

4
The case for all-out pacifism

Robert E. D. Clark

Resisting evil · Who should resist evil? · Can war ever be right? · Is there a criterion for justifiable war? · Christians in the armed forces? · Are some methods of war totally wrong? · On glorying in war · Bible teaching · Early Christian history · Examples set by other Christians

Those of us who agreed to participate in this Symposium have been asked to address ourselves particularly to answering a series of questions posed by the Editor. I shall therefore start by quoting these questions and answering them to the best of my ability from a Christian pacifist point of view. After that I shall consider, more directly, the teaching of the Bible on Christian pacifism.

In answering these questions I am, of course, giving a personal point of view. The need for brevity will perforce make some of this section seem unduly dogmatic. So please add to all I say, 'It is my opinion that. . .'.

Resisting evil

(a) *Do you agree that 'evil should be resisted – if necessary by force – or is force (violence) always wrong? Should evil in society be countered by society only by "overcoming evil with good"?'*

Yes, evil must be resisted. But the question 'by whom?', to which we shall return, must also be asked.

Is force (violence) ever right? Yes, I think it is. It might be necessary to use it to stop cruelty to a child, or an animal, or to restrain an insane person. In emergencies it is also sometimes difficult to see how evil can be overcome by good with sufficient speed to stop disaster.

But 'force' is an ambiguous word. As a boy I was at one period lazy at my lessons and was soundly caned for it: that caning did me a world of good. I knew that the master concerned wished me well and within a few days I felt quite grateful to him! I still am. But even as a schoolboy I reflected that the force (violence), to which I had been subjected, differed from the violence which the boys in the Officers' Training Corps were trained to use. I imagined what my feelings might have been if, when I got my sums wrong, I had my fingers cut off one by one by way of punishment. *That* was what war was about – about men blinded, gassed, maimed and left to suffer all their days for the 'sin' of having been born foreigners, for joining the forces of their fatherland, for condoning the sins of which their rulers were guilty, or for just living in a house which happened to be bombed or shelled.

Yes, force (violence) can be right if it is compatible with the Golden Rule ('Whatever you wish that men would do to you, do so to them', Matthew 7:12), but hardly otherwise. Anger, too, can sometimes be right (Jesus could be angry), but not if it is prolonged or leads to lack of self-control. 'Be angry but do not sin; do not let the sun go down on your anger' (Ephesians 4:26).

We have been thinking of force in two senses: force which is compatible with the Golden Rule, and force which at the personal level is wholly incompatible with this Rule. No-one, for example, wants to be killed or wounded by a foreign army, guerrilla or thief.

Today, however, force is often thought of in yet a *third* sense, especially in the poorer countries. Ellul[1] extends its meaning to cover extravagant life-style in places where many are in need of the essentials of life. The landless, homeless and hungry, like Lazarus of old, may feel forcefully, indeed violently, suppressed by the luxury-loving rich who in effect seem to deny them the essentials of life. The behaviour of the rich is (or can be) evil, but it may be permitted by the law of the land. Often it cannot be resisted without breaking that law. Whence terrorism and bombing.

The Christian is in no position to resist evil of this kind by force or violence. He has no God-given warrant to kidnap corrupt rulers and law-makers, or the rich pluto-crats of industry. 'Vengeance is mine: I will repay' is God's word. When the kingdom of God has come in its fullness and Christ is king of all the earth, he will invite his saints to rule the nations with a rod of iron (Revelation 2:27, *etc.*). If we attempt to forestall the future we shall make mistakes ('. . .lest in gathering the weeds you root up the wheat along with them. . .', Matthew 13:29).

We see, then, that the seemingly simple question, 'May a Christian use force (violence)?' can be interpreted in three ways, according to the three interpretations we place upon force. The use of force in the first sense is or may be right; the other two definitely wrong.

'Should evil in society be countered *by society* (*sic*) only by overcoming evil with good?' This question lies outside our terms of reference. I take it that we are trying to discover the duty of a Christian who seeks to follow the Lord. Society, in general, though it includes Christians, is not Christian. Christians, like agnostics, Jews, Muslims and others, can make useful suggestions as to how society should react to evil. If, however, ways and means too obviously Christian in character are proposed, they are likely to be rejected. We shall return to this question later.

Who should resist evil?

(b) If *evil should be resisted in society, even if necessary by force, then by whom should it be resisted? Can the Christian share in this task as a minister of God's wrath? In practice, can a Christian be a policeman or a judge, traffic warden, prison officer or even a schoolteacher charged with discipline and punishment?*

The word 'can' is inappropriate. Of course a Christian *can* do more or less as he pleases, but his work will be tried by fire (1 Corinthians 3:13). The required word is *may*, not *can*.

If evil should be resisted, by whom should it be resisted? We shall answer, of course, 'By the servants of God.' But who are God's servants?

The Bible distinguishes clearly between *two* classes of people who do God's will, two classes of servants or ministers of God. Godly Israelites and Christians are servants of God and are so spoken of repeatedly. But because God rules over the affairs of men, those who act wickedly often do his will unknowingly and so are also his servants. In the Old Testament Joseph's brothers were God's servants in that they sold him into Egypt; later Joseph could say to them, 'It was not you who sent me here, but God' (Genesis 45:8). Pharaoh was God's servant raised up so that the name of the Lord should be proclaimed in all the earth (Romans 9:17).

Nebuchadnezzar is called God's servant (Jeremiah 25:9; 27:6) and so is Cyrus (Isaiah 45). Such men were raised 'for the sake of my servant Jacob, and Israel my chosen'.

The teaching of the New Testament is the same. It is God who gives Pilate the power to release or to kill (John 19:10–11). It is God who sends both 'the emperor as supreme' (even Nero!) and governors 'to punish those who do wrong and to praise those who do right' (1 Peter 2:13–14). So we must be 'Submissive to rulers and authorities' (Titus 3:1), even though their official positions are seemingly but creations of men (Romans 13:1, Gk). We are to pay to Caesar what is Caesar's when taxes are demanded. In short, it is our duty to live as servants of God, to honour all men, to love the brotherhood, to fear God and to honour the emperor (or his modern equivalent) (1 Peter 2:16–17). In the wider biblical sense all who serve God, knowingly or unknowingly, are servants of God – wicked rulers as well as saints.

Paul argues that, because secular authorities are sent by God, those who resist them will incur judgment, for the authority is 'the servant of God to execute his wrath on the wrongdoer' (Romans 13:1–7). The church benefits from the disciplined society created by those whom God has set up to govern. On more than one occasion Paul owed his life to the intervention of the Roman power. All of this is basic Christian teaching and it seems obvious that the authorities Paul refers to are servants of God in the same sense as were Joseph's brothers, Pharaoh or Nebuchadnezzar. It would be perverse to argue that, because Joseph's brothers served God in selling their brother, I should be justified in behaving as they did. And equally perverse, surely, to argue that because servants of the state, even wicked emperors, administer the wrath of God, I should be prepared to administer it too! On the one occasion on which the disciples began to think along this dangerous line Jesus replied at once, 'You know not what manner of spirit you are of' (Luke 9:55).

May a Christian join the professions named? I think the answer must depend upon the motives. If, in joining one of them, I say, 'I want to help God as minister of wrath', then the answer is No. But other motives are possible. The would-be policeman or prison officer might make choice of his career in order to help and to love criminals whom otherwise he would not encounter at all. He might have to punish, but it would go against the grain and he would always act in such a way (like my schoolmaster) as to make it obvious that he did not enjoy that side of his work, and that justice was more than balanced by kindness and consideration. Despite his official position, he would not think of himself as a minister of God's wrath, but of God's love. For fine examples of true practical Christianity on the part of wardens at Grendon prison, who shamed at least one hardened criminal by sheer goodness, see A. K. Munro's *Autobiography of a Thief* (1972). Peter Thompson[2] tells of a prison officer who would turn on the light for him early so that he could read the Bible and who would often come and pray with him.

May a Christian be a judge? Here the case is probably different, for the judge's job may consist of judging and little else. Also Jesus says that his disciples are not to judge – 'Judge not, that ye be not judged' (Matthew 7:1). We must not be confused here by the use of words, for we use the verb 'to judge' in two senses. Judging as a judge judges involves passing a sentence, or punishing; but judging in the sense of forming an opinion as to whether someone has acted rightly or wrongly does not. The first usage is the one usually associated with judging in the Bible and I see no reason to doubt that this is what Jesus meant. In the second sense Jesus himself, though he said that he had not come to judge the world, certainly judged the Pharisees; Paul also judged the Judaizers and John the Baptist judged Herod. Jesus could hardly have meant that his disciples were not to form opinions concerning evil or were not to speak against it! We may fairly conclude, then, that it is wrong for a Christian to be a judge.

If I were a judge I should certainly find the strain intolerable. In judging others I should think of what Jesus said, 'Let him who is without sin among you be the first to throw a stone' (John 8:7). Remembering *that*, how could I be impartial in my judgments? Only, surely, by turning myself into a Jekyll-Hyde sort of personality, one part of me ignoring the existence of the other. If that is not to serve two masters, which Jesus says is impossible, what is?

Add to that the duty of a judge to administer oaths in court (save to such as wish to affirm) – oaths which Jesus expressly forbad (for to take an oath is to invite God to judge you if you falter, whereas a Christian when he sins should seek God's forgiveness, not his judgment) – and it is hard to see how a judge who follows Jesus can live with his conscience undefiled. Even so, there may be exceptions and all things are possible with God.

There are those who would say that because Christians have higher standards than other men, they will make better judges *etc.* than others. I fancy the reverse is true. Secular historians, such as Gibbon and Lecky, held that in the Middle Ages the influence of Christianity was such as to make the world a worse place than it might otherwise have been. If they were right, it is because the church, mixing its morals with those of the world, becomes Babylon the mother of harlots in whom is 'found the blood of prophets and of saints, and of all who have been slain on earth' (Revelation 18:24). It is said that in our own day the Russians have researched into the methods of the Inquisition in order to find more effective and crueller ways of torturing men – ways invented by the church, not by godless men.

Can war ever be right?

(c) *If we agree that, within the state, evil must sometimes be resisted by force and evil-doers restrained and punished, does this extend to international peace-keeping? Could it ever be right to wage war, for instance to defend the Jews from extermination by Hitler, or for a state to fight a purely defensive war against invasion?*

Since the duty of the Christian and the duty of the state do not always coincide, these questions are not questions to which the Christian, as a Christian, need look for pat answers. The Christian should make known what he believes, and in this way exercise influence, but his advice may be unheeded.

If he seeks to advise secular authorities, the Christian must bear in mind that it is no use for the state to try to enforce moral demands if the standard of ethics presupposed is unlikely to commend itself to a majority of people. The ethical standard assumed when new laws are made should be the highest acceptable to the population at large; if the standard is set higher than this, laws will be disregarded. If, for example, divorce, abortion, smoking and drinking alcohol were made illegal, divorces, abortions and smoking would continue clandestinely, while illegal stills would multiply with disastrous effects – as once happened in America. The passing of good 'Christian' laws rarely raises moral standards – if, indeed, it ever does. It is the hearts, the desires, of men that need changing and this is where Christianity comes in.

If it is generally accepted that force should be used on occasion, its use (after every effort at diplomacy) in international peace-keeping might well be 'right' from a

Robert E. D. Clark

national and secular point of view. The same might even
be true of a purely defensive war if we were invaded.
However, such a war would almost certainly escalate into
something much more terrible. If the foreign invader were
armed with the scientific weapons of today, how would it
be possible to repel him without sinking to his level, or
even below this level if guerrillas came into action? No
Christian should join in such a defensive war.

A purely defensive war being unthinkable, Christians
should try to persuade people that the safer, wiser, more
moral and more Christian policy would be to welcome
the enemy, feed him, afford him opportunity to express
his views, ask his advice where he thinks we are in the
wrong, respect his officers, and co-operate with them in
every possible way that is right and ethical. The presence
of foreign soldiers would be uncomfortable for a time:
there would be instances of rape (enemy officers might
help to prevent it). Unfortunately sexual offences are
common whenever men are dragged away from their families; our own soldiers when abroad are sometimes far from
guiltless. Above all, foreign Christians must be befriended
by our churches. Other like-minded people might also be
linked up – such as Jews, Muslims, and members of fringe
Christian sects. There would be suffering and inconvenience, for sure, but immeasurably less than would be caused
by retaliation using weapons. It would be necessary to
comply with many orders issued by a foreign army, but
(with the aid of trade unions) an absolute refusal to do
what was wrong – such as the making and transporting
of munitions of war – would be imperative. Some might
be killed for their refusal to comply with demands, but
perhaps not many. But to make such a method effective
it would be necessary for well over half the population to
agree to try the experiment. Even if only a few started a
shooting war, that war might escalate. Armed home troops
would have to be kept well away.

In view of the truly dreadful consequences which might
follow if a shooting war were to start again, advice such
as the above, which is based not on ethics but on self-

interest, is perhaps the only advice which a Christian can give to a nation which, like ours, is not Christian. It must be admitted that, at the present time, such views, though spreading, rarely meet with a favourable response. If as a nation we persist in refusing to obey the Lord's command to love our enemies, it may well be that the slowly grinding mills of God will have to grind again. 'If thou hadst known, even thou, at least in this thy day, the things which belong unto thy peace!' (a peace which now rests on the satanic nuclear deterrent) 'but now they are hid from thine eyes' (Luke 19:42, AV).

What about a war to defend others – 'the Jews from extermination by Hitler', for instance? Here fighting would merely make matters much worse. Before the Second World War Hitler tried to export Jews from Germany, to turn such as remained into second-class citizens and to prevent marriages between Aryans and Jews. Escape from Germany was easy and, though some Jews suffered in concentration camps, there was as yet no thought of the 'final solution'. The mass exterminations which followed would have been impossible, but for the fighting. War fanned Hitler's hatred of the Jews who, to his way of thinking, were on the side of the Allies. Fighting created the conditions necessary for the holocaust. Does fighting protect minorities?

The arguments we have been thinking about are of the secular kind. They might possibly be used to persuade a secular power not to go to war, but they will not seem compelling to a Christian who believes that his Lord has absolutely forbidden the sword to his followers. Jesus says that it is no use calling him Lord, Lord and ignoring his commands: to do so is to build one's house on the sand (Luke 6:46–49).

Is there a criterion for justifiable war?

(d) *Can we discover a criterion for what is a justifiable, and what is not a justifiable, war?*

Just possibly we can. But what possible use would

discovering it serve? If, at the start, the war was justifiable, the means by which it was conducted would soon fall foul of the criterion. The Nobelist scientist R.P. Feynman was invited to help at Los Alamos in the making of the atomic bomb. He reflected on the horror of misusing science in this way, but in view of what seemed at the time to be the very real danger that Hitler might have the bomb first, he consented. Hitler was defeated before the bomb was made, but Feynman has recounted on TV how that, although the *only* reason for making the bomb now no longer held good (there was not the remotest possibility that the Japanese would develop it before the Allies), the need for rethinking his position did not even occur to him. When the bomb was dropped on Hiroshima the Los Alamos scientists were beside themselves with joy: they spent the night drinking and shouting. No matter what the original justification for a war might be in the first place, does not all war develop independently of justification?

In 1939 a war against Hitler seemed justifiable enough. I tried earnestly to dissuade a student friend of mine from joining the RAF. It was useless. Then I said, 'Suppose it comes to the point and you are ordered to bomb women and children in Germany. Will you do it?' I shall never forget the look of horror in his eyes as he looked at me, in astonishment. 'I am absolutely certain', he said, 'that the British government will *never* order me to do such a thing.' Today Martin Middlebrook[3] calculates that about half the entire effort of the RAF in the Second World War was devoted to the night bombing of German cities. There, the young men had been called up: those left to take the brunt were old people, women and children. Little children were roasted alive in their thousands. Firestorms raged in the streets, blowing away the burning clothes of those who fled for refuge and incinerating the naked victims, their feet stuck in the burning molten asphalt of the roads. Schoolboys, not soldiers, were left to man the guns.

In private some of the air crews remarked to one another that if England lost the war, they would be branded as war criminals. One member of a Hamburg bombing crew reflects: 'What ever statesmen and braided air marshals may say and write, it was barbarous in the extreme. "Who ever harms a hair of one of these little ones . . ." I expect no mercy in the life to come. The Teacher told us, clearly. We disobeyed.'

Everyone knew what was happening. Newspapers were emblazoned with headlines about 1,000-bomber raids. Talk of an eye for an eye . . .! − On one single night at Dresden the RAF killed more than twice as many civilians as were killed in all the German raids on British cities put together. For the first time ever the dead were so many that there were not enough of the living left to bury them. Church leaders did nothing. Of the non-pacifist Bishops only Bell, the Bishop of Chichester, protested and was fiercely denounced for his efforts − Archbishop Temple gave him no support. Bishop Barnes of Birmingham, a pacifist, also protested strongly: there were no others.

Of what possible value is a criterion for a justifiable war, when war can develop like this? And next time it will be worse. In 1945 there were but two nuclear bombs in all the world. Men and women are *still* dying as a result of their use. Today there are 50,000 such bombs and much more powerful ones at that.

Criterion for a justifiable war . . .? It has been well said that much of what is now being written about the just war in relationship to Christianity might have been written 2,000 years ago. Augustine's code of war was taken from that of Plato and Cicero. Historically the purpose of formulating the idea of the 'just war' in a Christian context was to place a restraint on war, not to justify it. 'It is a perversion of the "just war" idea to describe it as virtually the same as a justifiable war.'[4]

The idea of the just war seems strangely out of touch with reality today, at least in so far as all-out war is concerned. It is more relevant to police action, or when one side is vastly more powerful than the other. The police should not use more force than is necessary to overcome the criminal; they must not attack those who are not

Robert E. D. Clark

themselves criminals, such as criminals' wives and children; punishments must not be excessive, and so on. Such rules are valuable at the police level: they regulate and limit the use of force, but they do not justify it.

Christians in the armed forces?

(e) *If it is right for the power to have armies for defence, can a Christian be a member of the armed forces with the obligation sometimes to kill members of the opposing armed forces? Alternatively, must the Christian leave these tasks to non-Christians while he remains thankful for what armies do to restrain evil and encourage peace in God's purposes of good for society? Should a Christian at most be a member of a non-combatant corps (e.g. an unarmed ambulance corps)?*

For 'can' read 'may', as before. 'If it is *right* for the power . . .': the implication is that if the state is doing what is 'right' a Christian ought to be prepared to help it in so doing. But the state is not a person like an individual, and 'right' and 'wrong' for a state and for a person may mean different things. As stated above, 'right' for a state can mean only the imposition of laws or standards which, morally, are the highest which a population will tolerate, but what is 'right' in this sense can be very 'wrong' by Christian standards – sometimes it might even be 'right' for the state to legalize brothels. No Christian should feel that he is under an obligation to help the state do what he believes is wrong!

The Christian thanks God for over-ruling the affairs of the world, for making the evil deeds of men work to the praise of God. It must always be wrong, however, for a Christian to sign a blank cheque, so to speak, promising to do what he is told by authorities who are not bound by Christian standards of right and wrong. To swear obedience to a civil or military authority is to make a promise to obey man rather than God if, or when, such a choice must be made.

'Must the Christian leave these tasks to non-Christians

...?' Must he rely upon fellow citizens to restrain the forces of evil, whether criminal or military, but refuse to help in the 'dirty work' which others do in order to preserve society from chaos? To this we may answer *Yes*, but without embarrassment. After all we do not *ask* anyone to act in ways of which we disapprove. The point is that we Christians are called upon to serve our generation in ways other than by resorting to violence. 'Take up your cross and follow me,' says Jesus. That cross, for all of us costly, for many has meant lives of poverty, suffering and danger chosen in preference to wealth and security, in order that others may reap the benefit. Accepted standards in our civilization (humane treatment of prisoners, honesty in examinations and commerce, education for all, care of the old and infirm, hospitals for the sick, and the like) owe a vast amount to the self-sacrificing lives of Christians. Rationalists, for instance, did little to help in the emancipation of slaves.[5] It was chiefly Christian influence which put an end to the thousand years of torture to which Chinese women were subjected by footbinding[6] or the burning of widows on their husbands' funeral pyres in India. Examples could be multiplied. Jesus calls his disciples to be the salt of the earth, to show by their example the goodness and kindness of God and to show it to the evil as well as to the good. This we cannot do if we, knowing that we are sinners ourselves, seek to participate in violence towards our fellow men.

Because, according to the Gospel (as we shall see later), we must show kindness to friend and foe alike: an unarmed ambulance corps would seem to fulfil this condition.

Are some methods of war totally wrong?

(f) *Are there any limits to the use of methods of war? Does there come a point where, although it could be right to kill members of the enemy's armed forces (usually conscripted) if they are trying to kill you, there are methods being used that are so evil in themselves, or in their effects, that a Christian must insist that the state must never use them—even if the result of that stand would be the victory of evil and the destruction of a great deal that is good? Are there, in effect, limits to the methods by which evil should be resisted? For example, is unilateral nuclear disarmament something that Christians should urge upon their government, and be glad to see implemented, even if it meant the almost immediate overrunning of the world by powers opposed to Christianity?*

In part these questions have been answered above – see section (d).

If, on moral or religious grounds, a Christian insists that the state must never use certain methods or weapons, he wastes his time. Even the most solemn promises made by governments are but bits of paper and will be so considered if expediency demands. The Russians are said to have broken every promise they made in connection with respect for human rights. The British government, twice over, gave a solemn undertaking that, whatever the Germans did, this country would not bomb women and children in German cities in the Second World War. Promises are soon forgotten. Christian insistence counts for nothing. Church leaders are soon compromised. Then ordinary Christians must stand alone.

Are there any limits to the methods we may use in war? All down Christian history the church has been looking for, and finding, such limits. In the tenth century soldiers began using the more deadly cross-bow instead of the short bow, and the church was scandalized. The use of the new weapon was formally condemned by the second Lateran Council in AD 1139; after that it was still permissible to kill your enemies with the older weapon, but the new weapon was so evil in its effects that it was never to be used. In the Middle Ages the Turks used pyrotechnic devices in battling with Christians. These were condemned as satanic and barbaric. The same was said of gunpowder when the knowledge of its composition reached Europe from China. This was the most wicked form of warfare of which man was capable – indeed the secret of how to make it had been revealed to mankind by the devil himself, who had materialized while an early alchemist had been mixing his chemicals and had pushed the man's arm while he was weighing out the saltpetre. Even the 'villainous saltpetre' (Shakespeare) existed only as a result of terrible sinning against the laws of God our Creator: it is formed 'out of the Saltness of the Earth where Beasts and men have promiscuously mingled' (Leonardus). The use of a gun was way beyond any legitimate way of killing one's foes. 'Christians do invade Christians with the Weapons of Hell,' cries Erasmus; 'who can believe that guns were the inventions of men?' The story is always the same. Submarines, poison gas, booby traps, high explosives, bombing of cities, chemical warfare, flame throwers, incendiaries, blockades and the rest – all have left Christians of their day with the impression that the ultimate limit had been reached. All to no avail. What passes as the ultimate limit of the allowable for one generation is accepted as the norm by the next. Once we start slipping down the slippery slope that leads to a hell on earth, once we reject the command to love our enemies, no earthly power can prevent the increasing misuse of God-given science.

'. . . Methods being used are so evil . . . that a Christian must insist that the state must never use them . . .' It is difficult to restrain a wry smile. In view of all the wickedness of the church in the past, would it not be equally sensible for Christians to sit on the beach in Canutian chairs and insist that the tide must not come in?

'. . . Even if it meant the almost immediate over-running of the world by powers opposed to Christianity.' Who are *we* to talk in this way? Do we think that the Kremlin is stronger than God? God is well able to protect those who do his will. But even if he does not, Christians must still be adamant, saying to the state, 'We will not serve your gods of guns, bombs and nuclear weapons' (*cf.* Daniel 3:17–18).

A Christian, however, must also stress another point.

99

Disposal of weapons (nuclear or otherwise) is not enough. It might even tempt a potential enemy to attack. National repentance – repentance of the terrible sin that we have harboured such weapons and even thought of using them – is also called for. The government that destroys its weapons must repent, must seek the forgiveness of God (in whom most people believe, if only vaguely), but also the forgiveness of potential enemy governments, for the sins of the past. Never mind what *they* have done, or may still be doing – for we cannot repent for others! It may be that in God's mercy the sense of sin will jump national barriers. Who knows? But without repentance disarmament will avail little, perhaps nothing at all. Well swept and garnished, the heart of the unrepentant wicked man who ceases to do wickedly may prove a haven for devils worse than the first (*cf.* Matthew 12:43–45).

It may well be replied that to expect such repentance by a non-Christian nation is unrealistic. Christians, however, can at least proclaim, loud and clear, that the making of scientific weaponry is a sin which shouts to high heaven. If Christians in all lands heard the clarion call and refused to make weapons or join national forces, politicans would find war-making very difficult – it would rarely be possible to shoot or imprison a sizeable fraction of the population. What hope is there for the world, however, when only a miniscule minority of Christians will take the stand which Jesus commanded (as we shall see below)? The salt has lost its savour (Matthew 5:13).

On glorying in war

(g) *Can a Christian ever glory in military victory or in war?*

Though his feelings will be tinged with sorrow, a Christian can thank God for accomplishing his will through the evil doings of man. Many a Christian, for instance, who views the return of the Jews to their ancient land as a fulfilment of prophecy, will have 'gloried' in ('been grateful to God for') their military victories over the Arabs. This does not imply lack of deep sympathy for the Palestinians or approval of any of the evil things that were done and are still being done. The Falkland War with Argentina is another case in point.

Again, in the last resort, at the end of the age, saints will certainly glory in the victory of Christ over his earthly foes. 'We give thanks to thee, Lord God Almighty . . . for destroying the destroyers of the earth' (Revelation 11:17–18).

Bible teaching – the Old Testament

Some Christians assume that if the Bible is the Word of God, or inspired, then what it commands cannot be wrong. Therefore since God sometimes told Israelites to fight, fighting must at least sometimes be right for us also.

Before assenting to this, we need to ask two questions. 1. Is it true that, if God has told men to act in a certain way in the past, that way must for ever after be right? 2. Can we fairly compare the wars of the Israelites in ancient times with war as it is today?

1. The answer to the first question must be an unhesitating No. In the New Testament, it is made abundantly clear that God's will was revealed to mankind in very early times, but that in view of man's perverseness and sin, other commands, often not in themselves good, had to be given later. The basic Christian message is that through the sacrifice of Christ God is able to forgive sin so that his people are now once again free to serve him as he originally intended. God made man and woman so that they might live together in harmony: divorce was allowed in later times but only because of the hardness of men's hearts. Jesus calls us back to what applied at the beginning. He says clearly that anyone who marries a divorced person commits adultery (Luke 16:18). Similarly, because in the beginning the Sabbath was made for man and not man for the Sabbath, the strict rules for Sabbath keeping of later times do not apply to disciples. Paul argues that because Abraham was justified by faith before circum-

101

cision and the law were given, it is now wrong for a Christian to be circumcised (Galatians 5:2).

The principle is of wide application. We cannot but contrast the beautiful harmony between God and man in the Garden of Eden, with the terrors of the giving of the law on Sinai, or the punishment meted out to Cain, the first murderer – exile but not death – with the capital punishment commanded in later days. Tertullian (*Exhortation to Chastity*) pointed out long ago that monogamy follows because God made one woman for Adam, not a plurality of wives! But later more than one wife was allowed.

The Bible abounds with examples of how God, in dealing with the perversity of man, often commands what is contrary to his will – his purpose being sometimes to teach mankind that disobedience brings its own judgment, sometimes to shame the wrongdoer, sometimes to awaken conscience by the use of irony. The Israelites rejected the Lord as their king: like other peoples they wanted an earthly monarch to fight their battles. God gave them their desire but warned them that forced levies, so necessary to maintain royal extravagance, would lead to discontent and rebellion. And so it happened. Balaam, forbidden to go with Balak's messengers, insists on going. So God tells him to go but turns his would-be curse into a blessing (Numbers 22). 'He gave them their request; but sent leanness into their soul' (Psalm 106:15, AV) summarizes God's dealings with the wayward.

Nowhere is the point brought out more forcefully than by the later prophets. 'I gave them statutes that were not good and ordinances by which they could not have life; and I defiled them through their very gifts in making them offer by fire all their firstborn, that I might horrify them' (Ezekiel 20:25-26). To Israelites who had vowed that they would burn incense to the queen of heaven, Jeremiah says, 'Go ahead then, do what you promised! Keep your vows!' (*cf.* Jeremiah 44:25). 'Do quickly what you are determined to do,' says Jesus to his betrayer (*cf.* John 13:27).

In short, biblical commands, taken out of the context

of human perverseness, are no sure guide as to how saints should behave! Nor have God's ways changed today. The Christian, bent on some course of action which is contrary to the teaching of Christ, can seek God's will in prayer and in the end feel assured that God has told him to do what he all along wanted to do. As of old, God will often bring good out of evil. Our wonderful God does not finally reject us when we are bent on doing evil, but we must not pretend that the evil he permits, or even sometimes commands, is good.

2. If God's people in old time were expected to fight on occasion, can we suppose that God forbids Christians to do the same today when their country and loved ones are in danger?

This argument overlooks the difference between law and grace. The basis of the law is that those who do good shall live: those who do evil will be destroyed. The basis of the gospel is that the just shall live by faith. The Christian knows that he is himself a sinner, but he trusts in Christ for forgiveness.

The Old Testament soldier did not see himself as a sinner: those against whom he fought were rebels against God, so it was reckoned right to kill them. The rebels were not always foreigners, either. They might be your own countrymen and then it might be your duty to fight and kill them – as happened when the Levites were commanded to 'slay every man his brother' because many of the Israelites had worshipped Aaron's golden calf, or when the other tribes were called upon to wage war against the tribe of Benjamin for failing to punish those who had been guilty of rape and murder. Foreign nations, too, were not to be attacked just at any time, but only when their sins had mounted high to heaven (*cf.* 'The iniquity of the Amorites is not yet complete', Genesis 15:16). In all this there was no question of 'my country right or wrong'. The true Israelite felt that he was the sword of the Lord, under obligation to fight the Goliaths of yesterday who defied the armies of the living God. When, as increasingly happened with the passage of years,

God's people realized that their own nation had sinned, many of them came to see that the Lord was no longer on their side. If they fought they expected the enemy to win and even realized with saintly Jeremiah that it would be wrong to offer resistance to the national enemy. Jeremiah openly told soldiers not to fight and risked death for his apparent disloyalty: 'Let this man be put to death, for he is weakening the hands of the soldiers' (Jeremiah 38:4).

If we accept the Bible as the Word of God, it is not for us to pick and choose. If we want to fight battles under the banner of the law, let us refuse to fight on the Sabbath (or perhaps Sunday); let us join the armed forces in war time but turn our guns on officers who take God's name in vain or behave immorally ; let us refuse to fight the national enemy if in our country sin is condoned; let us join forces with other Christian soldiers to fight against home towns and villages where sin and vice are rampant and unrebuked. This is the kind of fighting which appeal to the Old Testament might justify. Fighting in a modern war is quite another matter. Remembering that fighting may now involve the use of nuclear weapons which punish generations yet unborn, the sheer incompatibility of the two kinds of war is obvious enough. It is impossible to use the one to justify the other.

Again, the Christian who reads the Old Testament yet fails to note God's hatred of human wars must be curiously insensitive. Abraham is appalled by the thought that a wicked city might be destroyed when it contains as few as ten righteous people – he can hardly believe that God could do such a thing ('Shall not the Judge of all the earth do right?' Genesis 18:25). David is forbidden to build a temple to the Lord because he had shed blood in wars (1 Chronicles 22:8). God was pleased that Solomon did not ask for the life of his enemies (2 Chronicles 1:11). Repeatedly God intervened in human affairs in such a way as to prevent or minimize fighting, as in the crossing of the Red (or Reed) Sea, or, when Ben-hadad's army, smitten with blindness, was simply sent home after partaking of a good meal (2 Kings 6). Often only very small contingents of soldiers were chosen to defeat an enemy, so that Israel might not trust in her own strength or the weapons of the day – bows and arrows, chariots, swords and horsemen. Israel was called upon to trust in God for deliverance, to stand and see the salvation of God. So long as they were faithful to their God, victory was assured without preparation for war. We cannot but reflect on the contrast between the Old Testament and the situation today with its trust in weapons, half the scientists and technicians in the entire world being engaged in full-time work on weapons to the terrible impoverishment of the nations.

To summarize, God showed his will in creation and in his early dealings with man. When men rejected his will, God sometimes allowed, or even commanded, people to do evil because of the hardness of their hearts. In the New Testament, which we now consider, Jesus offers forgiveness of sins and a return to man's unfallen state. He is clear in what he demands: no longer is the divine will for our lives to be watered down by the evil in our hearts.

Bible teaching – the New Testament

We turn to the New Testament. Here again, as with the Old, some Christians make use of astonishing arguments in favour of fighting which in no way bear on the issue. A common one is that of alleged silence. We are told that the New Testament nowhere forbids Christians to enlist as soldiers. It is conveniently forgotten that the same argument might be used in support of slavery, polygamy, polyandry, gambling or the use of harmful drugs, none of which is explicitly forbidden.

The commonest contention always disguised in one way or another (because Jesus condemned it) is that it is right for a man to serve two masters – Christ and the state. A Christian man may safely forget about obeying his heavenly Master and behave in a quite contrary way when the state so demands.

A terrible example of this is afforded by the betrayal of the Communist-hating Cossacks who fought on Hitler's

side in the Second World War and were taken prisoner by
the British. Churchill, with Eden's approval, and Roosevelt
had secretly agreed at Yalta in February 1945 to Stalin's
demand that the Cossacks, with all other Russian prisoners, should be handed over to Russia. When the war
with Germany had ended Major W. R. Davies was put in
charge of about 30,000 Cossacks in Austria, who were
encamped there with thousands of their wives and children. The deeply religious Cossacks, under General
Domanov, were on very friendly terms with the British
against whom they had not fought and they trusted the
English, especially Davies, implicitly. Davies received an
order from Col. A. D. Malcolm, who had orders from
Brig. (later Sir Geoffrey) Musson, who had orders from
Field Marshal Alexander, who had orders from Churchill,
to hand the Cossacks, including the women and children,
over to the Russians. To avoid trouble Davies ordered the
Cossacks, on pain of death, to hand in their arms. He
gathered their officers (nearly 1,500 of them) in a field
ostensibly to meet Alexander himself, promised Domanov
on his word of honour that this was no trick and that
they would not be handed over to the Russians, and then
broke his word, not without feelings of anguish. Suicides
on the journey were common and all the Cossack officers
went to their death.[7] This is but one episode – over two
million prisoners, including great numbers of white
Russians for whom Stalin had not even asked, were
handed over to the Russians, deceit being commonly used,
and the fate accorded to almost all of them was terrible.
The Official Secrets Act was invoked lest the story should
be told too soon. The British authorites were well aware
of what would happen. Such is war. In view of what
happened it seems incredible that any Christian today can
promise, willy nilly, to obey military orders, let alone to
keep his mouth shut when he knows of atrocities which
ought to be exposed. Jesus said: a man cannot serve two
masters.

'Love your neighbour,' says the Bible. But can we love
those whom we are seeking to kill or conquer? Yes, it is

quite possible so to do, says the soldier-Christian. But this is not the teaching of the Bible. Love does no wrong to his neighbour (Romans 13:10) and if the parable of the Good Samaritan teaches us anything, it teaches that our neighbour is all mankind. Success in war depends upon espionage, deceit and lying, but the gates of the external city are for ever closed to everyone that 'loveth and maketh a lie' (Revelation 22:15, AV). How can soldiers defeat an enemy without deceiving him about when and where an attack will be launched?

The Christian is told, not only to love his neighbours, but to love his enemies. 'Love your enemies and pray for those who persecute you.' By so doing, says Jesus, disciples become sons (as distinct from children) of their Father in heaven, 'for he makes his sun rise on the evil and on the good, and sends rain on the just and on the unjust.' The love he refers to is not then a matter of sentiment but of active kindness (Matthew 5:43–48).

In a last desperate attempt to salve his conscience the soldier-Christian who seeks to serve two masters will argue that the enemies to which our Lord refers are personal enemies, not enemies of his country. Of course personal enemies are to be loved, but the context makes it clear that Jesus had national enemies very much in view.

Again and again Jesus contrasts the teaching of the Law with what he is saying – 'but I say to you'. In so doing he is not overthrowing the Law but establishing it, as we have already seen. He is seeking to bring men back to the basic principle of the Law of God, that God and man should walk in harmony. Owing to the hardness of men's hearts the Law made provision for man's frailty. It is these provisions to which he refers, quoting from the Old Testament in each case (save one), but urging men to return to the will of God on which the Law is based (see Matthew 5:21–48).

'You shall not kill,' said the Law. But Jesus wanted men to realize that anger and hatred which lead to killing lie behind this command. 'You shall not commit adultery,' said the Law; but the target of the prohibition was the

Robert E. D. Clark

impurity in the heart which leads to adultery. You must not swear vainly and rashly, says the Law, and if you swear to do something you must keep your oath. God, however, looks for truth in the inward parts, and disciples are told that on no account may they ever swear, for anything stronger than 'Yes, Yes' or 'No, No' comes from evil (or the Evil One). The Law said, 'An eye for an eye and a tooth for a tooth.' This rule, not taken literally by the Pharisees (with one notable exception), spelt out the limit to which revenge might go. 'Do not resist one who is evil,' said Jesus; in other words, cut out revenge altogether.

Finally, according to Jesus, it was said, 'You shall love your neighbour and hate your enemy.' Here for the first time there is no such passage in the Old Testament. 'Love your neighbour' is there, but not 'Hate your enemy'.

How can we explain this? An all too common explanation found in Christian commentaries is the statement that Jewish rabbis had added the offending words: this is stated to illustrate the dishonest way in which the Jews misinterpreted their own Scriptures. They taught their followers that personal enemies were to be hated and in contrast Jesus said that personal enemies must be loved.

This explanation is totally wrong and highly offensive to Jews. The Old Testament abounds with statements that personal enemies are to be loved. Even the well-known New Testament passage about heaping coals of fire upon the head of a personal enemy by acts of loving kindness is a quotation from the Old Testament (Romans 12:20; Proverbs 25:21–22). Many similar statements are to be found in the writings of the ancient rabbis, but none in defence of personal hatred. Christians have no right to slander Jews in this hurtful way.

How, then, do Jews explain the passage? The common view is that Matthew, filled with anti-Jewish prejudice, invented the slander which Christians repeat to this day. For this view, again, there is no evidence.

How, then, are we to explain our Lord's words? It appears that there is only one possible answer. Although the actual words 'Hate your enemy' are not to be found

108

The case for all-out pacifism

in the Old Testament, this is nevertheless a fair summary
of the attitude of the Law (as modified because of the
hardness of men's hearts) towards the national enemy.
There are many passages in the Old Testament which say
just this in effect. Here are some examples: 'Remember
what Amalek did to you. . .; you shall not forget' (Deuteronomy 25:17–19); it is said of Babylon, 'Happy shall
he be who takes your little ones and dashes them against
the rock!' (Psalm 137:9).

Our Lord lived in occupied territory and the national
enemy, hated by many of the Jews, was Rome. Rebellions
against the Roman yoke were common; Roman governors
and tax gatherers were hated. The law said 'Hate that
national enemy'; Jesus commanded 'Love. . .'. In telling
his disciples to love the hated enemy of his nation, he tells
all Christians down all the ages to love the enemies of
their nation.

When we think also of our Lord's words to Peter ('Put
your sword back into its place; for all who take the sword
will perish by the sword', Matthew 26:52) it is surely clear
as crystal that Jesus condemned participation in war, even
defensive war, by his disciples. As Tertullian put it, Jesus
disarms every soldier. And for centuries this is how the
Christian church interpreted his teaching.

Early Christian history

Attempts have sometimes been made to argue that early
Christians freely became soldiers: these are quite unconvincing. There are few writings save those of the New
Testament telling us about the Christian church in very
early times. There are, however, many inscriptions on
graves. After long research Hornus tells us that he knows
of only eleven inscriptions covering about two centuries
which apparently refer, directly or indirectly, to Christians
with army connections. Some have claimed larger
numbers, but only by including those who were not Christians at all, or who lived centuries later. The hagiographies
of later times which tell of Christians joining the army

and being martyred for their faith are pure romances. In one martyrology, Hornus tells us, lists of names are given, each being followed by MIL and a number. The figures give the miles travelled by hermits in moving from one shrine to another. So anxious is the writer of the martyrology in question to show that there were Christian soldiers in the Roman armies that he interprets MIL as milites (soldiers), and the numbers following as giving the number of fellow Christians martyred at the same time!

In the mid-second century the pagan writer, Celsus, in Rome, investigated the Christian religion but could not discover a single instance of a Christian serving in the legions. He opposed Christianity on the ground that if the Empire were converted to the new religion, the pagans would conquer Rome because of the pacifism of the Christians and all would be lost.

It is known that men in the legions when converted normally left the army and were sometimes martyred for their refusal to carry weapons. Early churches refused to baptize or receive into membership those who maintained army connections. It is true that army life might involve participation in idolatry, but that this was not the primary objection to such an occupation is clear from several of the testimonies of the early martyrs.

In later times some Christians remained in the Roman legions after conversion, but we need to remember that the army in those days functioned in peace-time rather like an extended civil service – it policed the state, guarded the mails in transit and even manned the fire service in Rome. For a century and more an army family might see nothing of war. At the Council of Arles (AD 314) Christians already in the army were told to stay, unless called upon to fight, when they were to resign immediately. In general the Canons of the early church say or suggest that a Christian should not volunteer for the forces, and that if conscripted he should not kill.

We need to remember that from early days Christians regarded all human life as sacred. Abortion in any form and the exposure of unwanted children were condemned.

Attendance at circus games where men killed one another was forbidden to Christians. 'We cannot endure to see a man put to death, even justly'; 'murder is always an offence, even if in self-defence it is a crime and should be punished.' Such are the sentiments of some early Christian writers. How inconsistent it would be, remarks Tertullian, 'to respect the life of a foetus and yet thoughtlessly to sacrifice the life of a man whom circumstances had placed in the ranks of an enemy army.'

The history of the subject can hardly be covered in a few paragraphs. It is now widely agreed, however, that Christianity started as a pacifist movement: not until the time of Constantine did Christianity and fighting begin to become reconciled. And for long after pacifist Christians remained to testify to their Lord's teaching on the subject. The literature is extensive, but for those who wish to read further two excellent books may be recommended – C. J. Cadoux, *The Early Church and the World* (1940), and the well-researched work of Jean M. Hornus, '*It is not Lawful for me to Fight*' (Paternoster Press, 1980).

Examples set by other Christians

To some of us who, like the writer, have had long family connections with the Forces, or have known, admired and loved fine saintly but non-pacifist Christians (I think especially of the late Bishop Taylor Smith, Chaplain General to the Forces in the First World War), it will be upsetting that a fellow Christian can write in so uncompromising a way about what they deem an honourable profession. But let us remember that the slave trade, likewise, was once held in high esteem by Christians. It was accepted by Christian bishops in the House of Lords and all the arguments now used in support of fighting in war were once used in support of slavery. John Newton was master of a slave ship transporting slaves from Africa to the New World for sale. His profession, Newton reckoned, was better than any other for 'promoting the life of God in the soul'. On the bridge or in his cabin he read his Bible and then, after he had used the thumb screw to torture some black slaves and they had sunk into helpless apathy, he interpreted their changed attitude as a change of heart produced by the God of peace. Only after illness prevented yet another voyage were his eyes opened and he was then able to help the abolitionists. 'Custom, example and interest had blinded my eyes. What I did, I did ignorantly, considering it as the line of life which Divine Providence had allotted me.'

The terrible story of witchcraft persecution is the same. Deeply devout Christians were often involved: they took it for granted that the Old Testament injunction 'Thou shalt not suffer a witch to live' (Exodus 22:18, AV) justified their merciless cruelties, including burning to death. In the depth of a European winter, when fuel was scarce, a poor woman sent her precious mite, a couple of faggots which she sorely needed for warmth, to help God in his glorious work of burning a witch. Calvin, from all accounts a kind and godly man, was implicated in appalling cruelties against witches. Roman Catholics and Reformers united to stamp out the so-called anabaptists. These last, for the most part saintly Christian pacifists who believed that infant baptism is no baptism at all and so baptized one another, were mercilessly sought out and murdered. Many were burnt to death. Some were mockingly displayed in cages made of iron rods of wide mesh, in which it was impossible for a man to sit or stand.[8] A common final punishment was by drowning in lakes, mockingly referred to as a third baptism.

Let us face it. These are the ways in which born-again Christians have too often behaved in the past. The Scripture is clear that if we decide what is wrong and what is right on the basis of the example set by other Christians, rather than the commands of Christ, we shall be judged for our unconfessed and unforgiven sins at the last day. 'Every one who hears these words of mine and does not do them', says our Lord, 'will be like a foolish man who built his house upon the sand; and the rain fell, and the floods came, and the winds blew and beat against that house, and it fell; and great was the fall of it' (Matthew 7:26–27). We have been warned (*cf.* 1 Corinthians 10:12).

My thanks are due to the Editor, Dr Oliver Barclay, to Professor John Ferguson of Selly Oak Colleges, Birmingham, and to Mr Malcolm Heath of Merton College, Oxford, for helpful criticisms and suggestions. The case for Christian pacifism is more fully developed in my book, **Does the Bible Teach Pacifism?** *(Marshall Morgan and Scott, 1983).*

Response to Robert Clark

John Peck

Robert Clark's main contentions make me wish that my own case against all-out pacifism, which follows, had stressed more fully that war may now have reached dimensions which disqualify it completely from achieving justice for the oppressed, and that certainly at least *some* Christians are called to witness plainly to that fact. Thus I gladly pay tribute to the power of his contribution to the debate. But Robert's reasoning disturbs me profoundly.

The fallacies are numerous, and there is space to deal with only a few. For instance, the comparison of beating a child with amputating a finger is faulty – the latter would be appropriate only to an adult offence, say, of poking out a small child's eye for sadistic pleasure. Again, no-one wants to be injured in battle, but criminals have been known to want punishment as some atonement for their wrongdoing. The reference to metaphorical 'force' is irrelevant: war is certainly not metaphorical violence! And Matthew 13:29 is about excommunicating hypocrites, not executing public justice. The exposition of 'servant' is dubious: as far as I know, neither Joseph's brothers nor the Exodus Pharaoh (or anyone else while in opposition to God) are actually *called* 'servant', and the argument hinges on that: his wider meaning to 'servant' makes it

114

mean little more than a human being. The context of Matthew 7 shows that 'judge' there means condemning others by a law you do not apply to yourself. A magistrate, of course, is under the law, and not to condemn a criminal would make him an accessory.

When I come to read Robert Clark's scenario for a pacifist nation's acceptance of an enemy, its implausibility strikes me. Maybe I have read too much of *The Gulag Archipelago* : but the picture of us 'affording' an occupying force 'an opportunity to express their views' is simply not credible. His reference to temporary discomforts, unfortunate incidents of rape, suffering and inconvenience, are similarly unreal. Did the Stalin government need war to persuade it to wholesale genocide? Accepting such occupying forces will be no mere experiment. We shall not just suffer inconvenience; we shall in effect be crucified. For every horror which Robert (rightly) associates with war one could match equal horrors in peace in aggressive totalitarianism. It is arguably the escalation in the efficiency of evil which has necessitated an escalation in the horrors of defensive war.

The weak argumentation, I suspect, however, is really produced by what seems to me to be an unsatisfactory methodology. I cannot so easily dismiss the Old Testament as largely an accommodation to an obsolete moral difficulty. As Robert himself admits, much of it was instituted for the 'hardness of men's hearts'. Precisely. God does not stop calling men to obedience because they cannot rise to the heights of Christian personal discipleship. (In fact, even for Christians there are some hints of it; *e.g.* 1 Corinthians 7:35ff.) No responsible exegete would apply Old Testament provisions without reference to their historical context; but surely it is the very fact of their realism in the face of human sin which makes it possible for the Christian to speak practically in the Lord's name to a morally crippled world. Our 'good Christian' laws do not have to be unrealistic, as Robert implies – and does he really think it makes no difference what sort of laws are passed?

New Testament thought is saturated with Old Testament attitudes: indeed, it actually universalizes their principles. Its stress on the response of the individual to God (fundamental to all else) should not blind us to the fact that it is not rejecting, but fulfilling, the Old Testament in all its varied communal relevance. It would take too long to argue this out fully; but the neglect of this forces Robert Clark to an all-or-nothing alternative: either a Christian pacifist nation, or Christians have nothing to do with it — not even to carry out justice on those who brutalize or exploit the weak. Robert cannot call a nation to a martyrdom for which great numbers of its citizens do not have the moral resources, since they inadequately appreciate the real issues and the cost involved.

Instinctively he knows it, and it shows. It is that very unrealism which I fear the unilateralist peace movements are fostering.

The Bible speaks of Christ, and him crucified, as Lord, claiming the obedience of more than just our religious and moral lives. He calls all men to a measure of obedience, however morally disabled they may be, and in whatever capacity they are acting; whether as citizens, rulers, thinkers, workers, artists, lovers, or whatever. He does not leave anyone in silence; he has a word for them as they are, that in obedience they might hear him call them to what they ought to be. Unless we introduce people to a truly biblical way of thinking, working, doing art and justice, and incarnate it in our own sharing of the burden of life, our exhortations will become more and more lofty, isolated and unreal.

5
The case against all-out pacifism

John Peck

War as related to nationhood · The obligations of the Christian citizen · Limitations on a non-pacifist view · The words and example of Christ · The vocational Nazirite

Pacifism is an issue that usually comes to the fore in relation to the prospect of war. The argument, however, often extends very quickly to the whole question of the use of force. During the Second World War I remember as typical this question being put to pacifists: 'What would you do if a German paratrooper was about to bayonet your wife (husband/child/grandmother)?' Of course any sane person, pacifist or not, would reply, 'I really don't know.' But the incidence of that kind of reasoning is significant. The situations that are being compared for the question are certainly different, and may not even be analogous. It is obviously easy to slide into inaccurate and emotive argument; some careful thinking is going to be needed.

It is notable too that Christians tend, just like others, to polarize heavily on the issue, and the individual's stance so often goes with a number of other attitudes on widely differing subjects to form a consistent pattern. This indicates that we are not dealing with mere opinion or even moral convictions, but underlying divergences of a philosophical nature. Progress in such a case is possible only by careful response to such questions as, 'What do you mean by . . . .?'

John Peck

War as related to nationhood

Pacifism, then, is commonly associated initially with the
possibility of engaging in war. So let us begin by
considering the nature of war. We could, I think, define
war, in the literal sense used in this debate, as physical
conflict between communities as they are identified by
their respective organs of governmental authority. War is
thus bound up with the phenomenon of nationality.
(Those who maintain that a World Government would
put an end to war could therefore be right. In so far as
by that they imply that hostilities between communities
would also stop, they are being hopelessly naive.
Governments alone never succeed in stopping violence.)

Now it is a further fact that war is seldom, perhaps
never, seen as an end in itself. It always requires justification by some goal believed to represent a moral ideal –
the righting of an injustice, restoration or maintenance of
national honour, preserving national institutions, ethos,
freedom, integrity, or whatever. In other words, war is
vindicated by the implication that the good of the nation
is *morally* significant. We do not fight for mere selfish,
personal advancement; we fight because our national well-
being has a claim that demands obedience from our
conscience. It follows – and here at last is the crunch –
that the issue of pacifism, as we find it, is closely connected
with the nature of nationhood.

The concept of nationhood in Scripture

It becomes necessary at this point, then, to consider the
biblical understanding of nationality. For if nationality,
and its normal corollary sovereignty, is something divinely
ordained, and if an essential element of it is its ability to
uphold its authority by force, then the case for an absolute
pacifism becomes virtually impossible to sustain. It seems
to me that that is precisely what is indicated in Scripture.

To begin with, there are apparently clear indications
that God has appointed human beings to live together in

118

national communities. In Deuteronomy – hardly the most nationalistic of Old Testament books – the song of Moses declares that 'the Most High gave the nations their inheritance', and 'when he divided all mankind, he set up boundaries for the peoples' and he did so (incredibly!) 'according to the number of the sons of Israel'.[1] The language of this seems to be echoed in Paul's address to the Athenians.[2]

It takes very little investigation to find that nationality is a dominant means in Scripture of identifying people. Repeatedly the Lord's dealings with mankind involve raising up nations, gathering nations, scattering and destroying nations. People who are personally innocent see themselves as sharing in the guilt of the nation.[3] The history of mankind in Genesis is told as of families becoming tribes, and tribes becoming nations, suggesting that this was a divinely planned pattern for the development of the human race.[4]

The climax of Old Testament redemption in the story of the children of Jacob is the creation of a nation; and the penalty of Israel's disobedience was deprivation of the marks of nationhood: the land, the kingship, the national symbols of religious faith (priest and Temple).[5] In the New Testament, too, people are repeatedly characterized by their nationality. Paul still speaks with a certain national pride, even as a follower of the Messiah whom his nation had rejected and humiliated.[6] And apparently the identity of the redeemed in heaven itself has reference to nationality. There will be no sun or moon or Temple, such as this earthly life needs; but it is 'nations' and 'kings' as well as just 'people' that walk by the light of God.[7]

It is instructive to note the occasions when our Lord addressed people in terms of their nationhood (*e.g.*, the Parable of the Sheep and Goats, and the Great Commission[8]). There was no linguistic necessity for this; he had other ways available to express his message when its particular application was to individuals.

There may be an objection that by the New Testament times the phrase 'the nations' (*ta ethnē*) had simply come to mean 'everybody in the world at large', and any

119

distinctively political significance in the phrase had worn off by constant use. This ignores the fact that in the first place the New Testament deliberately adopts Old Testament language, speaking within its semantic tradition, using Common Greek in a slightly archaic and specialist sense derived from the Septuagint; and secondly that the distinction between the Jew and the 'world at large' was in fact one of nationality. No Jew could possibly forget that, even if he became a Christian. It seems that the pacifist Christian outlook has lost sight of this dimension of human identity. Thus nationality, like personality, sexuality, social function, can be seen as one of those categories whereby God's creative and redemptive activity heightens both our community and our individual variety.[9]

Nationality, then, is seen in the Old Testament as a divinely ordained institution; and the New Testament does not abrogate this. If anything, it gives it new significance, as it does with other aspects of human culture, raciality and sex. In this respect at least it ranks with the family and the church as divinely ordained institutions, entitled to a Christian's loyalty, support and defence.

The nature of nationhood

The expression of a Christian's commitment to his nationhood must of course depend on the nature of that institution. It would be easy to appeal directly to the teaching in Romans 13 for this – and we shall certainly be considering it – but my concern here is to show that our understanding of that passage is not simply a matter of drawing on texts as armaments in a battle, but of seeing them in the context of an overall view of life as found in Scripture.

There are, I suggest, three ingredients that go to make a normal national consciousness. One is a common homeland, a territory. The second is a unifying history. The third is a distinctive corpus of governmental law. Now it is possible to imagine a nation existing without these three elements, but if the lack of them were accepted as normal and inevitable for any length of time, then first the sense of nationhood, and finally the fact of it, would disappear. Conversely, a newly-formed nation immediately brings itself under a body of law. It quickly appeals to, embroiders, and may even fabricate a unitive folklore about its past, which frequently becomes ritualized and symbolized in art. (The function of Virgil's *Aeneid* in the New Rome is an obvious example.) A people that does not look to a territory as its homeland at best survives as a tribe or a subculture.[10]

Of these three factors, the corpus of governmental law is specially significant for our purpose. Law in government has to be enforceable, or it is seen as a mockery. Hence any re-assertion of national consciousness always includes a cry for self-government. We may object to such a necessity as short of Christian ideals, and no doubt in heaven our national sense will be freed from it. Truly Christian ideals, however, take account of sin in this world, and the restraint of wickedness is a dominant task of government here on earth.

Government is not quite the same thing as sovereignty. Sovereignty is the institutional source of governmental power, and nationhood can function fairly well without possessing it (albeit usually with some discontent.) The Jewish nation in our Lord's time did not have sovereignty, and knew it. Its authorities were willing to trade sovereignty for a measure of self-government.[11] So they had their own courts (there were both civil and religious Sanhedrins) and their own Temple police. They could levy taxes, and even mint their own coinage.[12]

Nevertheless, nationhood always depends on sovereignty. It is its normal and natural concomitant, and in the history of Judah and Israel, loss of it was seen as a divine punishment for national apostasy. In such a case, the governmental life of the nation depends on the sovereignty of some other nation to which it is subject. Jewish government depended on Rome for its effectiveness, as the accounts of the suffering and death of Christ illustrate. And it was the nation which had the sovereignty, the

121

power, 'the sword' as Romans 13:4 puts it, that could claim the loyalty of a subject nation, since it provided the power-support for that nation's governmental existence. The fact is that, whether in sovereignty or subjection, nationhood always functions by this inescapable principle of *law*, sanctioned by *force*. The exhortation in Romans 13:1 is to the 'higher' powers, that is to say, those that have the ultimate resources of *force*. The merits of the laws involved are not considered. Paul, like any other Jew, would never allow that Roman law was better than Jewish law; but he counsels subjection to Roman power for all that. In our somewhat squeamish society it needs to be emphasized that our security under the law of this nation is based on the fact that the state has the sheer physical ability to force people into prison. And this is what is asserted in Scripture as the function of government as God has willed it.[13]

Now this principle applies in two directions. It applies to a nation's ability to overcome threats to its governmental law from within the nation, in the form of crime, violence, disorder.[14] But it also has to overcome threats from outside, in the form of military attack. The wise practice in western democracies of using two distinct organizations to meet these two commitments should not blind us to the fact that they are but two sides of the same coin – the uses of force to preserve national sovereignty. The police do not simply keep order; they implement the law of the *nation*. War is not waged simply to save life or comfort (!), but to defend a nation from an alien sovereignty. (It may of course, illegitimately, attack another's, too.) The functions of the two can be interchangeable in emergency. Civil police may round up military deserters; martial law can be proclaimed. The crime of treason can take either of two forms: subversion from within, or support to outside enemies. It is quite impossible to accept one aspect of the use of force and reject the other.

All this means that God has appointed, in nationhood, an institution in which the use of force plays a special and essential part. This divine acknowledgment of force is, to many people, disturbing; but I suspect that it is largely emotional. We take the use of physical force for granted in many areas of life; we accept it even applied to human beings in many cases – in surgery, the saving of a drowning man, the restraint of the violent insane. Curiously, we shrink from its use when people knowingly and deliberately threaten our welfare. That is, if we think of it, very strange.

The obligations of the Christian citizen

So Christians are called upon to acknowledge the claims of an institution defined by its power to exercise the use of force. Under Christ's teaching, there was even an obligation to go beyond the call of duty in this matter: if a government agent required escort for a mile, the disciple was to provide for two, even though any despatches he might carry would most likely be about troop movements or the treatment of wrongdoers.[15] Our Lord's remark about rendering what is Caesar's to Caesar, cryptic though it is, at least implies that Caesar has claims on the Christian.[16]

In particular, soldiering is always treated with respect in the New Testament. When John the Baptist spelt out to soldiers what repentance would mean for them in practice, he did not include any hint that they should abandon their profession.[17] Jesus fully concurred with Pilate's claim to the right to use force, adding that it was given him 'from above'. In John's Gospel, such a phrase could not merely refer to Caesar's authorization.[18]

Now it is often argued that all this calls only for passive support for the work of government, and it is quite another thing for Christians actively to take part in it. Such arguments are precarious, to say the least. In the first place, distinctions between 'active' and 'passive' are difficult to maintain. Passive submission to an authority becomes active when that authority requires you to be active. Suppose a magistrate were converted. Paul's words about his office, in Romans 13:3–6, inform him that as a magistrate he is a servant of God doing a commendable task. How could the *mere fact* of his becoming a Christian require him to give up such a task? (There might be extraneous factors, of course, but that is not to the point.) Then, at the next assize, dealing with a dangerous criminal convicted of murder, he could hardly instruct the police to persuade the man to receive his punishment (or even restraint), but on no account to use force! Secondly, the idea of a passive submission which supports the use of force without being personally prepared ever to exercise it, is morally suspect. New Testament teaching is that we should pay our taxes – and expressly for that purpose, says Paul in Romans 13:6. Biblical morality never recommends a person to pay someone else to do what would be morally wrong for him to do himself. We might look at the argument in reverse: Paul instructs us to pray for magistrates 'that we may lead a quiet and peaceable life, godly and respectful in every way'.[19] He can hardly be thinking that Christians should by non-co-operation withold the very resources for that prayer to be answered. If magistrates are indeed God's servants, then surely one might expect his people to be best fitted to such a task rather than to be disqualified.

The teaching of Romans 13 deserves further careful consideration in this respect. The immediate message clearly supports what we have been saying – God has appointed the civil authorities as instruments for carrying out forcibly his judgments against evil-doers, and it is the Christian's duty to support these. This follows on immediately from the exhortation at the end of Romans 12 not to resist evil, but to leave it to the 'wrath of God' – the very phrase applied to the judge's task in 13:4! But the language of the passage takes us further still: it calls not just for measured support, but for a positive commitment to the business of citizenship. Christian obligations are shown there with a surprising concern for what we would regard as rather fussy detail; the distinction between giving 'fear to whom fear is due', and 'honour to whom honour', implies that Christians should care about the niceties of protocol. Anyone who has been involved in the touchiness of bureaucratic rank will know the difficulty of distinguishing between conscientious respect and oily sycophancy at this point. It certainly requires more than an offhand compliance. As we have seen, taxes are to be paid, and again distinction is made between types of tax. These detailed obligations are only part of a total commitment: 'render therefore to all what you owe'. Of course, in Paul's day, the duties of citizenship seldom went beyond doing what one was told, but even then, higher authorities did demand from some citizens that they should render more; they might be directed into governmental positions where they would be called upon to render further dues, such as political counsel or military responsibility. Nowadays, in a modern democracy, where sharing in government is the privilege, and therefore the duty of the common citizen, we shall find it even more difficult to allow others to do our dirty work. The Christian at least owes the due of an intelligent vote. To take part in choosing one's rulers cannot really be regarded as passive compliance with the claims of government. The fact is that citizenship, as Paul envisages it in this passage, is potentially as fully a dimension of a Christian's life as language, logic, or the stewardship of wealth. And it is inescapably involved in the use of force, with the possibility of conflict, killing and war.

The thrust of the evidence in this line of investigation, leading from the Old Testament to the New, indicates a general duty on the part of the Christian to participate in the use of force exercised by the sovereignty of that state in which God has called him. There appears to be no case for *unqualified* pacifism.[20]

Limitations on a non-pacifist view

The Bible does not give a case for an unqualified militarism, either. The Bible does not glorify war, though it does glorify victory in a war waged righteously. The almost universal sense that war is not a moral ideal gains a clarity of focus in Scripture. War is no part of an ideal world; it is a necessity brought upon mankind by sin, and this is emphasized both by teaching[21] and by certain symbolic events.[22]

War in the Old Testament was always related to judgment on wickedness. In some cases this was by divine command, against a corrupted people – though in applying this idea to a modern situation account has to be taken of the fact that Israel was a special people and the subject of a unique promise. What is so striking is that, in spite of that promise, the actual subjugation of Canaan was not a mere exercise of power, but an act of judgment which waited some 400 years for its execution to be seen to be just.[23] There were other cases in which war was justifiable: for the preservation of national integrity[24] and even the vindication of national honour[25], or to aid allies under attack.[26] But there is no approval for wars of self-aggrandisement, or for the exhilaration of battle. The special resources of war were not particularly appreciated by the Lord of all.[27] Notably, Israelite law forbad the accumulation of aggressive armament,[28] and the presumption is that war was to be conducted only in self-defence or, in rare and exceptional cases, in an act of retribution. There was no approval of war waged to gain national independence once it was lost, and resistance was recommended only when the conquering enemy had broken faith.[29] In one case, the prophet Jeremiah expressly maintained that Israel deserved to be attacked, and ought to take her punishment rather than resist.[30] All this indicates that the concept of a 'just war', as a painful necessity in the face of human sin, had a stringent application in the Old Testament. Here, again, we can see how war against others was governed by the very same principles as those controlling the exercise of justice within the nation against crime and disorder. The principles which lie behind the necessity of force in restraining evil within the state are also operative when we consider its use between states in war.

Summary so far

In so far as the pacifist issue is about war, Christians have the same obligations relating to warfare as they have to the maintenance of law within a nation. Force may be used, even to the point of using 'the sword', but only on threats against the law of the nation, with due regard to the innocent, and subject to the law of God.

Relationship of such teaching to the words and example of Christ

So far we have pursued the question only along the lines of the general ethic and rationale of scriptural testimony. It goes without saying that if Christ himself explicitly repudiated such attitudes, we should have to grant them very limited authority, perhaps regarding them as pedagogic preparation for a higher morality.

The trouble is that any view which interprets Christ's teaching as negating that of the Old Testament comes up against insuperable difficulties. There is his own express statement that he did not come to abolish the Law and the Prophets, but rather to fulfil them.[31] There is the awkward fact, as we have seen, that, especially in respect to soldiering, the tone of the New Testament attitude is hardly distinguishable from that of the Old. This is reinforced by the fact that the New Testament is saturated so much with the language and thought-forms of the Old. In addition, Old Testament texts are so commonly cited in support of Christian ethical principles.[32] Indeed such principles are often explicitly supported by reference to specific Old Testament laws.[33]

Nevertheless there is a strong 'pacifist' element in Jesus' moral teaching which can at first sight seem overwhelmingly decisive. To Christians who are strongly conscious of the revolutionary quality of Christ's ethic, and who instinctively feel its rejection of the world's ways, this element may fill the whole horizon of their moral consideration.

'Turning the other cheek' is often the subject of humour, but Jesus obviously meant it seriously enough, and carried it out to its logical conclusion in his own life, even to death on a cross. He expressly stopped his disciples acting in his defence.[34] He rejected outright the idea of calling on the powers of heaven to his rescue.[35] (To suggest that this was because he was determined to die makes his death into a contrived demonstration.) Especially to the point, he maintained that his kingdom was not of this world, and *therefore his servants would not fight.*[36]

The early church seems to have understood Jesus' words in this matter in a strongly pacifist sense. There were cases of converted soldiers refusing to carry their swords. Relatively few records (for instance in epitaphs) remain of Christians as soldiers of this period: refusal to fight or join the army was widespread. Origen (early 3rd century) reacted to Celsus' criticism of Christians on this count, not by denying the fact, but by vindicating it. The early Fathers used to say that 'Jesus, in disarming Peter, disarmed all soldiers'.[37]

We cannot ignore the fact that Jesus' teaching had very plain 'pacifist' connotations, any more than we can ignore the way in which New Testament moral attitudes are in general consistently woven with Old Testament threads of thought pointing in a different direction. So what do we make of it all?

A reconciliation of the evidence

It seems to me that Jesus is here working within a view of human life under God that penetrates the entire biblical revelation. That view is that a human being in this world functions simultaneously in more than one 'sphere of operations'. The laws and principles of each sphere overlay each other and interact, but never violate each other. So, for instance, a human being functions as an animal in having appetites and instincts that bring their pressure to bear on him just like any other living creature made of the dust. Lack of food makes him hungry, and at the sight of it he salivates. Yet alongside this instinctual life he also has a rational life, using analysis and logic. He is also an economic being, whose life is qualified by making, saving, exchanging and consuming.

Now he is also a citizen, functioning in politico-legal relationships such as we have already been discussing. As we have seen, however, those relationships are themselves dependent upon a whole range of moral ideas focusing on that of justice. So man is also an ethical being, and his life in that sphere functions by different (though analogous) principles from those of his citizenship. A person, for example, may be immoral, but legally unimpeachable. Still further: a man's ethics will be qualified by his religious life – yet another sphere of his humanity. His place in the kingdom of God, of course, will relate him to a realm that is not only infinitely greater than any of these spheres, but will inevitably include all of them within it.

So to be a good citizen in that kingdom means living obediently in every sphere of human existence, and not merely in those which are conventionally thought of as 'the higher' or 'more spiritual' realms. (It is obvious that *such* a kingdom could hardly be benefited by a mere clash of arms!)[38]

Here we need to concentrate on two of those realms of human living in particular: that of man's moral experience, and of his citizenship. They are alike at certain points: they certainly interact, but they are not identical. The laws of citizenship are predominantly about inter-social behaviour, and they are governed by the dominant notion of justice – an equitable relationship with one's fellow men without exploitation or subversion. But his moral life is concerned with the motives and priorities that direct his behaviour, and in that the dominant idea is 'loyalty love', for so the Bible word might best be translated. The two realms completely overlap. The law of the land is at its best when its justice allows the fullest freedom of expression of man's loyalty love; man's life of love has to be built on a foundation of just and lawful dealings. The trouble with fallen man is that he so easily confuses one with the other. In particular, there is the tendency to think of morality as if it were a special kind of legal system. A typical example is found when Peter asks how much he should forgive his brother. He talks about numbers – 'seven times?' But Jesus' reply demonstrates that this is a moral question, not a legislative one, and numbers are irrelevant.[39]

Now when God called the people of Israel into being, they became a nation, and that required governmental law. What so many Jews of Jesus' time were doing was to think of morality as if it were a kind of governmental principle; a matter of measurables, of minimum requirements; a definition of behaviour alone. It was understandable: rabbinic Judaism developed a system of social order which was in many ways unsurpassed as a reflection of divine judgment and mercy. The best is always in danger of being an idol. Jesus' prophetic concern was to attack this deep-rooted idolatry in man. He insists that man's moral experience is a different thing from his citizenship. It is concerned with man as a motivated, choosing individual, relating by choice to other individuals. So when a man faces his enemy, his behaviour is not to be governed by retaliation or revenge, whatever he may have to do. When he has wronged someone, he is to seek reconciliation immediately, not wait for a court verdict.[40]

This does not override his civil obligations, however. The Sanhedrin still has authority over him.[41] Jesus stresses that being his follower will not exempt a person from the claims of the law.[42] What Jesus, then, is saying is that, when the determining factor in the situation is your personal interest or welfare, your attitude should be a 'pacifist' one. It is noteworthy, though, that Jesus' view of this attitude is an extremely positive one, involving the extra moral dimensions of caring and praying, loving and accepting. As we have seen, it will involve more than compliance with the law; it will mean making life easier for the person who is making the legal demand.

If this understanding of the situation is correct, then Jesus' 'pacifist' teaching is not directly about our obligations as citizens at all, but rather, if anything, about the attitudes in which we might fulfil them. The 'pacifism' that led him to the cross results accordingly from the moral and spiritual purposes of his ministry and calling. He was not called, in this incarnate life, to be a governmental figure such as a king or magistrate.[43] This fact governed his course of action.

Special considerations

Examples might soon come to mind in which one's moral obligations as an individual might well conflict with one's obligations as a citizen in this fallen world. Peter and John had to tell the authorities, 'We ought to obey God rather than men.' And the Bible is, as we have seen, not unqualified in its support for war! There are forms of warfare which no Christian could be free to participate in, such as unprovoked aggression. There will be many cases in which a government may persuade itself and its citizens that wrong is right in this matter. In such a case, those that know the truth are responsible for the actions of those that cannot. Christians have a special obligation to find out as much of the truth of any situation as we can.

There are other considerations in Scripture, however, which might affect our attitudes. One is the limitation placed on the accumulation of aggressive armaments in Deuteronomy 17:16. This suggests to me that the principle of such a law would ban the accumulation of missiles designed for the possibility of a pre-emptive strike. Another issue is the ecological one, derived from the fact that the earth is not man's, but the Lord's. There is an interesting exhortation in Deuteronomy 20:19 against cutting fruit-bearing trees for a siege. The implication is that nature is not to be indiscriminately ruined for the sake of war. Now, undoubtedly, modern weapons of war are overwhelmingly weapons of mass-destruction (though I suppose, of all things, the neutron bomb might escape these strictures!). A third is the principle of biblical law against dehumanization, even of guilty law-breakers.

Modern war involves civilians directly and necessarily in destruction; its methods of intelligence work and psychological pressures, its reduction of casualties to computerized statistics, may well be seen as an unacceptable violation of this.[44]

All this suggests that warfare has now developed in character to a critical point. The influence of biblical thinking, and indeed of other religious thinking, has in the past always placed war under certain constraints derived from some transcendent value. The secularization of this age has meant that *total* war is an immediate possibility. The ideal of military success accordingly functions as a god, ruling the practice of war entirely by its own values. The question now is not whether a Christian should take part in a war, but whether he should take part in war *in its present form*. The whole issue has come to a head in this age rather in the same way that slavery did in the eighteenth and nineteenth centuries. Scripture nowhere condemned slavery; rather it takes it for granted. In Old Testament law, and in the New Testament principle of gospel fellowship, however, it placed conditions upon it which radically modified the institution. For Christians, nothing but the institutional shell was left. The gospel presented standards which ultimately challenged that beyond possibility of avoidance. Once such ideals pervaded a society, slavery either had to go, or break loose from all constraints in defiance of those ideals. As a result, slavery took on exploitative forms in such stark contrast with the gospel ethic that no compromise was possible. Warfare has now taken a similar course. The form it takes is surely reaching an unacceptable point for the Christian.

Obviously Christians are going to differ as to what is precisely an 'unacceptable point'. We had better expect to get *some* point of consensus, or it may be too late to make any witness at all!

The vocational Nazirite

There is another possibility, however, for some Christians

at least, whether that point is reached or not. The Bible does recognize that some people may have functions in life which could debar them from taking part in warfare. Newly-married men, for instance, were to have a year to set up home.[45] There were also in Israel, however, people whose place in society was to symbolize certain religious and moral ideals. They were a continual visual reminder that, though the activities of this world were good and could be sanctified, there were ultimately transcendent goods to which the claims of life here eventually have to surrender. Such a person was the Nazirite, debarred from taking wine or trimming his hair. Similarly, apparently, Jesus spoke of those who would be celibate for the sake of the kingdom of God.[46] There may well be Christians who, especially in this age, are called, peremptorily, to bear testimony to the paramountcy of the kingdom of God over the claims of any earthly citizenship. I suppose, in fact, that the law exempting ministers of religion from bearing arms in war is a fumbling attempt to implement this idea. What is more likely, to be effective, is that some Christians may be recipients of an overwhelmingly lucid insight into the truth about what war has become in this age, or so grippingly aware of its corrupting effects, or so overcome by the paramount claims of that eschatological vision of peace, that they cannot but stand apart from that which for the rest of us, with our commitments and relationships in the world, is our common duty. This is nothing so glib as 'feeling led', nor so heady as a higher spirituality, but a constraint to a particular kind of obedience. Such a compulsion is not so 'normal' in Christian experience as some would ask us to expect, nor is it some sign of greater sanctity. Its compulsion may be due to the necessity inherent in God making a disciple follow a course of action more than ordinarily against the stream.

In conclusion

The complexity of the moral situation must make us hesitant to pronounce absolute moral judgments. So much of any Christian's convictions will be related to the extent of his knowledge and insight. Some factors in this will be a matter of spiritual experience, even of a power of imagination which makes possible a clearer projection of the problems involved. Some of it will be a matter of plain divine calling. In a world whose very sense of moral values is torn in conflicting directions, God undoubtedly has many very different things to say at once to, and through, his people, and no one man or group can expect to say all of it at once. Whether we believe it to be right to go to war or no, two attitudes are vital to our integrity as believers. One is that there must be an integrity of motive, that we do what we do as servants of Christ, and not as slaves to our own impulses, or to the will of the world around us. The other is that we act as those who cannot claim to be absolutely right, but rather who are grateful for being accepted for Christ's sake in 'those things whereof our conscience is afraid', or uncertain. Only obedience to Christ in his Word will keep us as a people of principle, and only his forgiving mercy in the cross will keep us open to others whose obedience differs in form from our own.

Response to John Peck

Robert E. D. Clark

John Peck very fairly puts his cards on the table. If nationhood 'is something divinely ordained, and if an essential element of it is its ability to uphold its authority by force, then the case for an absolute pacifism becomes virtually impossible to sustain'.

How so? In my paper I draw attention to the elementary point that God has ordained two kinds of servants to do his will. Pharaoh, Nebuchadnezzar, Cyrus, Nero and others were God's servants in that God used them to fulfil his purposes. Christian saints are also God's servants, though not of the same kind. John Peck, who often quotes Paul's words in Romans 13 where the reference is obviously to servants of the first kind, rests his case on the assumption that servants of the second kind can with impunity hop into the shoes of those of the first. This assumption seems to me unfounded.

Let me press the point further. John Peck says, 'Jesus fully concurred with Pilate's claim to the right to use force, adding that it was given him "from above".' Agreed. Pilate was a servant of the first kind, acting according to the foreknowledge of God. But would a disciple have been justified in aiding Pilate to judge Jesus? Of course not. But is not this the kind of conclusion to which John's argument must drive us?

I ask again, is not the plausibility of the argument, as John Peck presents it, due to the fact that Romans 13:1–7 has been taken right out of its context? Paul has just said, 'Bless those who persecute you . . . live in harmony . . . overcome evil with good' and the like. Then Paul says, 'Let every person be subject to the governing authorities' (13:1), and shortly after, 'Love does no wrong to a neighbour' (13:10), and so on. Now it is perfecty possible to be subject to authorities in good faith for 99.99 per cent of the time, but John seems to be arguing that, because Paul inserts no footnote to the contrary ('the merits of the laws are not considered'), the percentage should be taken as precisely 100 per cent – even though subjection to authorities for the residual 0.01 per cent would (or might) be flagrantly inconsistent with Romans 12 and 13:8f.

Another point – is it fair to draw conclusions from what nationhood might involve, yet to ignore other kinds of '. . . hoods'? What about parenthood? 'Children, obey your parents in everything' (Colossians 3:20). Or slave-master-hood? 'Slaves, obey in everything those who are your earthly masters' (Colossians 3:22). Do such passages justify a child who steals because his parent tells him to, or a slave who murders at his master's command? Of course not. Then what conceivable ground is there for justifying participation in war, an activity which *does* do wrong to a neighbour, on the basis of a similar command in Romans 13:1?

John Peck allows that certain classes of citizens are rightly exempted from actual fighting. Does he forget that in the New Testament *all* believers are priests, 'a kingdom of priests'?

Lastly I will quote from the end of John's paper. 'The complexity of the moral situation must make us hesitant to pronounce absolute moral judgments.' How is it possible to square this with our Lord's beautiful words about the single eye? 'If your whole body is full of light, and no part of it dark, it will be completely lighted, as when the light of a lamp shines on you' (Luke 11:33–36, NIV). Does not our Lord connect the bad eye, which makes the whole body full of darkness, with the attempt to serve two masters (Matthew 6:22–24)? – in the present context these are God and the state. Are not the words 'the complexity of the moral situation' a euphemism for 'the bad eye'? Jesus is saying, is he not, that if we serve two masters we shall be fuzzy-headed in our moral judgments? Simple issues willl appear complex. What else *can* he mean?

6
The just war revisited

Jerram Barrs

*The justice of God · Justice on earth · The penalty of
death · Government in the New Testament · Justice at
home · Should we not trust in God rather than in
weapons? · Does the Just War theory still apply? · Is
war the worst alternative? · The destruction of the world?*

'Blessed are the peacemakers, for they will be called sons
of God.' 'Do not resist an evil person.'
   Many Christians argue that these words of Jesus rule
out the possibility of a believer taking up arms to resist
evil, whether on the personal, the national or the international level. Jesus taught non-violence in the Sermon on
the Mount. He practised non-resistance of evil in going
to the cross. The pacifist teaches that if we want to remain
'in the perfection of Christ' we must never be involved in
the use of physical force to restrain evil. The use of force
is essentially carnal and worldly and Christians are called
as individuals and as communities to show the world a
new way.
   The early Anabaptists understood that, taken consistently, this position required that no Christian should take
any office in the state, for all states back up their power
and laws by force. The Anabaptist Articles of Schleitheim
of 1527 stated that the magistrate's office 'is carnal' and
'outside the perfection of Christ'.[1] These articles also
totally rejected war, and said that rulers of nations should
not resist sedition or invasion.
   Pacifists acknowledge that in the Old Testament God
sanctioned the use of the sword in civil justice and even

war on occasion. They deal with this in one of two ways. They declare that God revealed his perfect will only gradually: wars were a condescension to Israel's limited understanding, rather like the polygamy of some Israelites; God's perfect will is revealed in Christ.[2] Alternatively, they regard the 'holy wars' of Israel as being battles showing God's power by miracle, battles in which Israel's military efforts were either unnecessary or incidental to victory.[3] On this view, the only lesson for us today is to abandon any confidence in modern weapons, and to put our trust in God for our defence.

Some argue that judgment is God's strange work, mercy his most fundamental characteristic, and that therefore the child of God should never be involved in the application of justice. The taking of human life, in particular, could never be justified, for our desire should be only for the repentance and conversion of the criminal, or the nation which practises aggression. Besides, they continue, every nation is evil; we have enough to be concerned about with injustices at home. We should simply trust God to vindicate our cause if it is right.

Others acknowledge that the Bible approves of the sword of justice both to punish evil at home and to defend a country against attack from abroad. However, they say, modern warfare in general, and nuclear weapons in particular, are so indiscriminate in their destruction, and so appalling in their nature, that we ought to abandon the prudence of nuclear deterrence, and please God by laying down our nuclear weapons in a unilateral gesture, whatever the outcome.[4] If we were overrun by an enemy, at least the church might be refined by any resulting persecution. This view of nuclear weapons leads us in practical terms to a pacifist position, for conventional arms provide no deterrent to an enemy with nuclear weapons.

These arguments of the pacifist are, I believe, mistaken from beginning to end. The fundamental issues involved in our discussion are the place and importance of justice and judgment, both for God himself, and among us as humans; the question of whether justice involves death;

139

the relationship of God's commandments to mankind in the Old and New Testaments, particularly the teaching of both Testaments on personal vengeance and judicial punishment; the calling of the church in the world; and the biblical understanding of peace.

1. The justice of God

One of the problems that trouble our society in the West is how to distinguish between good and evil. Many thinkers in our century have recognized that it is meaningless to speak of good and evil, or moral responsibility, if we are only developed animals, complex chemical bio-organisms.[5] We do not accuse computers of criminal behaviour, though the complexity of our brain is compared to them; nor do we bring animals to trial, though we are said to have evolved from them.

This inability to distinguish finally between good and evil has produced terrible results throughout the world. In the West it has been one of the major factors leading to the breakdown of sexual morality and of family life; and also to the killing of unborn babies and handicapped newborns. In the communist world we see this 'lawlessness' in the very fabric of government because the rejection of absolute moral standards is a fundamental aspect of Marxist-Leninist teaching. Brezhnev repeated in 1970 some words of Lenin: 'Our morality is completely subordinated to the interests of the class struggle of the proletariat ... Morality is that which serves to destroy the old exploiting society ... We deny all morality that is drawn from some conception beyond man, beyond class. We say that it is a deception ... a fraud.'[6] The consequences of this can be seen most clearly and perfectly consistently in the Cambodian revolution in which between one-third and one-half of the population was killed to bring about a new society.[7]

Christians should not have this problem of uncertainty about good and evil – God's own character defines for us what is right and good, and all human behaviour must be measured against his character. God's law, given to us in Scripture, expresses God's righteousness, and man, made to be the image of that righteousness, is called to obey the law and to judge his life against it.

All human beings are created with a moral conscience, the law of God written on the heart, but this can become confused or hardened, either by cultural tradition or by the individual's sinful choices. Beyond this, however, we have an absolute basis for knowing what is good and evil, for we can check all human ideas about morality against God's revelation of his character and law in Scripture.

As well as answering the dilemma of moral uncertainty in our culture, the Christian also has a firm basis for determining what to do in his own life. Beyond this he has a basis for withstanding the immorality of those in power, either in a democracy, or a dictatorship, and for withstanding the will of the 51 per cent in western society, where morality changes with the consensus of the day.

Knowing with certainty the principles for human life which God has given in his law, we ought to provide a living example of righteousness to our society. We ought also to bring these principles to bear on our society to improve its laws and institutions.

The doctrine of judgment follows on necessarily from God's revelation of his righteousness. As his character is the moral foundation of the universe, so any falling short of his perfection is found wanting, exposed for what it is and judged. Rather than being embarrassed by the judgment of God, as Christians often are in this age where evil is explained away and excused, we ought to glory in it. Judgment means that in the end it really makes a difference whether we are kind or cruel, merciful or brutal. The book of Ecclesiastes sees the judgment of God as the one factor which makes sense of a world in which the wicked often prosper and the righteous perish.

We are taught in the twentieth century to see punishment of any kind as cruel and vindictive. As Christians we ought to re-educate ourselves according to Scripture and see punishment as good and right.

God's judgment is a revelation that evil is evil, and is destructive to human life, and therefore it must be exposed and dealt with according to its nature. We ought to lament, as Christ does himself, that people are so foolish as to turn away from him and live their lives in disobedience (Matthew 23:37). We ought also to imitate Jesus by giving ourselves in service to others, so that they might be moved by our love and come to repentance and faith. Yet we must, in a sense, be glad for the doctrine of judgment which declares once and for all that good and evil are different, that it does finally matter how people live their lives. God's punishment of sin, his just wrath against the evil-doer, must be seen as right and good.

2. Does God require justice to be practised here on earth?

As we look at Scripture, we have to answer 'Yes' to this question, as against the early Anabaptists who saw the practice of justice as carnal and worldly. Government is not simply a human invention organized by men to preserve order in society, or to give power to a few. God himself established the institution of government that there might be some reflection of his character as judge in human society.

In Deuteronomy we are told how Moses appointed wise and respected leaders chosen by the people to rule and judge.

I took the leading men of your tribes, wise and respected men, and appointed them to have authority over you – as commanders of thousands, of hundreds, of fifties and of tens and as tribal officials. And I charged your judges at that time: Hear the disputes between your brothers and judge fairly, whether the case is between brother Israelites or between one of them and an alien. Do not show partiality in judging; hear both small and great alike. Do not be afraid of any man, for judgment belongs to God. Bring me any case too hard for you, and I will hear it (Deuteronomy 1:15–17, NIV).

In this passage we see the direct relationship Moses makes between the judgment of God and the justice he requires to be practised on the human level. Because judgment is God's prerogative, the God of perfect justice requires that all human judgment be fair and impartial to all people, whatever their place in society.

Later in Israel's history, we read how the people wanted to have a king like the nations around them, for they were dissatisfied with the Lord as their king (1 Samuel 8:5–8). In response God allowed the rebellious people to have a king, first Saul, and then the line of David. Some have argued from this that therefore all human government and practice of justice is a 'second best', a 'carnal' alternative, permitted by God because of the unspirituality of the people of Israel. This argument is then used to reject any involvement by Christians in the armed forces, the police force, the government or the judicial and penal systems. Christians in any situation which includes the administration of justice by force are necessarily going the way of the 'world'. This argument, however, is without foundation, for, as we have seen in Deuteronomy, God had judges appointed long before the Israelites asked for a king. It was their desire to be like the nations around that was unspiritual, not the fact of government, or its forceful administration with penalties of various kinds.

The king, in fact, was called, like the judges, to revere God, to read and obey God's law himself, and to rule by it (Deuteronomy 17:18–20). God delighted in those kings who loved him and who ruled justly according to his commandments (2 Samuel 7:8–16; Psalm 89:1–4, 19–37).

Many times in the Old Testament the relationship between divine and human justice is made clear. One example comes from the time of Jehoshaphat, when he appointed judges after a period of wickedness and lawlessness.

He appointed judges in the land, in each of the

fortified cities of Judah. He told them, 'Consider carefully what you do, because you are not judging for man but for the LORD, who is with you whenever you give a verdict. Now let the fear of the LORD be upon you. Judge carefully, for with the LORD our God there is no injustice or partiality or bribery' (2 Chronicles 19:5–7, NIV).

What were the purposes for which God established human government? There are three which stand out in the Old Testament, for they are repeated many times.

1. Maintaining justice in the fear of God according to his holy law and his wisdom. (*Cf.* the passages mentioned above; also Deuteronomy 16:18–20; Proverbs 8:15–16.)

2. Punishing disobedience to the law justly and impartially, 'Acquitting the guilty and condemning the innocent – the LORD detests them both' (Proverbs 17:15, NIV; see also many passages in Exodus and Deuteronomy, especially Deuteronomy 16:8–13).

3. Defending the poor and needy who have no advocate against aggression and injustice, and ensuring equity for them. 'Speak up for those who cannot speak for themselves, for the rights of all who are destitute. Speak up and judge fairly; defend the rights of the poor and needy' (Proverbs 31:8–9, NIV). God requires this attitude to the poor and oppressed from those in authority, because it is his own attitude (Psalm 146:7–9).

It should be clear from all these passages that God values justice on earth very highly, and that those who rule wisely and punish wrongdoers are honoured and approved by him. So highly does God place the maintenance of justice that human rulers are given the title 'gods' in Psalm 82. This Psalm pictures God presiding over the assembly of human rulers from all the nations, and calling them to account for their failure to judge justly and rescue the poor from the wicked who oppress them. It is because of passages like this that Calvin could write: 'civil authority is a calling not only holy and lawful before God, but also the most sacred and by far the most honourable of all callings in the whole life of mortal men.'[8]

3. Does justice on earth involve the final human penalty of death?

I add the word 'human' here, for of course the final penalty is the eternal judgment of hell which only God can pronounce (Luke 12:4–5). God has, however, given to men the responsibility to pronounce the death penalty in certain circumstances. 'From each man, too, I will demand an accounting for the life of his fellow man. Whoever sheds the blood of man, by man shall his blood be shed; for in the image of God has God made man' (Genesis 9:5–6, NIV).

In our society we are taught to think of the death penalty as cruel and unusual, as barbaric. Human beings are so precious that no-one ever has the right to set him- or herself up as judge and deprive another of life, so the argument goes. Granted, human life is precious, and the Christian above all people should regard every human life as sacred, whether born or unborn, handicapped baby or fragile old person, weak or strong. However, it is this very dignity of the human person, that we bear in our very being the image of God, which is the basis for God's decision that the life of a murderer, who despises this image, should be forfeited.

This requirement of the death penalty for certain crimes is repeated many times in the Mosaic law, for example Deuteronomy 19:11–13 (NIV):

> But if a man hates his neighbour and lies in wait for him, assaults and kills him, and then flees to one of these cities [of refuge], the elders of his town shall send for him, bring him back from the city, and hand him over to the avenger of blood to die. Show him no pity. You must purge from Israel the guilt of shedding innocent blood, so that it may go well with you.

Christians will often point out that the Ten Commandments forbid killing. It is clear, however, that the

145

commandment 'You shall not kill' means 'You shall not murder'. In the context of this commandment in Moses' law, judicial killing is also commanded; so the death penalty is not prohibited by the law, in fact it is required. In our culture we are taught that the primary purpose of punishment is the rehabilitation of the offender, and a secondary purpose is the protection of society; all notions of requital or avenging are regarded as vindictive, barbaric and uncivilized. We need to re-educate ourselves according to Scripture. Neither the punishment that God requires men to hand out, nor those that God himself imposes, are primarily educational. They are seen rather as just vengeance required by God.[9]

This is a difficult idea to grasp in the twentieth century, but we have only to consider the plagues with which God punished Egypt, the destruction of Sodom and Gomorrah, the perishing of the whole human race (apart from Noah's family) at the flood, to see that God as judge of all the earth is acting rightly and justly when he takes life. Human wickedness in some situations becomes so great that God will no longer endure it, and he consequently judges with terrible judgment.

The death penalty is prescribed by God not only in cases of individual wickedness, but also in the case of war between nations. Where Israel suffers unjust attack and oppression at the hands of other nations God sanctions wars of self-defence, of relief from oppression and of the punishment of wickedness. For example Israel required to destroy the Canaanites in the land of Palestine because of their great wickedness (Joshua 6:21; 8:1–2). When Israel was oppressed by the Midianites, God raised up Gideon to lead the people to overcome their oppressors (Judges 6:7). There are many examples of such wars of self-defence, and wars against oppression, throughout the history of Israel.

When Israel's own rulers became wicked tyrants God sanctioned revolution against them (Jezebel and Athaliah provide two examples of this: 2 Kings 9 and 11).

Because God so clearly sanctions war in certain circumstances the psalmist could write:

> Praise be to the LORD, my Rock,
>   who trains my hands for war,
>   my fingers for battle (Psalm 144:1).

> May the praise of God be in their mouths
>   and a double-edged sword in their hands,
> to inflict vengeance on the nations
>   and punishment on the peoples,
> to bind their kings with fetters,
>   their nobles with shackles of iron,
> to carry out the sentence written against them.
>   This is the glory of all his saints (Psalm 149:6–9).

4. Has God changed his attitude towards government in the New Testament?

Is it right to say: 'God revealed himself as judge in the Old Testament, but now in Christ he has revealed himself as he more properly is, the God of love and mercy'? On this view the practice of justice is a worldly calling which the Christian who models himself on God's Son must reject.

The simplest response to this is that God's character does not change; he is the same Lord, yesterday, today and for ever (Hebrews 13:8). God does show his mercy to us supremely in the death of his Son on our behalf. However, this revelation of the mercy of God does not set aside his character of justice and holiness. Judgment *and* mercy are for ever characteristics of God. Even our salvation through Christ's death has not been brought about by God abandoning judgment in favour of mercy, but rather through upholding it. Jesus died, himself bearing the punishment for our sins on the cross, and this is our salvation. God showed his mercy by the Son bearing the judgment, so that, as Paul expresses it, 'he did it to demonstrate his justice at the present time, so as to be just and the one who justifies the man who has faith in Jesus'

147

(Romans 3:26, NIV).

Jesus was full of mercy indeed, but he also spoke some of the strongest words of judgment recorded in the whole Bible: 'But if anyone causes one of these little ones who believe in me to sin, it would be better for him to have a large millstone hung around his neck and to be drowned in the depths of the sea' (Matthew 18:6, NIV; see also verses 7–9).

The same Jesus who was full of mercy and compassion, who let himself be led as a lamb to the slaughter, is the one who will one day return to judge justly, and to wage war. Jesus is the one who will rule all the nations with an iron sceptre, the first king ever to rule with perfect justice. The prophets and psalmists looked forward to such a king (Psalm 2; 72; 110; Isaiah 11; Zechariah 9); the New Testament declares that the reign of justice will begin with Jesus' return to destroy his enemies with terrible judgments (Matthew 24:30; 25:31–46; Revelation 2:27; 6:16–17; 19:11–21). God then is still the judge of all men. We shall be praising him in heaven for the justice of his judgments; therefore we should be ready to praise him now as Judge as well as Saviour (Revelation 11:15–18; 15:3–4).

Because justice is still important to God, we find the New Testament making affirmations about the place of government that are similar to those of the Old Testament. Jesus, in answering the accusation of blasphemy for claiming to be God, appeals to the Old Testament. He argues from the lesser to the greater: 'If rulers were called "gods", how much more fitting is it for me, God's Son, to take that title?' (*cf.* John 10:35–36). Jesus quotes Psalm 82, which was referred to above. He quotes it with approval; indeed, when referring to the designation of human rulers as 'gods' he says, 'the Scripture cannot be broken' (John 10:35).

In Romans Paul writes of the authority of governments. This is a particularly helpful passage, because in Romans 12:14 – 13:10 Paul addresses both the place of government and justice, and also the matter of personal vengeance. At the end of chapter 12 Paul virtually quotes Jesus' words in the Sermon on the Mount about loving enemies, responding to evil with good, not taking vengeance (*cf.* Matthew 5:39–48 with Romans 12:14–21). Many Christians have read the statements of Jesus in the Sermon on the Mount and said: 'Here is a perfect illustration that the concern for justice of the Law of Moses has been replaced by a readiness to suffer evil and not require vengeance.'

If we look carefully at what Paul writes as he refers to Jesus' teaching, it is clear that this conclusion is unjustified. Certainly Paul forbids the taking of vengeance on the personal level: 'Do not take revenge, my friends, but leave room for God's wrath, for it is written: "It is mine to avenge; I will repay," says the Lord.' Two things should be noticed here. First, Paul is not saying justice is unimportant now. Second, he says that God will avenge wrongdoing and quotes Deuteronomy 32:35 to prove his point. We should note too that personal vengeance is forbidden in the Mosaic Law (Leviticus 19:17–18).

Some Christians will respond: 'Paul says that we are to leave all justice to the end of the age; justice and vengeance are God's business, not man's.' Paul, however, does not allow such a reading of his words. He immediately, perhaps to prevent any misunderstanding of his words, turns to government and declares that all human authority has been established by God to rule and judge mankind (Romans 13:1–7). Paul writes of the one in authority: 'he is God's servant to do you good. But if you do wrong, be afraid, for he does not bear the sword for nothing. He is God's servant, an agent of wrath to bring punishment on the wrongdoer' (verse 4). No personal vengeance, yes, but God has appointed government for the very purpose of punishing wrongdoing here in the present. Paul requires the Christian to have a high view of justice and those who judge in this age. They are God's ministers, *diakonoi*, to bring justice in society, just as others are God's ministers, *diakonoi*, to teach the word of God in the church. It is striking that the same word is used for both callings. If God has graced the ministry of justice with the same title as the ministry of the gospel, how can his children declare the ministry of justice to be 'worldly', 'unspiritual', unfit for the believer's participation? The more Christians in government, in the armed forces, in the police, on the judge's bench, among the jury, the better; the more likely there is to be justice after God's own heart, the less likely to be injustice, partiality, corruption.

The pacifist will argue that it is illegitimate to draw such conclusions from Romans 13. The passage was addressed to a persecuted church, he will claim; the Christians in Rome would never have thought that Paul was making statements about the nature of government for the church in future ages, which would encourage Christians to see the ministry of justice as a positive calling. My reply to that is twofold. First, Paul's statements are very strong. Second, Paul's teaching does not come in a vacuum. Paul himself knew very well that the Old Testament upheld this very same view of government, and so did the Christians in Rome to whom he was writing. Paul's teaching was not a 'one-off' word for a persecuted minority, but a word in continuity with the whole of God's revelation already known to the church.

Consequently we find Paul encouraging Christians to pray for governments (1 Timothy 2:1–2), acknowledging the legitimacy of the Roman courts, asking them to rule justly, appealing to a higher court (Acts 16:37–39; 24:10; 25:8, 10–11). We find no suggestion that anyone in governmental office or in the army be required to leave their position on conversion (Matthew 8:5–13; Luke 3:13–14; Acts 10:1, 2, 30–48). We find the analogy of the life of a soldier used as a positive picture of the Christian life (2 Timothy 2:3–4). None of these things would be in the New Testament if in fact it were wrong for Christians to take part in the work of justice, either within a nation or between nations. But their presence makes perfect sense in the light of the continuity between the Old and New Testaments' view of the need for human justice.

There is, of course, discontinuity between the two Testaments. The church and Israel are not exactly the same. The Old Testament people of God were required to put to death those within Israel who were false prophets and idolaters. The true worship of God was sanctioned with severe penalties. It is clear from the New Testament that in this age the punishment for false teaching is church discipline and putting out of the church, rather than the death penalty (1 Timothy 1:19–20; 2 Timothy 2:17–18). We are not to spread the gospel by the sword, but by the Spirit, the Word, prayer and righteous living. Nor are we to resist persecution for our faith with the sword, though we may demand just treatment from the courts when we are persecuted for being Christians (Acts 16:37–39; 24:10; 25:8, 10–11).

No country today can claim to be the new Israel and claim to be God's nation in the world in the way Israel could. God does not tell any nation today to wage holy wars in the same way that Israel was told. However, this does not mean that we can abandon all that is said in the Old Testament about government, justice and the waging of war. Jesus explicitly rejects such a view when he declares in the Sermon on the Mount:

> Do not think that I have come to abolish the Law or the Prophets; I have not come to abolish them but to fulfil them. I tell you the truth, until heaven and earth disappear, not the smallest letter, not the least stroke of a pen, will by any means disappear from the Law until everything is accomplished. Anyone who breaks one of the least of these commandments and teaches others to do the same will be called least in the kingdom of heaven (Matthew 5:17–19, NIV).

Neither the church nor any nation is in the position of Israel; but all the principles of government, of law, of punishment, of just war are fully applicable, and are important to God today. God desires justice within nations and between nations, and so should we his people.

Two reservations need to be made about what has been said about the Christian's attitude towards government. First, we are always to obey God rather than men when there is a conflict between what a government demands and the commandments of God. A high view of government does not mean that the Christian should automatically assume that government is right, and should therefore be obeyed at every point. We regard government as honourable because it has been ordained by *God* to uphold justice and righteousness. Where a government commands us to do evil, and ceases to be a terror to evil works, it can no longer be obeyed. It is God whom we honour first as the source of all true justice, and as the final judge before whom we and all kings will one day stand.

The apostles resisted government when they were commanded not to preach the gospel (Acts 4:19–20; 5:29). This principle is equally important in other situations. The Hebrew midwives refused to kill the newborn babies; Joseph disobeyed Potiphar's wife; Rahab hid the Israeli spies from her own rulers. In this century we can think of Corrie Ten Boom in Nazi-occupied Holland, disobeying the government there, and hiding Jews against the command of the state. The New Testament speaks of a state which is the enemy of God, and of his people (Revelation 13). The Christians are singled out as those who refuse to obey the beast, or to take his mark.

Second, we need to ask, if justice is still a matter of importance, what does taking up our cross mean in practice? If, like all other men, we should be concerned for justice in society, what is distinctive about the Christian? Every Christian is called to follow the example of Christ, to give our lives in love for the sake of others. This will mean that we are to go many extra miles, to turn our cheeks many times, not to rebuke and slander when we are slandered. It is all too easy for us to call 'enough' far too soon, to refuse to give, or to share our lives when it costs us more than pleasant feelings, to return any angry word with immediate interest. All such behaviour is forbidden to us. It is just at this point that we are called to be an alternative society, demonstrating the love of Christ to our world. There is always need for such a demonstration, and the life of every individual Christian, and every church, ought to be such. In our families, at work, in every social situation, we are not to be characterized by giving as little as we can and taking as much as we can, but rather by spending ourselves and being spent for the sake of those around us (2 Corinthians 12:15).

How, then, can we be concerned for justice too? An example should show how both principles can be applied. Consider abortion. Out of love we should be prepared to care for those who seek abortions, to provide an alternative for them, a place in our home, support as they struggle with the pressures on their life. Yet at the same time we may work hard to change the law to make abortion illegal, out of love for the unborn child. Love and justice go hand in hand, as they do for God himself (Micah 6:8; *cf.* Matthew 23:23).

> He has showed you, O man, what is good.
> And what does the LORD require of you?
> To act justly and to love mercy
> and to walk humbly with your God.

5. Should justice at home be our only concern?

Some pacifists argue that a righteous nation does not need to fear enemies from abroad, for God will vindicate the righteous. Therefore it is unnecessary to devote money and arms to defence, or to maintain the armed forces and weapons stock at a level which will deter the aggression of any potential enemy.

In response to this, it should be noted first that, if the pacifist acknowledges that justice at home is important and a legitimate concern for the Christian, he is in effect conceding that it is right and necessary to resist evil with force. For there will be no justice within a country's borders unless its laws have teeth, unless they have the sanction of punishment, whether fines, imprisonment or the death penalty. As we observed earlier the pacifist traditionally forbad all use of force, all involvement in government, or the application of law, as unspiritual. If a pacifist

153

moves from this traditional position to acknowledge that the resistance of evil by force is legitimate within a country, he has no basis any longer for declaring resistance of evil by force to be illegitimate when it is used against enemies of a nation who seek to destroy its citizens, steal its land, remove freedom, or oppress the poor and defenceless elsewhere. What difference in principle can be demonstrated between the use of armed police against a gang of criminals just inside a nation's borders, and the use of armed forces against an army bent on destruction from outside a nation's borders? The Scripture makes it clear that both are matters of concern to a government, and it is clear that there is no difference in principle, only in geography.

Second, every Christian must agree that our first concern must be justice in our own land. As in the life of an individual, righteousness must begin with oneself and then be practised in the family, in the church, in one's local community, and only then can one's desire for justice be expressed on the national level; so in the life of a nation the commitment to international justice will seem hollow if injustice is rife at home. With what integrity can a nation's leaders call other countries to account for removing civil rights, destroying freedom, imprisoning unjustly, ruthlessly crushing opposition, if their own prisons are filled with people who have done no wrong, if dissenters have no freedom of expression? So, as Christians, our longing should be first for the practice of justice within our own land. We ought to be actively committed to bringing the principles of God's law to bear on our society, for we know that God's law is fitted to all men, to every society. The law of God is given for the good of mankind (Deuteronomy 4:5–8; Psalms 1;19;119; James 1:25).

Along with this commitment to justice at home, a nation will quite rightly be concerned to protect its people against aggression from an enemy, or to answer the requests for help from other nations which are being attacked unjustly. A country, like an individual, ought to love its neighbour as itself, rather than look only to its own interests. So if Holland or France is invaded by an enemy, Britain should be prepared, both out of a commitment to justice and out of love, to go to its aid. Such readiness to resist aggression will of course be costly in money, time and people, just as the maintenance of justice at home is costly.

6. Should we not trust in God rather than in weapons?

In support of this view various passages from the Old Testament are quoted

No king is saved by the size of his army;
   no warrior escapes by his great strength.
A horse is a vain hope for deliverance;
   despite all its great strength it cannot save.
But the eyes of the LORD are on those who fear him,
   on those whose hope is in his unfailing love,
to deliver them from death
   and keep them alive in famine
                  (Psalm 33:16–19, NIV).

It is better to take refuge in the LORD
   than to trust in man.
It is better to take refuge in the LORD
   than to trust in princes (Psalm 118:8–9, NIV).

The pacifist will argue on the basis of such passages that our calling is to pray for peace, to trust in God, and to put no emphasis on developing, stockpiling and being prepared to use sophisticated weapons of deterrence. Israel's defence was God's concern: their actions in war were basically irrelevant or unnecessary. God gave victory to Israel by miraculous intervention so that the victory was the Lord's alone. This should be our model for today.

There are two problems with this position. God did sometimes deliver the Israelites by miraculous means without their having to fight; for example, the drowning of Pharaoh's army in the Red Sea. However, it is untrue to say that Israel's actions in war were always superfluous if they were faithfully trusting God. When Jericho was captured, God brought down the walls by his power at the sound of the shout and trumpet blast. Yet it was the Israelite army which had to kill with the sword every person in the city (Joshua 6:20–21). The same is true on many other occasions. In the battle against the Amalekites, Moses prayed all day, and the army fought under Joshua's leadership, so that the text declares both that the 'Lord is at war against the Amalekites' and that 'Joshua overcame the Amalekite army with the sword' (Exodus 17:8–16). Even Psalm 118, quoted above, continues: 'All the nations surrounded me, but in the name of the LORD *I* cut them off' (verse 10).

The pacifist's argument here makes a false antithesis between God's action and human action. It is parallel to those who teach that in the Christian life we do nothing, the Holy Spirit does everything; our calling is simply to trust and watch the Spirit at work. Neither on the personal level, nor on the national level, can such an antithesis be supported biblically, no matter how spiritual such an approach appears to be. Rather, in every area we are called both to pray and to act.

Secondly, we cannot draw an exact parallel between Israel and any modern nation, as we noted earlier. God's miraculous dealings with Israel were unique in history, for Israel had a unique calling. We do not have the right to expect God's direct intervention into the courts of civil justice, though Israel was promised this (Exodus 28:30; Numbers 27:21; Deuteronomy 1:17). Nor do we expect that God will call us to 'holy' wars, as he did the Israelites when they entered Canaan, and many times in their later history through the period of the judges and the prophets. The pacifist cannot have it both ways. He cannot insist *both* that the Old Testament does not apply at all, that the forceful resistance of evil is for the Old Testament only, *and* that miracle will be the normal means of God's delivering nations today, as he argues it was for Israel in the Old Testament. My contention instead is that God's concern for justice is basic in both Testaments, and that the principles for the practice of justice seen in both Testaments must apply both nationally and internationally.

We are to work for a sound defence, and we are to pray for the Lord's help. We know at the same time that the nations are in God's hands, and that if he desires to judge our nation there is nothing we can do about it except work and pray for repentance that such judgment be averted.

7. Are today's weapons so appalling that the just war theory no longer applies?

This is the position put forward by the nuclear pacifist: nuclear weapons are so destructive, they would involve the killing of so many civilians, that the rules of the just war are irrelevant. Therefore, it is said, the only right Christian response is to work for unilateral disarmament and totally reject the making of, dependence on, or use of nuclear weapons. It would be better for us to be overrun by an enemy than to continue maintaining a nuclear deterrent. The principle of the sacredness of civilian populations must take precedence over the prudence of being armed with a nuclear arsenal.

This argument rests on the assumption that nuclear weapons are qualitatively different from other weapons used in history. But are they? Surely they are quantitatively different, capable of greater destruction than conventional weapons, but not of a quite different order. Man has shown, again and again, that he can kill millions of people with quite simple weapons (Julius Caesar's wars in Gaul are one example). The ability to kill many with one bomb is not qualitatively different from killing many with swords or guns.

The just war theory required that war be directed against combatants, not against civilians. However, while the desire to keep civilians out of battle is obviously praiseworthy, we have to recognize that this is sometimes difficult. Have there in fact been any wars in history in which civilians have not suffered? Even within a country, as soon as the police are faced by an armed gang instead of by one individual, it is almost impossible to avoid the involvement of non-combatants. As the level of attack increases so the problems increase. A situation where a government is faced by guerrilla attacks from within ordinary communities is an obvious example of this. A government should not abandon the pursuit of justice in such situations and stand idly by while the killing continues. Rather it has to recognize that the guerrillas are representatives of the people among whom they hide, and by whom they are supported, and so reprisals have to be taken which cannot be precisely discriminate.

In war the same holds true. Weapons ought to be aimed at military targets, munitions factories and the like, but the inevitability of civilian involvement increases with the level of force necessary to resist an enemy.

Of course everyone wishes that nuclear weapons had not been invented. Everyone longs for multilateral disarmament. The question that must be faced by all is how to deal with the threat of an enemy armed with nuclear weapons, and with the danger of nuclear destruction. The nuclear pacifist must recognize that he is for practical purposes a total pacifist, given our moment of history. Unilateral disarmament by the United Kingdom might have the effect of destabilizing the situation in the world, rather than furthering peace. Further, those who suggest unilateral disarmament ought to consider the consequences of their advice, as George Will said in a *Newsweek* article: 'When the subject is nuclear weapons, everyone, and especially persons propounding radical and dubious new religious duties inimical to deterrence, should remember the duty to be clear in their own minds about where their logic leads, and to be candid with others about the probable real-world consequences of the behaviour they favour.'[10]

This issue of the awfulness of modern welfare raises a further question which must be considered in relationship to it.

8. Is war always the worst alternative?

In many disussions of war today it appears to be taken
for granted that we should strive for peace at any price,
that war is always the worst option. Is this necessarily
true? Vladimir Bukovsky, an exiled Russian dissident,
comments on the First World War and the Revolution in
Russia. 'The Russian people were in any case so fed up
with the war by then that they did not care. Anything
seemed better or at least not worse. After three years . . .
in which some 20 million people were slaughtered or died
of starvation, cold, and typhoid (i.e. *ten* times as many as
were killed at the front during the whole of World War
I) the war came to seem a trifle by comparison, a sort of
frontier skirmish somewhere in the Byelorussian
swamps.'[11]

Vietnam is a more recent example. Twice as many
people have been killed in Vietnam in the years since the
war ended than were killed in the whole 30 years
previously, and yet one still finds statements such as: 'At
last America withdrew its troops and peace could finally
be established.'

Such a statement should make us ask: 'What is peace?'
As Christians, we have to answer that peace is not simply
the absence of war. Peace cannot be had in the world
simply by protesting against war, or by disarming unilaterally. Of course we should pray for peace, and work for
peace, but peace cannot come unless, and until, there is
justice. This is why there are far more prayers for justice
in the Bible than there are prayers for peace (Psalms 94;
96; 97; 100). As in our relationship with God peace came
through Christ's receiving our justice, so in human society
it is impossible to have peace where there is injustice.
This is true within a nation: there can be no peace while
criminals are at large. It is true internationally: there can
be no peace in the world while the world is full of injustice.
Peace is not the absence of war, it is the restoration of
justice in relationships.

If, therefore, we long for peace in the world, our prayers

and our efforts ought to be devoted to the establishment
of justice. That will mean both the preparedness to be
armed with whatever weapons are necessary to deter an
enemy, and also the readiness to fight wars to resist evil
when no other way forward can be found. Bukovsky
expresses it this way: 'The issue now is not "peace versus
war", but rather "freedom versus slavery". Peace and
freedom appear to be inseparable, and the old formula
"Better red than dead" is simply fatuous. Those who live
by it will be both red *and* dead. Whether we like it or not,
there will be no peace in our world, no relaxation of
international tension, no fruitful cooperation between East
and West, until the Soviet internal system changes drast-
ically.'[12] '. . . There are 400 million people in the East
whose freedom was stolen from them and whose existence
is miserable. It so happens that peace is impossible while
they remain enslaved . . . The fate of Solidarity should
open our eyes.'[13]

9. The destruction of the world?

Many people are terrified by events in the world, by
nuclear build-up and by international tension. This terror
is one of the factors pushing people to join the cry for
'peace at any price'. As Christians, how are we to respond
to this fear? We do have to pray for, and encourage, our
governments to be responsible in dealing with international tension. We also have to recognize that some
things are worth fighting and dying for. We ought also to
have confidence in a biblical view of history, that this
world will not be destroyed by a nuclear holocaust, but
will still be here when Jesus returns.

Meanwhile we are not to set aside all our principles
when the stakes become high. It would be like the police
force giving in when it is faced by a heavily armed gang
threatening retribution on civilians, rather than by one
man armed with a pistol. God has established the power
of the sword to be his instrument of wrath against the evil-
doer. He has given us principles for justice and government

throughout this age. Our responsibility is to see that this calling is fulfilled in our own time, and to trust the outcome to him who is just in all his judgments.

Response to Jerram Barrs

Neil Summerton

Jerram Barrs' analysis shares assumptions with other contributions in this volume: in particular, that war is a species of judgment; that justice is fundamental to judgment and therefore to divinely-acceptable government; and that peace is a consequence of doing justice.

1. The effectively exclusive emphasis on judgment distorts God's requirements of human government. As is recognized at one point but not pursued in respect of government, God is *both* just *and* loving and merciful. So, while Micah 6:8 is cited, it is not explained how in government, particularly in war, one is to do justice, love mercy and walk humbly with God. (It is interesting that the prime example given of the requisite union of these characteristics – the cross – was in fact an act of submissive suffering.) God the Judge also goes the second mile and turns the other cheek in his government and the question is, therefore, what does this mean in human government? It simply does not do to regard mercy as a divine attribute to be applied only in personal life and not by the state.

2. While Christian pacifists often tend to the opposite distortion, it is palpably unfair to identify them with the atheist moral relativists of the twentieth century. To hold

that judgment should always or on occasion be delayed until the Last Day does not automatically imply carelessness about, or inability to recognize, evil.

3. Hermeneutically, Jerram makes the New Testament subservient to the Old, and, following Calvin, human government is given an inflated status. Government is certainly one mechanism – among many others – seen by Scripture as keeping fallen man within bounds in the absence of Jeremiah's heart of flesh. But for fallen man, even when Christian, the process of just, loving and humble government, particularly by means of war, is a good deal more difficult than appears to be supposed. Arguably the message of Psalm 82 is that, as a matter of fact, all rulers are under divine judgment for the way they govern in practice, whether the 'gods' of Psalm 82:1 are human rulers or the principalities and powers which influence them (see, *e.g.*, the Tyndale Old Testament Commentary on *Psalms 73–150*, pp. 296–297). Similarly, the New Testament condemns as unjust virtually all the rulers to which it refers, from Herod the Great through Herod Antipas, the chief priests, Pilate, the governor of Damascus (2 Corinthians 11:32), the city authorities of Philippi and Ephesus, Felix and Festus, to Herod Agrippa II. Paul had reason to be grateful to Sergius Paulus (who was converted anyway), Gallio (who is portrayed as bored rather than just), Claudius Lycias (who passed the moral buck), and the centurion Julius. But Romans 13 is most naturally interpreted principally against Paul's own experience of government as summarized in 2 Corinthians 11:23–33. Thus in recognizing the biblical status of government, his dominant purpose (as in 1 Timothy 2:2) is to enable the Christians to avoid just, and if possible also unjust, punishment by the authorities (see also 1 Peter 2).

4. Justice being the principle, its implications are not recognized when applied to war. Why is the slaughter of the innocent unjust in the case of abortion, but apparently just in the case of war? The only answer given is that such discrimination, while desirable, is impracticable in

163

warfare. Under the criterion of necessity, not only non-combatant casualties are regarded as acceptable but reprisals as well. In this, the end of justice has been so magnified that the means are automatically validated. It would be well, however, to ponder the parable of the wheat and tares (Matthew 13:24–30 and 36–43), where the Master's advice is that, if his servants cannot pluck up without harming the good, they should leave matters to final judgment.

5. Those who reject nuclear weapons on the grounds of the just war are not 'making the assumption that nuclear weapons are qualitatively different from other weapons used in history'. They are indeed so, in the phenomenon of radiation – their least significant attribute for most military purposes. But just war teaching long antedates nuclear weapons and its proponents would wholly agree that technology *per se* is not the criterion: the critical questions are, who is harmed and to what extent? Much conventional warfare is condemned by the teaching, which is why it is so often dismissed on grounds of necessity.

6. It is not necessary (Section 9) to postulate the end of the world in a nuclear holocaust to be concerned about the moral implications of the present strategic situation. General nuclear war today would not result in the end of the world (90 per cent of the world's population would probably survive the immediate fighting), though the effects on world history would be cataclysmic. Confidence in the biblical view of history, and recognition of the fearful possibility that before Christ returns there will be a major nuclear war, are entirely compatible – after all, God sanctioned the Black Death, which devastated Europe swiftly and comprehensively in the fourteenth century, and the comparable horrors of the Thirty Years' War. The question remains, could those who initiate (or indeed threaten) nuclear, chemical or biological war be regarded as acting justly within the terms so sharply defined by Jerram Barrs?

7

The just war:
a sympathetic critique

Neil Summerton

*War and peace · The holy war · The just war and Scripture ·
Alternative biblical interpretations · The 'Augustinian',
'vocational' and 'apocalyptic' interpretations*

The starting theses which the writers of this volume were
asked to consider address in essence two questions. In the
biblical understanding, is war a legitimate instrument of
state? And if it is, may the Christian consent to and participate in its use?

In logic, there are three possible sets of answers: both
questions may be answered 'No' and he who answers thus
may be defined as a thoroughgoing Christian pacifist. Or
the first question may be answered 'Yes' and the second
'No'. This set of answers identifies what may be described
as a *vocational* Christian pacifist. Or both questions may
be answered 'Yes'. That set of answers may be given
both by the Christian 'realist', and by the adherent of
the dominant Christian teaching on war since the fourth
century AD, that of the just war. The difference between
the Christian 'realist' and the adherent of the just war is
that the latter feels bound to add to his set of answers the
indispensable qualifications, 'in certain circumstances and
under certain conditions'.

The burden of the two questions is whether the state
ought to make war; and whether, if it does, the Christian
ought to approve and participate. Lest theological bearings
are lost, however, it is worth considering first a separate

group of questions about war and peace as phenomena in human affairs. How does the Bible understand and explain war and peace? What are the causes of war and peace? What is God's purpose in permitting war?

The phenomena of war and peace

War is a characteristic human activity. In the liberal intellectual tradition it is an aberration in social behaviour, a fundamentally senseless activity which would be entirely avoidable if only man would begin to behave rationally.[1] In the tradition of Machiavelli, Hobbes and Clausewitz – so important for interpreting European thought since the Renaissance – it is an inevitable human activity, *'a part of political intercourse, . . .'*, 'an instrument of policy', 'a continuation of political commerce, a carrying on the same by other means'.[2]

Both these approaches can be discerned in the biblical understanding, but in themselves they are incomplete as a summary of it. In interpreting at least a millennium of Near Eastern history, the Old Testament sees war primarily as one of God's temporal judgments (*i.e.* his judgments in history as distinct from final judgment) upon human sin, alongside famine, pestilence and on occasion natural disaster. In the prophecy of Jeremiah, for example, the words 'famine, pestilence and the sword' form a kind of refrain in his utterances of judgment. In this triplet, Jeremiah knew however that he was heir to a tradition of some antiquity already: 'The prophets who preceded you and me from ancient times prophesied war, famine, and pestilence against many countries and great kingdoms' (Jeremiah 28:8).[3] Some 100 or so years earlier, Micah had already defined precisely the sins giving rise to this judgment: Jerusalem's overthrow in war was to be specifically a consequence of greed manifested in government, in the administration of justice, and in the exercise of the priesthood (Micah 3:5–12).

In this, the latter prophets lay squarely in the traditions of the Levitical and Deuteronomic law. There, the scourge of war had been held out as a warning to Israel, should they fail to keep their obligations under the covenant, particularly the provisions restraining the exploitation of others and the physical abuse of the land of promise (see Leviticus 26:15–35 and Deuteronomy 28:15–68). These temporal judgments were not reserved for the covenant people alone. It would be surprising if they were, when the relationship between God and Adam, and the terms of the Noachian covenant with all mankind are considered (Genesis 9:1–17). Leviticus therefore, for example, suggests that the judgment of the Amorites – in the holy war upon Canaan – was a consequence of wickedness unrelated to Israel, viz. sexual sin institutionalized in religious practice, and Yahweh spoke of the land as vomiting the Amorites out because of their defilement (Leviticus 18:24–25; see also Genesis 15:13–16).

The concept is developed in the latter prophets. Isaiah asserts that Yahweh's hand 'is stretched out over all the nations' (14:26) and he, Jeremiah and Ezekiel in particular promise woes to the nations for their iniquities, especially injustice, oppression and tyranny (see Isaiah 13 – 27; Jeremiah 46 – 52; Ezekiel 25 – 32; 38 – 39). War is prophesied as the principal instrument of that judgment. The ultimate fulfilment should of course be regarded as eschatological (see Revelation 6:12–17; 19:17–21), in the last judgment; but the prophets themselves looked for an earlier, partial fulfilment which can sometimes be identified in the events of pre-Christian history in the Near East.

Like the companion judgments of famine and pestilence, war can be expected to be a feature of human society while sin remains. Jesus' guidance to his disciples was that war would be characteristic of the 'last days' ushered in by his first coming (Matthew 24:6). His followers were not therefore to be alarmed by the fact of the phenomenon: 'for this must take place, ... nation will rise against nation, and kingdom against kingdom, and there will be famines and earthquakes in various places:...'. Jesus was however explicit that these were not so much signs of his coming as characteristics of the fallen world: '. . . but the end is not yet . . . all this is but the beginning of the sufferings' (Matthew 24:6–8).

But the Yahweh of the Old Testament is not only one whose justice demands judgment; his loving kindness and mercy also require blessing. Early in the book of Genesis, Yahweh is revealed as one who would rather destroy the earth which he had created than see man's violence continue to corrupt it (Genesis 6:11–13). Increasingly, through the utterances of the prophets, peace is revealed as one of the great goals towards which God is moving in history. In the New Testament, of course, that peace is understood to have a supreme spiritual dimension manifested within the individual Christian and in the church, and brought into existence through Christ (*cf.* John 14:27; Ephesians 2:11–22; Colossians 1:20–22). But we need not therefore exclude the idea that that peace should be reflected in practical human relations at both the individual and collective levels. The prophets certainly saw the peace which they foretold as including an end to war. So, Isaiah sees a 'Prince of Peace' whose government and peace shall increase without end, when 'every boot of the tramping warrior in battle tumult and every garment rolled in blood will be burned as fuel for the fire' (Isaiah 9:5–7). Both he and Micah in a famous passage prophesied of a time when the nations 'shall beat their swords into ploughshares, and their spears into pruning hooks; nation shall not lift up sword against nation, neither shall they learn war any more' (Micah 4:3–4).

This peace (*shālôm*) is one of the great and growing themes of the Old Testament. By it the writers understood not only, or even principally, spiritual peace, for they saw man as a unity of body and spirit. Moreover, the breadth of the concept covered by the term was such that a variety of English words is needed to convey the meaning, including tranquillity, integrity, right relationships, wholeness, well-being, welfare and prosperity (including material prosperity).

Shālôm is seen as a consequence of other virtues. Just

as war is understood as a woe resulting from unrighteousness and injustice, so peace is seen as the blessing flowing from righteousness and doing justice, particularly in the social setting. Thus, the law which warned that covenant-breaking would lead to war also held out peace and prosperity as the reward for keeping the covenant (Leviticus 26:3–6). This theme is developed also by the latter prophets. A psalm ascribed to Solomon (Psalm 72) understands that, as Yahweh gives his justice to the king, as the people are judged with righteousness, as the cause of the poor is defended, and as the needy are redeemed from oppression, so peace and prosperity would abound. When 'the Spirit is poured upon us from on high', says Isaiah, 'and the wilderness becomes a fruitful field ... Then justice will dwell in the wilderness, and righteousness abide in the fruitful field. And the effect of righteousness will be peace, and the result of righteousness, quietness and trust for ever. My people will abide in a peaceful habitation, in secure dwellings, and in quiet resting places' (Isaiah 32:15–18; *cf.* Psalm 81:13–16; Isaiah 48:18–19). And after the exile, Zechariah exhorts the returned remnant, 'Speak the truth to one another, render in your gates judgments that are true and make for peace, do not devise evil in your hearts against one another, and love no false oath' (Zechariah 8:16–17).

Implications of the biblical understanding of war and peace

From this analysis, a number of general principles of abiding importance may be deduced. The first derives from the biblical balance between salvation and judgment. Sin is characteristic of 'this present evil age' (Galatians 1:4, RV). It is an aberration in God's order. And as judgment is necessary only because of sin (in the absence of wrong, the notion of judgment becomes meaningless), it follows that judgment too may be regarded as an abnormal phenomenon in the divine order, a necessity of 'this present evil age'. In the words of Isaiah, judgment is God's 'strange'

169

act, his 'alien' work (Isaiah 28:21 – in this case, the judgment of his own people at the hand of those not his people).[4] On a wider biblical canvas, judgment may indeed be seen as an act foreign to God's preference, while salvation reflects the primary desire of the divine heart. Thus the continual emphasis of the Old Testament is that God bears long with the sins both of his people and of the nations. His judgment is an act of last resort undertaken with deep reluctance when extensive opportunity for repentance has been given and other means of dealing with sin have been exhausted. Therefore, if war is judgment, then man's use of it (if permissible) must perforce reflect the principles which God observes in executing judgment. It follows that the Christian today may regard war as a legitimate instrument of state, and his participation in it as legitimate only when it is employed as a last resort (a principle which Christians are bound in my judgment to follow in all situations of conflict and potential conflict, whether personal, domestic, social or economic).

Secondly, while war is a permanent feature of 'this present evil age', it does not at all follow that we should simply accept it without making any attempt to mitigate its effects or restrain it. This is an inference which is often drawn from Jesus' words, '. . . you will hear of wars and rumours of wars;. . . for this must take place . . .' (Matthew 24:6). This requires, however, an assumption that Jesus was implying, 'So there is nothing that you could or should try to do about war.' But on the face of the text, Jesus' words were in themselves no more than a statement that, in the period up to his coming, war would be a permanent feature of history. The Christian should not therefore expect to see war entirely or even extensively eradicated until the parousia. But it need not be further inferred that the Christian is thereby absolved from concern about it. Most Christians do not similarly consider themselves absolved from feeding the hungry and healing the sick, *i.e.* from mitigating the effects of other manifestations of temporal judgment.

Thirdly, God's purposes for peace as revealed in the Old Testament, and the very character of the gospel itself, require that the Christian should be a peace-maker. In contrast to 'this present evil age', peace is a fundamental characteristic of the 'age to come', of its kingdom and its king. The gospel is *inter alia* the gospel of peace, with reconciliation at its heart. The purpose of Christ's atoning death was precisely to reverse the effects of the Fall and because that death establishes justice and righteousness in the 'age to come', peace (*shālôm*) may be expected to flow 'like a river' (Isaiah 48:18). It is only to be expected therefore that the Christian, as the citizen (Ephesians 2:19; Hebrews 11:14–16) and ambassador (2 Corinthians 5:18–20; in this capacity, carrying the message of reconciliation) of the new age, should be called upon to be the feeder of the hungry, the healer of the sick and the maker of peace. Jesus himself calls the Christian to be a peace-maker and thus to bear witness to his relationship with God (Matthew 5:9). There is no hermeneutical reason why the profession of peace-maker which Jesus had in mind should be limited to the spiritual as distinct from the practical sphere, or to the interpersonal and national as distinct from the international sphere. Indeed, the all-embracing scope of Christ's reconciling work as revealed to Paul (Ephesians 1:10; Colossians 1:19–22) is such that it would be surprising if the peace-making obligations of the Christian were not required to be demonstrated at all levels in human society. That an individual Christian is a politician, a diplomat, a soldier, or a military administrator would not relieve him of the obligation to make peace not only through war, but in other more peaceful ways if possible.

Fourthly, the Christian peace-maker has clear guidance as to how he should set about his task. For biblically peace is not to be brought about irrespective of other considerations. The Christian is not called to a process of papering over the moral cracks in the belief that war is in principle worse than any conceivable set of circumstances (though in practice it has often been so and in modern

171

conditions it may perhaps inevitably be so). While the cessation of hostilities is perhaps always a desirable first step in the process of peace-making, it should not be regarded as more than a first step. The aim should be to deal not only with the symptom (war) but also its causes. To achieve lasting effect, the process of peace-making should seek to bring the hostile parties (of which he may be one, but still obliged to seek peace) to understand the issues of justice and injustice, and of righteousness and unrighteousness, which underlie the situation, and seek to regulate them.

Finally, war and peace are seen in the Old Testament in relation to, and under the judgment of, high moral categories. The moral environment in which the phenomena are to be understood is that of righteousness, justice, injustice, exploitation and oppression, both within and between states. It is sometimes argued that moral issues are, or should be, irrelevant to the conduct of international affairs; and that foreign and defence policy should be conducted strictly on the basis of the balance of power and concern for one's own country's interests alone, whether political, economic or military. In the extreme version of the position, moral questions can be regarded as an annoying and irrelevant complication. It must be recognized that consideration of national interest and morality are often intertwined. When they are, however, the biblical approach would require that policy should be shaped wholly in relation to the moral considerations and not at all in relation to those of national interest *per se*. Indeed, where it is difficult to disentangle considerations of morality and self-interest, it may be that a country's cause can never be regarded as just, with the implication that a just war be fought only in defence of the just interests of other nations and not of one's own.

Morality in international relations

Some Christians would of course be inclined to argue that the state may legitimately act on the principle of self-interest on the grounds that its primary duty is to protect the lives and property of its citizens. Those who hold such a view would claim that both the Mosaic law and the references of the apostles Paul and Peter to the duties of civil government sanction action by the state which is not permitted to the private citizen, or to a sub-national body or grouping. Even if it is granted that the state enjoys such a sanction, care should however be taken in the deductions which are made from it. It is one thing to argue that biblically it is permissible for the state (but not the individual) to take life, or indeed exact any other penalty, in retribution (judgment) for action it judges worthy of such retribution; it is quite another, however, to assert that, in defence of the lives and property of its citizens, there is available to the state a different set of moral principles from those available to the individual which may determine when the right of retribution may be exercised.[5]

The latter deduction seems debatable quite apart from biblical doctrine. It begs the question as to why this alternative set or sets of moral principles should be available only to the governments of sovereign states and not to bodies at a higher or lower level.

At best the argument is likely to be that of dire necessity. Nor is it clear what the content of the alternative set of moral principles will be if the state is to avoid guiding its actions purely by *raison d'état* and *realpolitik*, by the principle that all actions are permissible if they serve the end of defending the state (whether defined as a separate entity or simply as the commonwealth of its citizens). Such a principle sanctions the phrase, 'All's fair in love and war' and enables it to be asserted, apropos the circulation of untruths to mislead the enemy, 'Anything I can do to help win is fair, and I would have thought that the media and the public want that too.'[6] Observation suggests that, while the public may certainly want that *in extremis*, most of the time even fallen mankind is inclined to bring to issues of foreign politics the same moral principles as they consider should apply to the actions of individuals and major corporations: try as the statesman may to evict considerations of conventional morality from foreign affairs, the public has a habit of reinstating them.

The argument that there is no alternative set of moral principles available to the state seems even stronger when considered biblically. The God of Scripture is a unity and *a priori* it would be surprising to find that the justice and righteousness required of the state were something different from the justice and righteousness required of its individual members. Jesus' strictures against the rulers with whom he came into contact are relevant here (*e.g.* Luke 13:32)[7], as is the fact that the Old Testament prophets, in the context of domestic law, condemned institutional oppression of the poor as sharply as they condemned the oppression of the poor by the private individual. It follows that an action is no less unjust because it is sanctioned by the courts than if it is undertaken by a private citizen – arguably, stricter standards should apply, since the biblical *raison d'être* of the administration of law is to approve what is good and to punish what is evil, and not vice versa (Romans 13:3–4).

The prophetic condemnations of Gentile rulers in the Old Testament testify that that principle applies equally in foreign policy and war, as may be seen, for example, in Habakkuk's condemnation of Babylon, even though they were God's chosen instrument of judgment: '. . . that ruthless and impetuous people, who sweep across the whole earth to seize dwelling-places not their own . . . they are a law to themselves . . . guilty men, whose own strength is their god . . . Woe to him who piles up stolen goods and makes himself wealthy by extortion! . . . Woe to him who builds a city with bloodshed and establishes a town by crime! . . . The violence you have done to Lebanon will overwhelm you, and your destruction of animals will terrify you. For you have shed man's blood; you have destroyed lands and cities and everyone in them' (Habakkuk 1:6 – 2:17, NIV; *cf.* Psalm 2:1–3, 10–11). Scripture therefore seems explicit that, even if war is permissible as an instrument of retribution, in use and threat of use it must be regarded as subject to the unitary system of moral principle in Scripture.

Old Testament holy war – use and misuse today

Jeremiah went so far as to exhort those who were to be
the instrument of judgment upon Moab not to spare the
sword (Jeremiah 48:10) and the concept of holy war is
fundamental for interpreting the whole Old Testament
history of Israel (see, *e.g.*, Leviticus 26:6–8; 2 Samuel 24;
and 2 Chronicles 14 – 16).[8] Some comment upon it is
essential, therefore, if only because many Christians point
to it and argue that, when linked with the New Testament's sanction of force in the context of civil government,
the divine approval of it continues to justify war today.

But we should be cautious about interpreting the Israelite holy war as licensing war in a wide variety of circumstances today. First, there is the radical spiritualization of
the concept in the New Testament, where the holy war is
seen principally as a theological type of Christian experience, particularly that of opposition to the gospel and
persecution, and secondly as having its equivalent in
excommunication as the means of preserving the holiness
of the gathered people of God. Secondly, in the New
Testament, the identity and character of God's covenant
people have changed. The old Israel were an earthly people
whose relationship with God was expressed largely in
physical ways. The evidence of divine blessing and cursing
was seen within the confines of human life at the physical
and practical levels (see, *e.g.*, Psalm 37). The blessings and
woes held out in Leviticus and Deuteronomy in return for
keeping and breaking the covenant were of a distinctly
material character, for example, in the earthly people's
relations with the heathen nations which surrounded
them. As Moses reminded God at Sinai, '. . . how shall it
be known that I have found favour in thy sight, I and thy
people? Is it not in thy going with us [to the land of
promise to drive out the Canaanites], so that we are
distinct, I and thy people, from all other people that are
upon the face of the earth?' (Exodus 33:16; *cf.* also vv.

1–3). This revelation was made known in part in the use of Israel as the instrument of divine judgment, *i.e.* in the holy war.

It followed that for a heathen people, under the supposed protection of their gods, to make war upon Israel was to make war upon Yahweh their God, and to call into question his very character and power.[9] This was well understood, for example, by both Rahab and the Canaanites at the time of the Israelite invasion (Joshua 2:8–11); the distinction between Rahab and the rest of the Canaanites was that she was prepared to submit to Yahweh, whereas her compatriots continued to resist Israel, and therefore Israel's God.

The position is now quite otherwise. The Israel of God is for the moment no longer an earthly people in the sense of a single nation or state marked out from other nations and states. It is rather the children of Abraham by faith, those whom the Lamb by his blood has ransomed from every tribe and people and nation (Revelation 5:9). It is therefore an international spiritual community which, *per se*, offers no direct threat to national governments (Romans 13:1–7) and which is led by a king who explicitly stated, 'my kingship is not of this world' (John 18:36) and who foreswore force, for the establishment of that kingdom (Luke 22:38, 51). Opposition to, and rejection of, God is shown *inter alia* by opposition to the church, his spiritual people, rather than in opposition to an earthly nation. Christians are certainly required to be pacifist in respect of the defence of the gospel and the Christian community.

This has important implications: it rules out the crusade in the strict sense of the word. With the coming of the church, war must in principle be regarded as having been secularized, and confined to matters of moral principle alone. At most, the sword of Romans 13:6 is to execute divine wrath upon the wrongdoer, not upon the infidel. This conclusion is also of relevance to wars for ideologies and belief systems, such as capitalism and Marxism, and for cultural entities such as Christian civilization.

When the fundamental religous dimension has thus been stripped away, the question arises as to how far the holy war may be taken as a guide for a Christian ethic of war. But if it is such a guide, the Deuteronomic holy war is by definition just (or justifiable) war, *i.e.* it must be regarded as compatible with the divine character as revealed in Scripture, particularly in judgment. The relevant principles of divine judgment are well displayed in the paradigmatic cases of temporal judgment in the Old Testament. Abraham's plea before Sodom and Gomorrah was, 'Wilt thou indeed destroy the righteous with the wicked? Far be that from thee! Shall not the Judge of all the earth do right?' (Genesis 18:23, 25). The subsequent deliverance of Lot (elsewhere in Scripture described as a righteous man whose righteous soul was vexed by Sodom's lawless deeds, 2 Peter 2:7–8), and his family, vindicated this line of advocacy and demonstrated the principle that the object of divine wrath is the guilty and not the innocent (see also the deliverance of Noah and his family, Genesis 6:9; *cf.* Hebrews 11:7 and 2 Peter 2:5; and the deliverance of Rahab and her family, Joshua 6:22–25; *cf.* Hebrews 11:31).[10]

The principle is consistently followed in Scripture, normally apropos civil judgment: 'You shall not pervert the justice due to your poor in his suit. Keep far from a false charge, and do not slay the innocent,' said the Sinaitic law (Exodus 23:6–7). The blood of the innocent cried out for judgment in the time of the prophets (see 2 Kings 21:16; Jeremiah 2:34: 7:6; 19:4). Furthermore, the degree of divine concern about the shedding of innocent blood can be measured by the elaborate prescription of the law for the protection of the individual who killed unintentionally and by accident (Numbers 35:9–15, 22–28); and for the ritual purging of the community from the 'guilt of innocent blood' when a dead body was found and the cause of death could not be ascertained (Deuteronomy 21:1–9). In the New Testament, the principle that judgment is reserved exclusively for the guilty is carried through into secular civil government: 'rulers are not a terror to good conduct, but to bad ... he is the servant of God to execute his wrath on the wrongdoer' (Romans 13:3–4; *cf.* 1 Peter 2:14). Something is fundamentally wrong if the ruler visits judgment upon good conduct as well as evil, thus rendering his sword as sword of injustice as well as, or instead of, justice.

Paul's reference to the civil power in Romans 13 has been widely used by Christian theologians, since the fourth century, as the fundamental basis in the New Testament for arguing that war is a legitimate instrument of state. But war justified on a text which refers immediately to the administration of domestic justice must show the same respect for innocent blood as is required in the exercise of the civil power. Such an implication was in fact already discernible in the Old Testament. It is powerfully illustrated by the case of Rahab of Jericho. The Deuteronomic regulation had been explicit, that in the cities of the land 'you shall save alive nothing that breathes, ... you shall utterly destroy them' (Deuteronomy 20:16–17). Yet in the first city that was entered, the innocent (by the obedience of faith, as we learn from the New Testament – Hebrews 11:31) were delivered (Joshua 2:13; 5:22–25).

If the holy war of the Old Testament is to be a guide to a Christian ethic of war, we should note, secondly, the regulation and limitation of both ends and means in the Law. The limitations on forming alliances, and on the military technology and organization permitted to the armies of Israel,[11] were required only partly for the spiritual reason of preventing Israel from relying on the ungodly, and on her own strength. Samuel's prophetic warning to Israel, for asking a king from him, emphasized the scale of the financial, economic and social damage which could be expected from the acquisition of capital weapons, and the concomitant establishment of permanent military forces (1 Samuel 8:10–17). In addition, strict limitations were implied in, for example, the requirement to undertake military service (Deuteronomy 20:5–8); in the means of appointing officers – the implication being that it was to be by acclamation of the people

(Deuteronomy 20:9); in the requirement to negotiate as an alternative to making war (Deuteronomy 20:10–11; *cf.* Judges 11:12–28); and in the regulation against genocide (with reparations being prescribed as an alternative, Deuteronomy 20:11–18); and on damage to the natural environment through war (Deuteronomy 7:22; 20:19–20).

The just war and Scripture

The doctrine of the just war has dominated Christian thinking about war since the fourth century.[12] It lies squarely in the tradition of natural theology and law,[13] and it has always drawn heavily on classical thought.[14] Earlier in this essay, however, an attempt has been made to assemble biblical material by which the tradition of the just war might be measured.

Some components of just war teaching are strongly congruent with Scripture. First, the terminology of the just war – that of the judicial process – is consistent with the biblical concept of war as judgment, *i.e.* the penalty prescribed for wrongdoing. The emphasis upon justice, and other moral categories, in relation to the *ius ad bellum* – to the cause of war, to war aims, and to the basis of establishing peace – is consonant with the requirement that war should be consistent with the divine character. The requirement that war shall be a matter of last resort harmonizes closely with the biblical understanding of judgment as an act of last resort on the part of a loving God, and therefore on the part of his servants also. Other components grouped under the heading of just cause command less biblical support. The rational calculus of whether victory is likely runs wholly counter to the central concept of the holy war, that military weakness will be no hindrance to victory for those whose just cause justifies their faith in their God. Secondly, the emphasis on self-defence, if it means of land and economic interests, does not fit well within the framework of Old Testament thought about war, let alone that of the New with its different emphasis on the importance of property.

The principles underlying the Old Testament understanding of war are particularly consistent, however, with that branch of just war doctrine which falls under the heading *ius in bello* – just means. In the light of the biblical teaching on the character of God the Judge, and on the supremacy of the requirement to love one's neighbour, the indispensability of pure intention cannot be overemphasized. It is a necessary condition, but not in itself a sufficient condition, of just means, however. For the deep concern of Scripture that judgment should bear only on the guilty and not upon the innocent strongly underwrites the just war's concept that the means of making war – strategies, tactics, weapons, *etc.* – must be discriminate. There are difficult questions here in the modern world as to how the guilty are to be defined: are they, for example, to be considered as only those actually under arms, or may those in the populace at large who consent to the injuries which are the just cause of war and who contribute to the war effort to be included too? That question must be answered in the light of the strength of the principle as revealed in Scripture. And the concern of the Old Testament about even the unintentional shedding of blood[15] must also call into question at least some versions of the just war doctrine of double (or side) effect, which suggests that the need to discriminate between the guilty and the innocent in war does not extend to those of the innocent who are accidental and unintended casualties of military operations intentionally directed only against those defined as combatants. This point is of much relevance to modern warfare, both nuclear and conventional.

Secondly, the limitations on means which were imposed by God even in the holy war strongly underwrite the just war concept of proportion of means. These limitations may be seen operating in three ways in particular. While the holy war entailed sweeping destruction for the guilty and their property (Deuteronomy 20:16–18), its regulations were designed to preserve the biosphere (Deuteronomy 20:19–20), with the implication that war should not be conducted in a manner which would have lasting environmental effects for either present or future generations. The purpose was of course to preserve the land of promise for the blessing of his victorious people. But as it was the original divine purpose that the earth should be to the blessing of all mankind and indeed all natural life (see Genesis 1 – 2), it does not seem unreasonable to extend the principle beyond the immediate context of the holy war. Secondly, the weapons, military organization and hence financial arrangements prescribed for the holy war were such as should avoid undesirable economic, financial and social effects attendant upon the professionalization of armed forces and heavy taxation. Thirdly, the kernel of humane treatment of enemy combatants and others may be seen in the requirement (of the regulations for war outside the land of promise) that on approaching the enemy's city the opportunity for surrender should be given and, if accepted, should lead to forced labour rather than massacre for the inhabitants; and in the preservation of women, children and cattle in the event of surrender after a successful siege (Deuteronomy 20:10–15).

Implications of just war teaching

In one section of the Sermon on the Mount, Jesus' method is to take various injunctions of the Mosaic law, to lay bare the fundamental moral principle underlying it, and to argue that the high moral standard embodied in that principle should now be applied with a startling rigour so that the Dominical formulation seems almost to contradict the Mosaic regulation rather than to build upon it (Matthew 5:21–30). If therefore the principles expounded earlier in this essay are to be made the basis of a Christian ethic of war, it seems reasonable that as a minimum requirement those principles should be rigorously applied. The Christian who considers that war is a legitimate instrument of state, and a legitimate activity for the Christian, must treat those components of just war theory which are consistent with the scriptural teaching discussed earlier. This must be done with the utmost seriousness, both in deciding when the cause is just, and what means are just.

Still less does there seem to be biblical warrant for dismissing just war teaching as impractical scholasticism and regarding war as legitimate in some, perhaps many, circumstances because it is the lesser and necessary evil. In this connection, there are some important distinctions to be drawn in an area in which muddle results from the confusion of the words 'evil', 'wrong' and 'calamity'. If war is to be justified biblically, it must be by the argument that there are circumstances in which it is morally right for one sovereign state to visit calamity upon another in retribution for morally evil actions. (Some might hesitate to describe such an action as 'good' rather than 'right', but that would require that 'good' be invested with the notion of 'pleasure', whereas just judgment acceptable to a holy, just and loving God might reasonably be defined as 'good' even when not pleasurable for the recipient; see, *e.g.*, Hebrews 12:5–11.) That is quite a different matter from embracing what is acknowledged to be morally 'evil' or 'wrong', because prudentially it seems the only course of action by which to avoid a worse evil. It seems highly questionable whether such a teleological approach should ever be acceptable from the Christian point of view. Certainly, the whole purpose of just war teaching is to provide the Christian ruler, citizen and soldier with criteria by which war may be limited to the status of a morally acceptable visitation of calamity, *i.e.* to the status of being a 'good', not a necessary or unavoidable 'wrong' or 'evil'. On this analysis, it would be preferable to describe war as the lesser 'good' rather than the lesser 'evil' and therefore as congruent with God's strange work rather than his proper work.

If those are the principles, in practice the closest guard must first be kept on intentions in assessing the validity of cause, in articulating war aims and in the actual execution of hostilities. Secondly, as any biblical justification of war is possible only within a forensic framework, it follows that every endeavour must be made to set it within the rule of law as the only safe way of ensuring that the retribution of war is just both in conception and execution. Serious efforts must therefore be made to develop the body of international law, and the instruments for administering and enforcing it. If wars are to be and remain just, each participant should as little as possible be judge and jury in its own cause, contrary to the position usually found in international conflict. Even in the present, relatively undeveloped state of international law and institutions, this argument and the doctrine of last resort would require that, where possible, matters of international dispute (such as territorial claims and other conflicts of material interest) should be submitted to international institutions for determination. There ought to be a willingness, on the part of the Christian participant at least, to accept those determinations. Less tangible issues of conflict would similarly need to be submitted to agencies of reconciliation and peace-keeping, again with primacy being given to securing justice rather than to preserving national interest *per se*.

Similarly, serious effort would need to be devoted to building up the laws and conventions of warfare in a manner consistent with biblical moral principle. According to our earlier analysis, those laws and conventions would have regard to three considerations; the avoidance of unnecessary suffering for the combatants; the rigorous avoidance of suffering, whether intentional or unintentional, for the innocent (*i.e.* non-combatants) in both the short and long terms; and the avoidance of anything more than short-term, local and remediable damage to the physical environment. Once what is regarded as a just war has been embarked upon, the Christian would be bound to require that his state should rigorously observe those laws and conventions (and, indeed, in so far as they are inadequate by biblical standards, require his state to go beyond these), in spite of the likely military consequences.

This proposition entails difficult problems under present arrangements of military discipline and conscientious objection in the western democracies, and still greater problems in closed societies. For it implies that there is a need for society to accept not only absolute but also selective conscientious objections. This is the right to refuse to participate in particular kinds of warfare with particular objectives, or entailing the use of particular kinds of weapons in particular ways, where that would be contrary to the relevant biblical moral principles. Such an obligation is in fact implicit in the development in the twentieth century of the concept of war crimes: in theory at least, the obligations of military discipline cannot be used to excuse those actions defined as war crimes. It may of course be than those who give the orders bear a heavier moral responsibility that those who obey them in response to the demands of military discipline. At least in countries accepting the rule of law, however, that argument cannot wholly absolve those whose duty is obedience. *Pace* some Christian interpretations of the New Testament, if man-made law conflicts with biblical moral principles, the Christian's duty to God must prevail over that to Caesar. It would follow that there rests on the Christian who accepts the biblical legitimacy of war a heavy obligation to work for the development of the law of war; for adequate adaptation of military regulations to that law; for proper education of both decision-makers and military agents in it; and for the recognition of a right of selective conscientious objection where that law is inadequate for whatever reason when measured against biblical moral principles.

Criticisms of just war teaching

Some will no doubt consider that these arguments are a strong echo (if not a considerable amplification) of medieval teaching on war as reflected in the canon law of the western church; and that they are as likely to succeed in limiting warfare as was that teaching; and that they invite the state to fight the most heavily armed and unscrupulous assailants with one hand, if not both hands, tied behind the back. These points are a convenient entrée to a critique of the doctrine.

The most fundamental objection can be stated briefly, but its force should not be underestimated for all that (though it must be granted that it may present less difficulty for anyone whose morality is of a thoroughgoing consequentialist character). It lies in the antithesis between the very nature of war, and the notion of limitation essential to the just war. War is in essence a contest between autonomous sovereign powers in which means are in principle wholly subordinated to ends: to achieve victory, it seems essential to deploy that quantum of force and those methods which are needed to overcome the opponent's will and means to resist. 'Violence', the philosopher of war, Clausewitz, wrote, 'arms itself with the inventions of Art and Science in order to contend against violence . . . he who uses force unsparingly, without reference to the bloodshed involved, must obtain superiority if his adversary uses less vigour in its application. The former dictates the law [*sc.* outcome] to the latter, and both proceed to extremities to which the only limitations are those imposed by the amount of counter-acting force on each side.'[16] Rationally, in such a contest all practicable steps must be taken to give victory with minimum effort and sacrifice whatever the consequences for the enemy; to do less, courts defeat (as Jesus himself observed in a famous parable, Luke 14:31).

Clausewitz was aware of, though he probably tended to underestimate, the extent to which even fallen man, for reasons of logic, convention or oversight, limits the possible uses of physical force. Nevertheless, it remains a matter of observation that war is in essence a contest without any recognized umpire. In it, *raison d'état* normally requires each contestant to take the precaution of using all necessary means of avoiding defeat and securing victory, with the result that it is highly unlikely that any multilaterally or unilaterally agreed limitations will be respected if the necessity arises. If this is the reality, it is not therefore surprising that, even in the most Christianized societies, the canons of the just war have generally been powerless to influence the conduct of war.

The second theoretical criticism arises from the first. If the fundamental character of warfare is as just described, to what extent is it reasonable to regard, or to try to place, war within the forensic framework presupposed by just war teaching? For in principle and practice, war in most circumstances is in nature far removed from the process of enforcing and administering the criminal law, and exacting due penalty within an established state. It seems more convincing to regard war as in essence a manifestation of anarchy rather than of the rule of law. This assertion is borne out by the chaos which infuses war and is the consequence of it; in that sense, it can be considered as bearing the demonic stamp. On occasion, of course, the breakdown of domestic order (quite apart from conditions of revolution and civil war) can reach such a pitch that the general arming of enforcement agencies to suppress commotion, rioting, looting and gang warfare may become necessary. Even then, the action would not normally be considered as extending beyond enforcement of order; apart from those killed in such enforcement operations, some species of trial, sentencing and retributive punishment of offenders could be expected to be carried out subsequently under due process of law. If it is correct to place warfare within the biblical framework of judgment expounded earlier, it implies the equivalent of simultaneous and integrated enforcement, charge, trial, sentencing and retributive punishment on the wrongdoing state. On this analysis it seems that the species of judicial process most comparable with warfare would be trial by battle, and there would be few Christians today who would be prepared to make a biblical case for that mechanism as an acceptable process of law.

In this context, it is relevant that, as will be considered at greater length later in this essay, the chief scriptures which may be called upon in the New Testament to convert the Deuteronomic holy war into the Christian just war deal immediately with domestic law enforcement. The sword of Romans 13 is explicitly that of police power and judicial punishment. Secondly, it is noteworthy that as a matter of fact, international peace-keeping operations bear a much closer resemblance to most domestic police activity that they do to warfare: normally, such operations are undertaken with the consent of the hostile parties, by lightly armed troops, and without the actual use of force (indeed, when such force becomes necessary, international peace-keeping forces usually stand aside, or are withdrawn). If warfare is so foreign to the framework and process of law and its enforcement, the applicability of just war teaching strictly interpreted is thereby called seriously into question.

A further difficulty of principle is that just war teaching entails the application of the criteria of just cause and just means to particular cases. Inevitably this entails the application of human, fallible judgment in each particular set of circumstances. Unfortunately, in practice it is usually each participant in a dispute who has to decide for himself whether his cause is just — with the danger that his judgment will be less than objective. Here again, if just war teachings are to be effective they point to the need for international institutions to assist in their implementation.

An objection of principle which applies particularly to the requirements of just means is the difficulty of fulfilling the obligation of pure intention. Since its inception with Ambrose and Augustine, just war doctrine has held it as imperative that in making war the high demands of Christian love must be met — that in initiating and conducting hostilities the Christian must continue to love his enemy as required by Jesus (it is a characteristically Protestant interpretation to argue that the injunction to love one's enemy applies only to interpersonal relations and not to international relations). It is axiomatic in the biblical understanding that the just and holy God, when reluctantly executing punishment, remains full of love and mercy; the purity of his intention is unquestionable, and indeed many of the judgments revealed in Scripture can also be seen to have a simultaneous quality of mercy. It must be granted that similarly it is possible for fallen man, reflecting the image of God, in measure at least to pronounce and execute judgment with reluctance, and with love for the condemned (though that is not to argue that human accusers, judges, juries, prison officers and executioners do not on occasion evince hatred or indifference towards the condemned). There is however a crucial difference between the circumstances of judicial punishment and those of warfare which has an important implication for the practicability of pure intention: in judicial punishment there is no risk to the life and limb of the judge or the executioner, whereas in warfare the position is quite otherwise. The psychological environment of battle is fear of the enemy. The desire for self-preservation and love for the enemy do not march easily together. This is especially so when considered in the light of Jesus' assertion that the greatest expression of love is to lay down one's life for one's friend, and in the light of Paul's statement that God's love was particularly demonstrated 'in that while we were yet sinners Christ died for us' (John 15:13; Romans 5:8). While a surplus of fear can paralyse, of course, the emotion is valuable, if not indispensable, in enabling most human beings to inflict suffering and death on other human beings. Hate, which drives out fear, will perform the same function. Equally, however, it is arguable that truth, love and fear are incompatible emotions (see 1 John 4:17–18).

Other mechanisms serve to overcome reluctance to inflict suffering and death in battle. First, there is the brutalization of the soldier which is found in traditional infantry training, and which is certainly of importance where fighting in close contact with the enemy is necessary. A related feature is the demonization of the enemy which is reflected in the infantryman's *patois* – 'Boche', 'Huns', 'Ginks', 'Charlie', 'Argies'. The depersonalization of the enemy is often needed, however, even where the character and power of modern weapons eliminate close contact with the enemy. Simple refuge in the fascination of the technology of warfare, and technical expertise, is a further means by which the fact that other human beings may get hurt is suppressed. The Christian requirement is, however, more than not to hate; it is positively to love, and the fact is that it is at best very difficult, even for the Christian, to love one's enemy and to do him harm at the same time.

The difficulty of observing the principle of pure intention has always applied. The principles of proportion and discrimination have borne more and more heavily, however, with the burgeoning application of technology to warfare. That is not to assert that their burden has ever been light. The effects of war in terms of economic depredation, famine, pestilence and environmental damage have always been more or less extensive and long-lasting. It is virtually impossible to argue that innocent blood is not shed, be it only unintentionally, as a consequence of any war. But ever since the application of combustion in the propulsion of delivery vehicles (firearms) and then in the projectiles themselves (shells and bombs), the risk of applying excessive force to combatants, and of shedding innocent blood, has increased exponentially with the range of the delivery system and power of the warhead (the latter always tending to neutralize the increasing accuracy of the former).

Many of the uses of modern conventional weapons fail against the standards of discrimination and proportion (*e.g.* obliteration bombing, defoliation and air-burst cluster bombs). The lack of control and long-term effects currently inherent in chemical and biological weapons certainly cause them to fail. And in use, the character of nuclear weapons as at present developed (whether battlefield, intermediate range or strategic) causes them to fail the standards comprehensively, whatever the targeting policy (*i.e.* counter-city, counter-value or counter-force).

The implication of these points is that in principle, and now in practice, the teaching of the just war may not succeed in justifying war. Even if the theoretical considerations do not carry conviction, the practical points seem sufficient in themselves to render most wars and military preparations unjust in the modern age. If so, two responses seem possible. The first is to abandon as impractical any attempt to place war under limitations on grounds of biblical morality, *i.e.* to abandon the qualification, 'in certain circumstances and under certain conditions'. This is in essence the Christian realist's position: the Christian lives in a fallen world in which power has to be managed, and in which it is therefore frequently necessary to accept less than the best; it is immature of the Christian to wish to keep his moral hands clean and his conscience unsullied.[17]As already indicated, this is to adopt a teleological, essentially utilitarian approach to the morality of war: the rightness of an action is to be judged by the consequences alone, and those consequences sanctify the means, even though they may seem to conflict with a biblically-adduced morality. As Edward Miall, the non-conformist political thinker of the mid-nineteenth century put it, war could be 'a *meanwhile* expedient to restrain the practical mischievousness of depraved human nature, until the gentler appliances of Christianity shall have healed its moral disease'; '. . . it requires the sacrifice of life, if necessary, to prevent the greater evil, the sacrifice of public safety and order.'[18] (There is of course a case to be argued – as it is by much of the humanist movement for nuclear disarmament – that many modern weapons are so horrendous in their effects that they fall by the canons of utilitarianism alone. This entails a difficult form of calculus, however, in which considerations such as the survival of populations and the avoidance of long-term damage to the physical environment have to be weighed against intangible goods, such as freedom, which are even less measurable. It is precisely when faced with this kind of calculus that utilitarianism begins to reveal one of its main practical shortcomings as a moral system. The differing views of the unilateral disarmament movement on the one hand, and the defence and political establishment on the other, derive largely from the differing weights which they give to these considerations in their fundamentally utilitarian calculuses.)

If the moral framework implied by the Christian realist position is regarded as unbiblical, two options remain.

The just war: a sympathetic critique

The first is to apply just war teaching rigorously so as to overcome at least some of the criticisms which have been stated. In doing so, it may be possible to admit some military action in the modern world as morally acceptable in certain circumstances. An example, perhaps, is police action by international peace-keeping forces to enforce international law or the duly decided policy of legitimate international institutions, provided that that law or policy passes the tests of just cause, and that the conduct of those forces satisfies the canons of just means. Much warfare will however be morally unacceptable, even that of a conventional character, for example, guerrilla warfare, bearing heavily as it does on the civilian population, and relying on the tactics of terror and reprisal. Such a proposition may seem to many to entail great political risks and the possibility, if not certainty, of much suffering for one's own people and for others. However, while certain forms of utilitarian calculus would reject the notion that suffering should be gladly embraced, there is of course no biblical undertaking that doing what is right will not entail suffering both for oneself and one's associates (*cf.* Revelation, *passim*). Some on the other hand may feel that the arguments deployed in this essay disqualify the just war doctrine altogether and therefore point to the second option of a thoroughgoing Christian pacifism.

Alternative biblical interpretations

The two options which are available to those who consider that the Christian realist's position is untenable lead back to the fundamental hermeneutical question which underlies these essays: do the Scriptures in fact enjoin non-violence on the Christian if not the state, or do they admit war at least in certain circumstances as an instrument of state in which the Christian may legitimately participate? The difficulty of this question lies principally in the fact that it is possible to discern two apparently inconsistent streams of thought in Scripture. The first is the tendency towards non-violence in the teaching of Jesus: that such a

191

tendency is at least apparent is witnessed by the widely-held view based on the sayings of Jesus that this was one of the distinctive characteristics of his teachings. Those teachings are closely paralleled by the apostles' writings, (*e.g.* Romans 12:14–21; 13:8–10; 1 Peter 3:9–18; Revelation 13:7, 9–10). Certainly, the early church interpreted both Jesus and the apostles as teaching thus. For this reason (as well as for reasons of eschewing idolatry), the church for the first three centuries of its history enjoined Christians not to join the Roman legions and, if they had turned to Christ while serving in them, to terminate their service if they were called upon to take life.[19] This stream of thought has continued to influence the church in one form or another. In recent years, a considerable body of biblical work has emerged supporting the thesis that non-violence was one of the fundamental planks of Jesus' moral teaching. The case is deployed in the earlier essay by Willard Swartley and Alan Kreider in this volume.

The second stream of thought rests on the biblical acceptance of the need in a fallen world for civil government entailing an element of coercion and retributive punishment. The recognition of this requirement in the Noachic and Mosaic covenants is explicitly imported into the New Testament by the well-known texts in Romans 13 and 1 Peter 2. Hence, while the Mosaic law was absolute and uncompromising in its injunction, 'Thou shalt not kill', it nevertheless enjoined killing as an act of judgment to maintain the holiness of the covenant people both internally in the shape of capital punishment of certain categories of evil-doer, and externally in the holy war against those who set themselves up against God and represented an external threat to his people's holiness. In the New Testament, when the covenant people had been transformed into an international spiritual community, the use of force within the framework of law is accepted as a legitimate activity for the now secularized government in an age in which evil will remain present.

The difficulty presented by these two streams of thought is that they appear mutually contradictory, and thus require some interpretative means of reconciling them. There are two differing reconciliations which are strongly represented in the Christian tradition, and a third which has been less widely adopted. The first may be traced to Ambrose and Augustine and, as such, is the most recent of the interpretative mechanisms, though it is now the most commonly held in the church. It solves the apparent contradiction by confining the *practical effects* of Jesus' teaching that we should love our enemies to relations between individuals (and perhaps between corporate bodies below the level of sovereign?). The sovereign state, to use modern parlance, is however called upon to use force if necessary to punish evil, and may call upon the individual citizen to assist with that task; if they are to discharge it, it follows that the command to love one's enemy must be internalized and applied only to the motive with which the state and individual citizen (*qua* soldier or supporter of the state) resorts to and executes force. Hence it is possible, as under the Mosaic law, to love one's neighbour as oneself and to execute punishment on behalf of God. The Christian may therefore both approve of war as an instrument of state and participate in it with a clear conscience at least in certain circumstances.

The 'Augustinian' interpretation

This 'Augustinian' interpretation, as it might be termed, resolves the apparent contradiction in a logically satisfying manner. There are a number of comments, however, which should be made upon it as an interpretation. First, it entails the hermeneutical procedure of interpreting the Master in the light of the apostles, rather than *vice versa*, as might be considered prudent in doubtful matters. Moreover, by this means a limitation is imported into the ambit of Jesus' words which is not present on the face of them and which, some have argued, Jesus did not himself intend; further, those words were, as has already been noted, echoed by the apostles themselves. Secondly the interpretation of Romans 13:1–7 with which we are here concerned requires two deductions from, or extensions of, the immediate argument of the text. The first deduction is that the text may be construed as giving lessons for the Christian *qua* ruler which are germane to the question of whether the Christian may engage in war. The apostle's immediate and overt purpose throughout the relevant passage (Romans 12:14 – 13:10) is to give instructions to the Christian *qua* citizen (*i.e.*, as subject). Indeed, the background to the passage is that of a Christian community under threat of persecution from society, if not also from the government, and the objective in Paul's mind is to recommend conduct which is likely to minimize the risk of persecution by the organs of government at least (*cf.* 1 Peter 2:12–17; 3:9–17; 4:12–19). He wishes to encourage conduct which will place the Christian community beyond the ambit of the organs of civil government or the relevance of the civil law (*cf.* Romans 13:8–10). In the circumstances of the church to which he was writing and from the text itself, it must be questionable whether the possible relevance of his words to the Christian *qua* ruler, or instrument of government, were even present to his mind as he dictated his letter. This is not of course to argue that the words have no such application. It may well be reasonable to construe the text in that way; it must however be recognized that it is the interpreter rather than the writer who consciously makes that use of it.

The second deduction from the text which is required by the 'Augustinian' interpretation is more serious. It is the argument that the origins and principles of civil government, as described in Romans 13:1–7, may be applied to justify war as well as the use of coercion in domestic government. Again, there is little room for doubt that the writer himself had in mind only the punishment by the ruler of the individual guilty of criminal acts. The proposal that this text should be taken as limiting the application of Jesus' teaching in Matthew 5 therefore rests on what might be described as a second-order interpretation. Moreover, the interpretation entails extending the

force of the text into a field in which circumstances and
processes are very different in the usual case from those
implied by civil government and the rule of law.

A further consideration of a different character is that
the interpretation of Romans 13 and 1 Peter 2 should
have at least an eye to those New Testament texts (in the
teachings of Jesus, the Acts of the Apostles and Revelation)
which emphasize the limits of the government's right to
command the allegiance of the subject. It is axiomatic
biblically that the state may require the subject only to do
right and that it may not require him to do wrong. As
already noted, there are no grounds for believing that
there is a special kind of morality which applies to the
exercise of power and not to individuals; the government's
mandate from God is to approve the good and punish the
evil. Also relevant in this context is the New Testament's
stress on government as a sphere in which Satan is particularly active in fomenting wickedness, and overthrowing
moral principle and law, in order to create chaos in God's
creation, and to threaten the good (*n.b.* the words of Satan
to Jesus on showing him the kingdoms of the world: 'To
you I will give all this authority and their glory; for it has
been delivered to me, and I give it to whom I will', Luke
4:5–8; see also Matthew 4:8–10; Romans 8:38; 1 Corinthians 15:24–25; Ephesians 6:11–12; Colossians 2:15).

Two conclusions follow from these comments on the
'Augustinian' tradition. First, because of the nature of the
interpretation of Scripture which underlies it, some
caution needs to be exercised in advocating it. Those who
consider that the burden of Scripture is to enjoin non-
violence may not be able to argue that their interpretation
is conclusive in the light of biblical teaching on temporal
judgment, and government's continuing role in executing
that judgment. Nor can the adherent of the 'Augustinian'
tradition argue the contrary case conclusively, however.
Secondly, as civil government is a temporary phenomenon
required by 'this present evil age', and seriously subject
to penetration and exploitation by the one whom Jesus
described as 'the ruler of this world' (John 12:31; 14:30;

16:11; *cf.* Luke 4:5–7), it follows that those who accept the 'Augustinian' interpretation should also accept the possibility of serious limitation, according to circumstance, on the scope for approval of, and involvement in, war. This of course is the essence of the just war philosophy.

The 'vocational' interpretation

The second means of reconciling the two strands of biblical thought may be termed the 'vocational' interpretation. Its essence is to recognize war as a legitimate instrument of state, but to deny that the Christian may participate in it; in effect it denies that there is any need to reconcile Jesus' teaching (which applies to the Christian) with the apostles' teaching on the function of government (which applies to rulers – who cannot be Christians if they would have to make war).

The 'vocational' interpretation must be acknowledged as holding a long and honourable position in the tradition of the church: it may be detected among those of the Christian Fathers who recognized the benefits of the *pax Romana* conferred by the Roman legions (though they were frequent disturbers of that peace!), but yet who rejected completely the notion that Christians might serve in those same legions if that would entail the taking of life.[20] A variant of the same tradition was recognized in medieval canon law in the western church which prohibited the bearing of arms by secular and religious clergy and yet which sanctified the crusade and the Thomist just war (the 'vocational' interpretation therefore applied to the religious, and the 'Augustinian' interpretation to the laity, a distinction which is difficult to justify on biblical grounds, as there is no reason for thinking that principles of the New Testament do not apply to all Christians). The tradition is also strongly represented in some pietist and quietist strands of Protestantism, notably in the premillennial and dispensational theology of the Plymouth Brethren, which took Anglo-Saxon evangelicalism by storm in the nineteenth century.[21]

The interpretation ought not to be too lightly dismissed on grounds of intellectual and moral inconsistency. Arguably, it does justice to the New Testament, both in giving primacy to the face value of Jesus' and the apostles' teaching on love for one's enemy in spirit and in practice, and in taking the words of Paul and Peter on the Christian's attitude to the civil power no further than they themselves explicitly took them. Secondly, the 'vocational' interpretation can appeal to the argument that there are a number of provisions of the Mosaic law which were permitted, not because they were ideal, but because they were necessary in a world in which fallen man found it impossible to live up to the full rigour of the ideals which represented the essence of the law. Examples would be the limited permission of the vendetta and of slavery, and the provisions for divorce. Jesus explicitly referred to the character of such provisions when he explained to the Pharisees, 'For your hardness of heart Moses allowed you to divorce your wives, but from the beginning it was not so' (Matthew 19:8). There is a temptation to read this remark as sanctioning divorce as a necessary evil – as sometimes the course with the least objectionable consequences among a number of courses with objectionable consequences. This is to interpret the verse through distinctly modern, utilitarian spectacles and to wrest it from its context. That context contrasts the divinely-commanded original standard with the regulation which Moses (rather than God) permitted, emphasizes that it was accepted only as the best that hard-hearted man could achieve under the law, and makes it clear that in the kingdom that Jesus was proclaiming a quite different higher standard was to be expected as the norm (*cf.* Jeremiah 31:31 ff.). Thus while there might have to be regulations adapted to fallen man in his hardness of heart, the Christian man is called to live out a different and more demanding ethic (*cf.* Romans 13:8–10).

A further argument in the same vein is that it is possible for evil men using evil instruments (*e.g.* war) unconsciously to accomplish divine judgment in a fallen world. That some war at least must be considered to be of that character is uncontrovertible in the light of texts in the Old Testament which describe aggressive and tyrannical Gentile rulers as the unknowing instruments of God's purpose: 'Thus says the LORD to his anointed, to Cyrus, whose right hand I have grasped, to subdue nations before him and ungird the loins of kings . . . For the sake of my servant Jacob, and Israel my chosen, I call you by your name . . . though you do not know me . . . I gird you, though you do not know me' (Isaiah 45:1–5; *cf.* Isaiah 10:5–19; Habakkuk 1 and 2).

Strong as these arguments are, however, there is a way of formulating them that seems to lead to absurdity. It is one thing to argue that war is inevitable in a Godless world, a judgment which may nevertheless offer glimpses of divine mercy, but that the Christian's calling is to separate himself from it to a set of higher ideals. It is another thing to suggest that war is acceptable, even desirable, for the Godless world as a calamity which maintains a measure of law, order and good, but in which the Christian may not participate. It seems even more difficult to lay claim to moral consistency if war is positively advocated as a legitimate and necessary instrument of state, in which the Christian can, however, have no direct part. There seems here to be a grave risk of trying to have one's theological cake and eat it at the same time. For the more extreme formulations of the 'vocational' position (as espoused in some dispensational theology) are open to the serious objection of implying one set of moral demands upon Christians and another, much less onerous, set of standards for the ungodly (a difficulty which cannot so easily be levelled against the 'vocational' interpreter who argues only that war is inevitable, but not in any sense desirable).

It is not immediately obvious why, if war is wrong for the Christian, it should not also be wrong for the ungodly as well. The dualist morality which appears to be entailed in some versions of the 'vocational' position is difficult to square with the rigorous unity of God in the Scriptures; with Jesus' assertion that he came not to destroy the law but to fulfil it, and his condemnation of the Pharisees for watering down the high moral standards of the law by their embroidery of it (Matthew 5:17–20); with Paul's understanding of the law as a high and changeless divine standard, met by justification in Christ, and to be fulfilled in Christian love for one's neighbour (Romans 13:8–10; *cf.* Jeremiah 31:31–34); and, perhaps most of all, it is difficult to square with his suggestion in Romans 2:14–16 that the man who is ignorant of God can by nature and conscience respect the requirements of the law. Moreover, in the face of the arguments from the holy war, and the description of the secular power as called upon to approve what is good and bear the sword (*i.e.*, deploy force) as judges of evil and 'ministers of God's service' (Romans 13:6, RV), it seems difficult to argue conclusively that force should always be exercised only by infidel rulers and citizens, acting only as God's unknowing instruments, and not also on occasion by the Christian.

The 'apocalyptic' interpretation

The third means of reconciling the apparently contradictory strands of thought in Scripture might perhaps be described as the 'apocalyptic'[22] interpretation. This might be so called because it implies that, in making war, the state is committing sin, and in that particular act is opposing itself to God. (Arguably, the first formulation of the 'vocational' position in the preceding section is in fact better viewed as lying within this interpretation.) The interpretative reconciliation is achieved by arguing that the teaching of Romans 13 may not legitimately be extended beyond domestic government, and that, at best, the sword of state is not the sword of war, but only of judicial punishment. Godless society is, therefore, as much required to love its national enemy and leave judgment to God as is the individual, even if in practice it cannot often be expected to do so. This is the interpretation adopted (whether he is aware of it or not) by the thoroughgoing pacifist, who argues that war is illegitimate for the state as well as for the Christian participant.

The exegetical and interpretative strengths of this position are the obverse of the weaknesses of the 'Augustinian' interpretation already noted. It depends much less on a deduction from Paul's immediate point in Romans 13, though some inference is still required – it is impossible to be *sure* that Paul was not thinking of the sword of war as well as the sword of internal justice, or to be sure that, even if he was not, the Holy Spirit does not intend the church to interpret the text as applying to war as well as to domestic government. The interpretation also implies a development, if not an actual change, in ethical teaching between the Testaments: put starkly, the 'apocalyptic' interpretation seems to imply that, whereas war under the old covenant was an acceptable mode of behaviour in which the people of God could regard themselves as called to be the knowing instruments of divine judgment, in the age of the new covenant it had become unacceptable.

Such an interpretation troubles Bible-based Christians, especially those unpersuaded by a dispensational theological framework: for it seems too convenient a way of drawing the teeth of inconvenient Old Testament material. But the possibility of modification of ethical teaching between the Testaments, and also in the course of the Old Testament, should at least be examined.

Some degree of development seems difficult to deny – or, at least, it is widely accepted by conservative, as well as more liberal, branches of Christian thought in our present century. It can be seen in areas of ethics which are by no means irrelevant to the central topic of this book. An evolution in attitude to capital punishment is, for example, discernible between the Testaments.

The Mosaic law prescribed death as retributive punishment for at least eight offences not entailing the taking of life (Exodus 21:17; 22:18, 20; Leviticus 20:9–16, 27; 24:16). It would, however, be difficult to adduce positive approval in the New Testament for capital punishment for offences other than murder (the New Testament analogy with capital punishment for many of the offences noted above is in fact excommunication from church fellowship as the means of preserving the sanctity of God's people). Indeed, apart from Paul's sword (Romans 13:4), it might even be difficult to adduce positive New Testament approval of capital punishment for murder (though Paul's remarks to Festus can be read as implying acceptance of it – Acts 25:11). Certainly, it is difficult to view Jesus' own commentary on the Mosaic tariff of judicial punishment as a development so much as a straight contradiction, or rescinding, of them. His exhortation that we should love our enemies, and pray for those who persecute us, may reasonably be interpreted as a dismissal of the scribal *misinterpretation* of Leviticus 19:18, 'You shall not take vengeance or bear any grudge against the sons of your own people, but you shall love your neighbour as yourself.' This was taken as meaning 'You shall love your neighbour' (*i.e.*, in the context of Leviticus 19:18, your Jewish compatriots) 'and hate your enemy' (*i.e.*, the enemy of the Jew – *cf.* Luke 10: 27, 29, 36–37) (Matthew 5:43). The scribal 'an eye for an eye and a tooth for a tooth' (Matthew 5:38) was, however, a more accurate citation of the Levitical tariff of punishment which was to apply equally to the native Israelite and to the sojourner in the land: 'He who kills a man shall be put to death. He who kills a beast shall make it good, life for life. When a man causes a disfigurement in his neighbour, as he has done it shall be done to him, fracture for fracture, eye for eye, tooth for tooth; as he has disfigured a man, he shall be disfigured' (Leviticus 24:17–20). In the face of this Mosaic judicial tariff, however, Jesus enjoins on his disciples not only mercy and forgiveness in place of judicial retribution, but also positive acts of benevolence. It is, moreover, difficult to see this purely as the response required of the individual, as Jesus included among his examples advice on how his followers should respond when called upon to do duty of *corvée* for the Roman occupying forces (Matthew 5:41). Even if this were to be viewed as applying only to the Christian community and not to the state, it could be adduced as support only for the 'vocational' interpretation, and not for the 'Augustinian' interpretation. Moreover, even if Jesus' words in this important passage were to be regarded as rejecting the institutionalized acceptance of the vendetta, rather than as applying to the Mosaic tariff of judicial punishments, that rejection would be all the more apposite to war, which may often be defined as a form of international vendetta carried out outside due process of law, as has already been argued.

If Jesus modified the obligation to carry out judicial punishment entailing physical harm to others, and the analogy between judicial punishment and war is crucial to the 'Augustinian' case, a considerable burden of proof rests upon the latter interpretation. In this context, we may also note an outstanding example of progressive development of Christian ethics. Slavery was brought under control in the Mosaic law (Exodus 21:1–11; Leviticus 25:39–55; Deuteronomy 15:12), was tolerated by the apostles in the expectation that Christian masters should seek to ameliorate its evils (Colossians 4:1; Philemon), and is now regarded virtually universally in the church as morally inconsistent with the principles of the gospel (with evangelical Christians in the forefront of the crusade against it).

Involvement and witness

This review of the hermeneutical problem has not been intended as conclusive. One purpose has been to indicate the limitations of each position and therefore the need for charity and humility among Christians who adopt the differing positions. The main intention of this essay has been to show that even the Christian who adopts the 'Augustinian' interpretation must accept the onerous limitations which it places upon war as an instrument of state, and upon the Christian's personal participation in it. In the final analysis, the issue discussed in this book manifests itself as a question about the degree of involvement that is possible in this area of human activity for the Christian who is enjoined to be salt and light in the world. The 'vocational' and 'apocalyptic' interpreters are both saying that there are never any circumstances or conditions under which the Christian may be involved, because such involvement would entail sin. The 'Augustinian' is saying that there are some circumstances or conditions under which it is possible. That implies in itself that there are some circumstances or conditions in which it is not possible. Separation from evil (a fundamental object of the holy war) is therefore as much a requirement to be respected in principle by the 'Augustinian' as it is by the 'vocational' or 'apocalyptic' interpreter.

The 'vocational' and 'apocalyptic' interpretations have a simple principle of non-participation which applies in all cases. The 'Augustinian' position implies a complex casuistry, in which from case to case it must be decided whether war itself and Christian participation are justified both initially and throughout hostilities – with the inevitable possibility of misjudgment in either direction. Some of the principles of this casuistry have been discussed earlier. In a fallen world, however, in which Christians are likely to be in a decided and perhaps tiny minority, it would not be surprising to find that there are many cases in which the 'Augustinian' finds that he cannot participate because he is not in a position to determine policy, and that policy is not in the event based on principles which he can accept.

This clash of principles is all the more likely because war is a corporate and social act, not an individual act. It is in this respect that many Christians today, including evangelicals, tend to be over-sanguine about the prospects of legitimate involvement in the enterprises of 'this present evil age'. Where sin is an individual act, holiness may be practicable, if difficult; for example, while all around may be giving themselves over to debauchery, it remains possible for the individual Christian to reject it. Where, however, the activity is of a corporate nature, the difficulties multiply exponentially, as for the theatre nurse assisting in gynaecological operations in many places in the western world. In such circumstances, it is doubtful whether it is adequate to argue, as Augustine did with respect to soldiers, that so long as orders are being obeyed, the individual is thereby relieved of personal moral responsibility.[23] The same difficulty may be faced in the business organization; and the moral difficulties can be expected to be particularly acute where the corporate activities are those in which there is good biblical reason to believe that 'the prince of this world' seeks especially to subvert Christian and non-Christian alike for his own chaotic ends, viz. government, international relations and war.

Thus in a secularized, post-Christian society the 'Augustinian' may well often find that, while just cause and just means might be possible in principle, they are not available to him in practice because he is constrained by the way in which those around him and above him choose to conduct affairs. In such circumstances, the 'Augustinian' may find that the demands of being a citizen of the heavenly city ('the age to come') in the midst of Babylon ('this present evil age') thrust him into precisely the same position of dissent as the vocational or thoroughgoing Christian pacifist has come to occupy by a different interpretative route.

This argument should not be dismissed simply as a sophisticated smokescreen for traditional evangelical quietism. While the biblical requirement of holiness has often been interpreted as a call to quietism or to the laagering of the cultural wagons of Evangelicalism, there is no reason why it must be so. For even when compelled to stand aside, the Christian community remains called to prayer, peace-making, and prophetic witness to 'this present evil age'. That calling to prayer needs no further comment, except of course to lament our neglect of it and lack of faith in it. The call to peace-making has already been discussed. Nor should the significance of prophetic witness be underestimated. Society may often require a word of judgment which can be heard without peradventure. Whether it is against war as an absolute evil, or as a conditional evil, may in present circumstances make little difference in practice – and the distinction may well be lost on many of the hearers! But prophetic witness should not stop there. To be truly biblical it should be a witness as well to the issue of justice and righteousness which lie at the roots of the particular conflagration; and to the coming kingdom of justice, peace and joy inspired by the Holy Spirit which Christ is bringing in (Romans 14:17–18, NEB).

Response to Neil Summerton

Jerram Barrs

It may appear unfair to Neil Summerton's sophisticated and complex discussion of war to summarize his chapter so briefly, but it appears to me that he has two basic methods of disposing of Christian participation in warfare today; the first is by defining just warfare in such a way as to make it impossible for Christians, or governments, or even God to resist evil; the second is to declare that Scripture itself is inconsistent.

A. The first method Neil uses is to give a set of principles for a just war, principles which he defines so carefully that it is clear no war ever has been fought on their basis, nor could any war be fought in which they were systematically applied. They are, in fact, principles which are purely theoretical and impractical. They cannot be found in Scripture, either in its statements about how war is to be fought, nor in its statements about how war was in practice fought.

1. For example, Neil assumes that it is wrong to shed innocent blood in any circumstances, and assumes that this means that war may be fought only against combatants. He allows the exception of a limited number of civilians who might be killed unintentionally. However, the forbidding of the shedding of innocent blood was a

principle for peacetime rather than for war. See, for example, the passage always quoted on this topic, 1 Kings 2:31–33. Joab is killed because he shed the innocent blood of Abner and Amasa. However, 1 Kings 2:5–6 makes it clear that their blood was innocent because they were killed in peacetime rather than in battle.

In practice in the Old Testament, not only soldiers, but also non-combatants, including women and children, were often killed in warfare, sometimes at the explicit command of God, as for example in Jericho, and throughout the wars against the Canaanites. God recognizes the solidarity of a nation when evil of an extreme kind has to be resisted and punished. The same is true in Sodom and Gomorrah, and in many other Old Testament examples of judgment and warfare.

2. In elaborating the theory of just warfare Neil suggests that it must come as close as possible to the practice of civil justice. There must be arrest, prosecution, trial, pronouncement of guilt, sentencing and punishment. Since these formal steps are not generally possible during warfare, Neil argues that war is therefore almost inevitably unjustly waged, and that it is in effect more akin to trial by battle, or worse it is the manifestation of anarchy, and anarchy of a demonic kind.

What Neil fails to recognize here is that even within a state, when respect for law and order breaks down, evil has to be resisted on the spot without recourse to formal trial. If I, or a policeman, see an armed man battering and robbing, or a gang of youths attacking someone, then love requires, and so does justice, that we use whatever force is necessary to stop the evil then and there. Is it wrong to protect the battered or robbed person by force because there is not time for a trial? Of course not. The same is true in warfare.

3. Neil also argues that patriotism makes it impossible for the Christian to discern clearly where the cause of justice lies; and that therefore we need an international body to determine which side is right, and whether it is possible for there to be a peaceful solution to the conflict.

While we may say in principle that this ought to be helpful, one does not have to be a cynic to recognize that international bodies are not necessarily any more fair-minded than a national government, and that their efforts at peace-keeping have not been tremendously successful. In the real world there have been, and still are, clear cases of tyranny and international aggression by totalitarian states which must be resisted by force, including warfare.

These are just three examples from Neil's discussion of the just war theory which illustrate that the effect of his principles is to tie the hands of Christians and of governments so that they are prevented from being able effectively to resist evil of major proportions. His principles seem more appropriate for a duel between Victorian gentlemen than a code of conduct for the real world where evil of a gross kind can and does exist, evil which must be resisted and deterred by whatever weapons most effectively do the necessary task.

Neil allows at one point near the beginning of his essay that man's use of war must reflect God's use of war. As is clear from the examples considered briefly above, his just war principles do not reflect the way God used war. Neil speaks disapprovingly of the *Christian* realist who is prepared to take part in warfare, even though the just war principles could not be adhered to strictly. My response is that the *biblical* realist ought to be prepared to participate in warfare when he sees that evil has to be resisted, as God resisted it, by violent means.

B. The second method Neil uses to discount Christian participation in war is to set the Old Testament against the New Testament, law against gospel, justice against mercy. He charges in fact that Scripture itself is inconsistent, and that therefore we must take Jesus' example of non-resistance as our guide, view differing interpretations charitably, and refrain from taking part in the application of justice in violent ways lest we be sullied by involvement in the demonic aspects of government and warfare.

1. Neil argues that in the early part of the Old Testament God is revealed in his character as judge, but that

in the progress of revelation this is replaced in the later prophets, and in the New Testament, by an emphasis on God's mercy, and his goal of peace for this world. In this way Neil opposes the law and the gospel of peace, so that a New Testament Christian must be on the side of peace-making by non-forceful means, rather than on the side of the application of justice by forceful means, including the waging of war against evil.

In response to this, I would argue that the peace to which the Old Testament prophets looked forward was not a peace which replaced God's judgment on the nations, but a peace consequent upon God's judgment of the nations. The book of Revelation, in the New Testament, makes exactly the same point; it is only after terrible judgments on the nations that oppose him and that follow the totalitarian rule of the anti-Christ, that Christ inaugurates his reign of peace in a world that is wholly his. The final peace of God comes both as a consequence of the gospel of blessing in Christ and also as a consequence of the judgment of God. If we are, as Neil says, to reflect God's means of inaugurating the new age, then we too must on the one hand proclaim and live out the gospel of Christ, and also proclaim and live out the justice of God.

2. A second opposition Neil makes between Old and New Testament is to argue that Old Testament believers had expectation of the manifestation of God's justice primarily in this life, so that their faith was rooted in the longing for material blessing in the here and now. He argues that they had no real understanding of the spiritual and eternal nature of fellowship with God, whereas in the New Testament we do have such an understanding. In this manner he again opposes law and gospel, justice and mercy, material and spiritual blessing, present hope of vindication and future hope.

This argument betrays a serious misunderstanding of the Old Testament, for Old Testament believers repeatedly state that their final hope is in the future life, and the judgment that comes after death. Though they longed for a present manifestation of God's justice, and for material blessings, they often did not experience these. In practice they lived on the basis of a spiritual fellowship with God, and by faith in God's promise of ultimate blessing and justice in the future life. This is the theme of Ecclesiastes, of many of the Psalms, and also the prophets. Hebrews 11 argues that Old Testament believers, from the time of Abel onward, looked for something in the future which they did not receive in their lifetime.

Even though they knew that their hope was a future one, they were still concerned for the application of justice in their day, for they knew that justice was pleasing to God. We too should have this same concern which fuels the commitment to resist evil at home and abroad, even though we know that there will be no perfect manifestation of justice in this life. It is, in fact, our longing for the justice and peace of God which lies behind both the hope we have beyond the grave, and also the pursuit of peace through gospel and justice now.

3. Neil is very strongly influenced by that tradition of interpretation which argues that the Christian's calling can never be the same as the calling of the state. The Christian is to imitate Christ; the state to apply justice. The real force behind this argument comes from the second and third centuries of the church where Christians did not participate in the armed forces: Neil appeals to this fact several times.

Two fundamental principles of interpretation need to be recognized here. First, Scripture interprets Scripture. Paul's and Jesus' teaching about the state are perfectly consistent with Old Testament teaching about the state; that is, that rulers are God's agents of justice in the nations, and that their work is pleasing to God, because it is God's own work. In the Old Testament believers were commended for doing this work, and nowhere in the New Testament are they commanded to refuse to participate in it. Where Scripture can clearly be interpreted consistently with itself, then Scripture must not be set against Scripture.

Secondly, church history does not interpret Scripture, but rather Scripture is to stand in judgment on church history. Consequently we must ask whether there were specific reasons why the Christians of the second and third centuries did not participate in the legions of Rome, when those of the New Testament era did. The answer is that Rome became increasingly totalitarian, so that those in the legions had to swear total obedience to Caesar, and acknowledge him as lord and god. No Christian could do this then, just as no Christian today can participate in certain political movements and tyrannical governments which make the same demand for total obedience. The Christian cannot forswear allegiance to Christ as his only Lord and God.

The existence of such totalitarian regimes, which in effect claim divine status, does not mean that in other circumstances and other nations Christians cannot be policemen or soldiers. Particularly where biblical principles have had some influence on governments and legal structures, so that there is respect for the rule of law, the Christian may and ought to participate. Even in a totalitarian regime where total obedience is required in members of the government, the judiciary and armed forces, the Christian should long for, and pray for, the end of such tyranny, so that believers can once again be salt in that part of society also.

Finally, I must add that I strongly reject the use of sophisticated arguments setting Scripture against Scripture which tie the hands of believers, and of governments, so that they are unable to offer any effective resistance to evil in this broken world. The conclusions to which Neil comes bear little resemblance to the teaching of Scripture, or to the practice of God as it is recorded in his Word. Neil's principles are of use only where evil exists on a simple level, and where the evil-doer retains a decent respect for law. They are of no value in the real world which the Bible addresses, and which exists all around us. If God had the same squeamishness about exercising justice, the world would have been reduced to total anarchy long ago. Thankfully God has resisted evil, and requires us to do the same.

8
In conclusion

Oliver R. Barclay

Three main questions that lie behind this debate were outlined in the introduction. It will be useful to return to these now and to summarize the discussion in terms of these questions.

1. Is it part of the duty of the Christian to help the state authorities to restrain and punish evil-doers by the use of force where moral persuasion is not effective?

It is not denied by any of our authors that God has appointed the state to punish evil, and that it may 'bear the sword' in order to do so. This at least implies the use of violent force.

The pacifists hold that, even if the use of violence is God's appointed weapon for the state, the Christian cannot use such methods because they are totally out of keeping with the standard of Christian character given to us in the Sermon on the Mount (Swartley and Kreider, pp. 39ff.). The Christian cannot, for instance, be an armed policeman; certainly he cannot in their view be a soldier or a judge; he may at best 'as a rule teach (in) school, hold public health positions'. They believe that Jesus forbad the use of violence in his followers. They are, however, not

212

quite clear in this book as to how far the state's use of force should go. Some do not believe the Christian can tell the ungodly state how to act anyway. They are, however, clear that the Christian must opt out of any civil responsibility that requires the use of such ungodly means as killing people. 'We are to obey God rather than men.'

The reply to this from the just war advocates is that there is a distinction between personal response to evil and the *God-given* duty of governments. (I shall refer to the non-pacifists in future as just war advocates. As becomes clear in the exchange between Neil Summerton and Jerram Barrs, the two sides hold very different views of the just war, but the non-pacifists argue that there can be a war in which the Christian can take part with a good conscience, and this is what I shall mean by the phrase, just war, in this summary.)

The just war advocates say that even when Paul has repeated almost pure Sermon on the Mount material on not resisting evil, in Romans 12, he goes on immediately in Romans 13 to say that *God* has appointed governments to resist and punish evil and to 'bear the sword' in doing so. The powers are ministers of God's *wrath*, and we must not hesitate to be his ministers in this respect. We must be willing to play our part in any government role such as judge or soldier, so long as we act justly and in love (for the whole of society and not only for the evil-doer). Not to punish evil is to be out of character if we are to be like God. Painful as it is to put anyone beyond the opportunity of repentance, that is God's way when other methods are inadequate. We must be tough against evil because God is tough and calls on the state to be so. The problem lies with really evil men. When they get into power the structures that are intended for good (law and order and peace) are hi-jacked by them for evil. (Hi-jackers can be dealt with by giving way, or by subduing them, often violently.)

These advocataes also believe that some people can be dealt with by force only at the risk of killing them, and that this is what the Bible requires both in the Old and

New Testaments. If the Christian is not to help the state to do its job, it is a very unusual situation. They are then to pray for God's will to be done, including the 'bearing the sword' by the authorities in the ministry of wrath. They are to pay taxes so that the government can do this work (Romans 13:6). Surely, they argue, if we are to pray, and to pay for the state to do these things, we must help to answer our own prayers, and see the resulting action as pleasing to God?

If we are personally not to 'resist' evil (or evil men, Matthew 5:39), that cannot be the duty of society and its authorities ('the powers'). To try to apply the personal ethics of the Sermon on the Mount to the duties of government is to leave evil almost unpunished and unrestrained – except by the sort of moral pressures on conscience that evil men do not acknowledge. Within the church such pressures are sufficient; outside the church God has given other means to deal with evil. There is then on this view a twofold duty laid on the Christian: to live according to the Sermon on the Mount in personal relationships, and to help the 'powers' to use the appropriate and God-given means (including 'the sword') in the restraint and punishment of evil in society as a whole. Hence, in the Old Testament, God commanded his authorities such as Moses and Joshua to use force, and not moral persuasion alone, as God's means of dealing with evil. The Christian must hold that it is God's will that evil men and women are not only restrained and reformed, but also punished. This is a clear biblical teaching, and none of our authors dispute it, though some non-Christian pacifists may do so.

The pacifists' reply to this takes two forms. First, the evil means forbidden by our Lord cannot become a right action for the Christian when done by the state. A Christian cannot help the state to do even its God-given duty when it involves foul means. Secondly, they argue that there cannot be a double standard – a 'higher' one for the church and a 'lower' one for the state. The traditional understanding of Romans 13, on their view, makes it contradict Romans 12 and the Sermon on the Mount. We must, therefore, have got it wrong, and they look for another interpretation of Romans 13. Neil Summerton's position is different, however: it does not exclude the death penalty.

Here there emerges a difference of view about the Old Testament. The pacifists make a far more radical break than the others between the Old Testament and the New Testament. As a result they can largely ignore the Old Testament view of the state (Swartley and Kreider, pp. 47ff.), and can argue that Romans 13 has been interpreted too broadly as laying down general principles when it may have been largely addressing a particular situation. The just war advocates argue not only that the positive Christian view of the state's role is more widely represented in the New Testament than Romans 13 (*e.g.* 1 Peter 2), but that we must take into account the more positive view of the secular powers, as an agent of God's righteous judgment, that appears in the New Testament, but is a constant theme in the Old Testament. The two Testaments, they say, teach the same positive view of the state and its duty, and clearly Old Testament believers were expected to be the agents of the state in this role.

There is often involved here, also, a difference of view about the place of the Law of God. That emerged particularly in Arthur Holmes' paper (pp. 18ff.). On most pacifist views the church has little place for the law, and some pacifist traditions have been explicit on this. On the just war view, the law is not a lower standard than the gospel. Both are God-given, but the law and its penalties are all that evil men will listen to (see 1 Timothy 1:8–11), while the Christian follows the Sermon on the Mount, going far beyond the law without in any way abrogating it. Christ *fulfilled* the law, so that the law remains to warn us of what God hates, and will punish, as Jesus himself stressed, even in the Sermon on the Mount (Matthew 5:22, 29–30; 7:2). This different view of the law is not essential to the debate, but is often implicit, and is raised by the just war advocates to explain their response to the charge of having a two-tier morality.

There is here, then, a division of view about how God intends evil to be dealt with, which involves two different attitudes to the state, and to human sinfulness. Romans 12 says, 'overcome evil with good', but then in Romans 13 it says that God has ordained the 'powers' to punish evil. Is it then God's will that Christians do not resist evil with other than moral force? Robert Clark would say Yes; Willard Swartley would allow that God intends the state 'powers' forcibly to restrain evil so long as there is no danger to life and limb. The Christian, however, should set a consistently Christian, Sermon on the Mount example, and should not be enthusiastic in helping the state in this duty.

On the other side, Arthur Holmes, Jerram Barrs and John Peck argue that the Christian should, with a good conscience, be an armed policeman, a judge or, presumably, a hangman. Neil Summerton would probably agree with them so far. Our proper desire to do all we can, short of violence, must not blind us to the fact that violence may be a duty to God. God himself uses violence in judgment, and will do in the final judgment. For us to do so in the course of justice or righteousness is not 'ungodly'. The Christian should not feel a bad conscience about being involved in such activities if he is satisfied that other less violent means will not be effective. On this view the Christian should be enthusiastic to help the state to carry out all its God-given tasks, and punishment is a matter of justice whether it restrains evil or not.

A basic divergence of attitude
There lies behind this a difference of view about the state, and an important difference of view about what means are necessary to curb the sin of man. The pacifists who write here have a somewhat negative, or at least a pessimistic, view of the state. If they do not think that it is 'worldly', they emphasize that it can be the embodiment of evil spiritual powers (Neil Summerton, Willard Swartley and Alan Kreider). Correspondingly, however, they have a more optimistic view of individuals than the just war

216

advocates. They have often held that moral persuasion and passive resistance should be enough to restrain even Hitler (Robert Clark). They value highly the residual moral sense that is in unbelievers, especially where there is a Christian background in their culture. They believe that the Christian way is to 'overcome evil with good', and that this excludes the use of violence, especially killing, even if (as in Christ's cross) the result is apparent failure.

The just war advocates have a less optimistic view of man, and believe that even God himself does not win all men over by moral persuasion and passive resistance. God himself uses violence and promises that in the end he will do so again to the unrepentant. The threat and execution of judgment is, on this view, a godly thing, and is even part of God's good and loving method of overcoming evil. It is not a 'strange work' in the sense that it is inconsistent, or less than God's love – only in the sense that it is, to mere men, a surprising part of God's love for his whole creation. As a result, they do not find it surprising that God himself has given the secular powers the duty and authority to act with violence in the interests of justice and judgment. The just war advocates have a more optimistic view of the state than the pacifists, believing that much good derives from a right use of force. God in his love has ordained this means of restraining evil. They agree that the state can become demonic, and that is equally true of the individual. Evil men, whether they have state power or not, deserve to be judged and punished when God requires that this should be done. So they hold a more pessimistic view of sin in man, and a more positive view of the state as one of God's means of dealing with it.

2. Is it part of the duty of the Christian to help the state to defend its citizens or its territory, to contend for international righteousness and to maintain law and order even, where necessary, by the use of violence including killing people?

The debate then moved on to the second question of

armed forces and war. If it is granted that force may be used by the state to preserve justice within its own boundaries, is this same duty extendable to its wider relationships to other states? For those who do not allow the use of violence within the state, the extension to war is obviously unacceptable. Willard Swartley and Alan Kreider allow that the state may wage war, but that Christians must have a different stand, and cannot help it to do this work. It is in their view not the churches' job to tell the state how to act in its capacity as a minister of wrath (page 51). That there is a responsibility laid on the government for defence is not questioned. The real disagreement then is about means. If a state disbanded its armed forces, even on the pacifist view it would still have a duty to enable its citizens to defend themselves against unjust aggression from without, as far as that is possible by non-violent means. Normally, no-one disputes the extension of the use of violence to international 'police' action if the use of violence is accepted within the state. Neil Summerton might do so, since, on pragmatic grounds, he believes war is wrong, even if armed police action is not.

The question of war then revolved round two lesser questions. If you accept the use of violence in some domestic contexts, for what purposes may violence be used for international purposes; and, secondly, are there limits to the means – to the kind of violence that should be used? The pacifists here stress that war creates all sorts of horrible evils. To shoot an armed criminal who may be about to shoot someone else is wrong in their view, but war is really a different matter, and different not only in scale. A good end does not justify evil means, and war is evil – they often say, 'sin', a usage that Arthur Holmes regards as assuming what needs to be proved.

Just war advocates argue that war must be 'just'. It should be used only for defence – defence of your own country, or some population that is unjustly threatened by evil powers (e.g. the Jews under Hitler). It cannot be used as a means of territorial aggrandizement, or imposing your will or culture on an unwilling population. Christians must be free to declare that a particular war is unjust, and to refuse to take part (as even some professional soldiers have done in the past). They argue that there is such a thing as a 'just war', and the fight against Hitler is mentioned as an example. They do not believe that there was any other way to restrain his evil and to punish his regime.

Willard Swartley, Alan Kreider and Robert Clark have as their ideal the 'vocational pacifist' – the one who believes that all Christians have a special vocation to refuse involvement in many 'worldly' roles, and to live a distinctive life as an example of non-violent contention for all that is good. Neil Summerton, although he is a practical pacifist, finds this option unacceptable; while John Peck, who is not a pacifist, believes that it could be an option for some, but not all, Christians. Neil Summerton and John Peck are left with no very clear practical policy in relation to the state, except in the matter of war itself, where they take opposite views. It must be admitted that the position of Willard Swartley, Alan Kreider and Robert Clark appears to be a more rigorously consistent pacifist option. The war issue is seen as only one application of a policy in relation to the state and its functions. On the other side, Arthur Holmes, Jerram Barrs and Sir Frederick Catherwood appear the more rigorously consistent in the opposite direction. They accept that the Christian should be willing to bear arms in a just cause, and should be positive about the duty of national as well as civil defence, and good law and order. All this arises again from their view of the state, and the means necessary to deal with evil in the heart of man.

3. If violence is justified in some circumstances, are there limits to the means that can be used?

The most acute problem arises over means. War has become a very different thing from conflicts between professional troops. Civilian populations will suffer, the destruction will often be far greater than was necessary, and so on. The pacifists argue that even if you granted the idea of a just war, the whole thing is absurdly unrealistic today. The criteria of a just war cannot any longer be applied (if they ever could), so that no war can be 'just', even if the use of violence was granted.

There is here a difference of stance that would make it difficult for the two sides to appreciate one another. To those pacifists to whom all killing is immoral, mass killing is simply inconceivable as a Christian option. The scale of evil in modern warfare is quite unthinkable. To the just war advocate, who accepts that evil is so vicious that extreme violent things are needed to deal with it, there is a certain 'toughness' that can face the possibility of war. That toughness accepts killing as not always the greatest evil. It accepts violent punishment as a means that God uses in the Old Testament, in history and in final judgment. It can therefore accept even the ravages of war as a shocking but necessary thing to deal with an even more shocking thing – rampant evil.

These differences are attractive to different temperaments. They are also the result of different overall theological emphases. Where God's implacable hatred of sin, and his violent judgment on it, have often been stressed, the just war option is easier to accept. Where the emphasis on love and caring for your neighbour has been paramount, the pacifist position is more attractive. Both emphases are, of course, biblical, but different traditions have emphasized or de-emphasized them in different degrees. Historically, this is illustrated in the kinds of church traditions that have taken the two views. For example, the backbone of the Resistance Movements under Hitler in occupied Holland (Calvinistic), and in Norway (Lutheran), were Bible-believing Christians in the main-stream Reformation tradition. The backbone of the pacifist tradition in the war was Quaker and Mennonite, creating ambulance and relief services. Both were willing to suffer and risk death for their beliefs.

As we have pointed out, there also cut across this discussion differences in the doctrine of the state, or at least the attitude to the state, and these differences emerge as a rule in other activities as well. It affects how far they get involved in the authority structures of the state, in politics, and the like. The pacifists are often foremost in social work, but not usually in social reform, because they doubt their right to tell the state its job. The just war advocates have often been prominent in social reform, but may be lacking in practical involvement at the grass-roots level. In each country one can probably think of examples. This suggests that in spite of sharp differences over war and violence, each side has something to learn from the other, even while they plainly disagree in principle.

4. Nuclear weapons

Finally, there is the question of nuclear weapons. This has not been argued at length in this book because the other issues are of wider practical application, and in some aspects it is only an extreme example of the whole war issue. Some of the just war advocates, however, are nuclear pacifists. They believe that nuclear war is so devastating to the whole population that it is simply unthinkable. Even if limited war is moral, this they feel would be totally immoral. To this, Fred Catherwood replies that, although we all wish that we could get rid of nuclear weapons and should try energetically to do so, to abolish them unilaterally would be an abdication of our fundamental duty towards justice and defence. He believes that the just war advocates who are also nuclear pacifists have really abandoned their duty to defence. They must be even 'tougher' than they are, and hold nuclear weapons as a deterrent, even while they aim to abolish them. If they do not, they may as well be thoroughgoing pacifists in today's world. Only a madman would use nuclear weapons when there is going to be a response with similar weapons. As soon as reprisals are not possible, nuclear weapons may well be used to destroy an enemy. The threat of reprisal is one aspect of 'bearing the sword', and in this case (as

Oliver R. Barclay

with the armed robber), if you are not similarly armed you invite violence. Alan Kreider judges that the arguments for nuclear deterrent are political rather than theological arguments, and, further, that the deterrent is likely to lead to the kind of use of nuclear weapons that Sir Frederick himself would not allow.

It should be remarked here that the nuclear pacifist is not necessarily an advocate of unilateral nuclear disarmament. Having got ourselves into the present position, it is possible to argue that we should put great energy into universal multilateral abolition of nuclear weapons, but that this cannot be done on a unilateral basis. This question – unilateral or multilateral nuclear disarmament? – has not been debated here, and is a further distinct question of political strategy. Nuclear pacifists would say that nuclear weapons should never be used, but the multilateralists would say that we should not unilaterally destroy them, but use them as a bargaining counter, to persuade everyone else to destroy theirs at the same time. The distinctive position of the nuclear pacifist is that we should declare that we will not use them, and therefore most nuclear pacifists are unilateralists. The two positions, however, are distinct.

The key issue

The one key issue in biblical terms is this: should the Christian be active in helping the state to do its God-given job, including acting as a 'minister of wrath'? If the answer is No, then not only war but being a judge, or a number of other aspects of state services, are closed to the Christian. He should not be involved in defence work or the police force that might necessitate taking life, or even violent reprisals on evil. The pacifists who write here do not distinguish in principle (only in degree) between armed police action and war. Neil Summerton is an exception, objecting only to war.

If the answer is Yes, then the Christian should do defence work with a positive sense of working for a God-given and necessary programme for restraining evil, even if it is a tragedy that this is necessary. He should be willing to be active in a just war, and some would go on to argue that he should be willing to hold nuclear weapons as a necessary defence against nuclear weapons – even while he seeks to get all nuclear weapons abolished.

No-one wishes to glory in war. It is a tragic last resort which, on one view, God uses and requires us to use in some circumstances because evil is so deeply rooted in some men, and so hateful and destructive for the whole of society. On the other view, war is a method that is so contrary to the Christian character that (even if the ungodly state may use it and so fulfil God's purpose), the Christian must simply repudiate it whole-heartedly.

Nuclear weapons are seen by some on both sides as simply an extension of the same principles. The non-pacifists hope to abolish them, and will never use them first, but believe that they are at present a necessary part of defence. To the pacifist they are the *reductio ad absurdum* of the just war position. Arthur Holmes, however, while believing in a just war, believes that nuclear weapons cannot be just and therefore takes a position between the two in this respect.

It is important for the Christian to think this issue through, and to try to arrive at a position which is thought out, and is consistent with his or her whole view of what is biblical Christianity. It is not good for anybody to be involved in work about which he or she has any niggling bad conscience. Either he or she should think it through and do it with confidence, or resign and do something else. We hope that this discussion will help people who are surrounded by jobs that have a bearing on defence, or who may, alas, be involved in taking part in war, so that, whatever they do in this situation, they do it with a good conscience before God, having thought and prayed it through.

Appendix
The just war:
a brief definition

Neil Summerton

Criteria defining just (or justifiable) war

1. *Ius ad bellum*: the resort to war – just cause
    a. Pure intention: the demand of Christian love
        War aim both initially and during war: a just peace; purpose of warring power must remain just for duration of hostilities
        No desire for revenge or aggrandizement either in response to initial injury or injury during war
    b. Authority
        1. Legitimate government must undertake
        2. Proper declaration of hostilities
    c. Just cause
        1. Unequivocal offence: response to real injury
            i. Self-defence *i.e.* defensive not aggressive war
            ii. Defence of others
        2. Last resort: All other avenues to just peace exhausted, *e.g.* negotiation, international judgment, arbitration
    d. Proportion
        1. Reasonable hope of victory: if just peace cannot be achieved or injury redressed, suffering would be to no effect

    2. Expected evils of war must not be greater than the evils resulting from the injury suffered, *i.e.* even where there is a reasonable hope of victory, the cost (to both sides and bystanders) may render war unjust

2. *Ius in bello*: just means

  e. Pure intention: the demand of Christian love
Avoidance of hatred, greed and brutality by those undertaking, directing and consenting to war

  f. Proportion
    1. No more violence than
      i . Warranted by the original injury
      ii. Necessary to war aims (achievement of just peace)
    2. Avoidance of unnecessary and long-term suffering for combatants
    3. Respect for established conventions and rules of war

  g. Discrimination
    1. Violence to be directed only against enemy combatants; non-combatant immunity, subject to 'double(side)-effect', *i.e.* permissibility of unintended civilian and non-combatant casualties
    2. Avoidance of long-term damage to the environment

Notes

1. A just war: defining some key issues · Arthur F. Holmes

1. *Harvard Theological Review* 45 (1952), 1, p.71.
2. Reinhold Niebuhr, *Christianity and Power Politics* (Charles Scribner, 1948), ch. 1. *Cf.* Elizabeth Anscombe, 'War and Murder', in *Nuclear Weapons: A Catholic Response*, ed. W. Stein (Merlin Press, 1961).
3. See Basil Mitchell, *Law, Morality and Religion in a Secular Society* (Oxford University Press, 1967); J. N. D. Anderson, 'Public law and legislation', in *Law, Morality and the Bible*, ed. B. N. Kaye and G. J. Wenham (Inter-Varsity Press, 1978).
4. Tertullian, *Apology*, 30–38. This and other historical sources cited in this essay are included in an anthology, *War and Christian Ethics*, ed. A. F. Holmes (Baker Book House, 1975).
5. Tertullian, *On Idolatry*, 19; *The Chaplet*, 6, 11, 12.
6. Origen, *Against Celsus*, 3.7; 8.73–75.
7. *E.g.* Peter Craigie, *The Problem of War in the Old Testament* (Eerdmans, 1978).
8. Martin Luther, 'Whether Soldiers Too Can Be Saved'.
9. See especially Paul Ramsey, *The Just War* (Scribner, 1968).
10. John Ford, 'The Morality of Obliteration Bombing', *Theological Studies* 5 (1944), p.261.

Response to Arthur Holmes · Willard Swartley

1. Numerous Church Fathers link the expression, 'the law of Christ', to the refusal of weapons of war and to the love of the enemy: Irenaeus, *Against Heresies*, 4.34.4 (*Ante-Nicene Fathers* I, 512);

226

Notes

Tertullian, *Against the Jews*, 3 (*ANF* III, 154); Origen, *Against Celsus*, 3.7 (*ANF* IV, 467); Arnobius, *Against the Heathen*, 1.6 (*ANF* VI, 415).

2. Pacifist Christianity: the kingdom way · Willard Swartley and Alan Kreider

1. Cited by Sidney Lens, *The Day Before Doomsday: An Anatomy of the Nuclear Arms Race* (Garden City, N.Y.: Doubleday, 1977), p. 251.

2. Carl von Clausewitz, *On War*, I, i, 3, trans. by Michael Howard and Peter Paret (Princeton, N. J.: Princeton University Press, 1976), p. 75.

3. Donald F. Durnbaugh (ed), *On Earth Peace: Discussions on War/Peace Issues Between Friends, Mennonites, Brethren, and European Churches, 1935–75* (Elgin, Ill.: The Brethren Press, 1978), p. 50. The classic historical documentation of this position and its expression during the two World Wars is to be found in Guy F. Hershberger, *War, Peace and Nonresistance* (Scottdale, Pa.: Herald Press, rev. ed., 1953).

4. Roland H. Bainton, 'The Early Church and War', *Harvard Theological Review* 39 (1946), 197; and the standard modern treatment, Jean-Michael Hornus, *It is Not Lawful for Me to Fight: Early Christian Attitudes toward War, Violence and the State*, rev. ed., trans. by Alan Kreider and Oliver Coburn (Scottdale, Pa.: Herald Press, 1980).

5. Hippolytus, *Apostolic Tradition*, ch. 16, in G.J. Cuming (ed.), *Hippolytus: a Text for Students* (Bramcote, Notts: Grove Books, 1976), p. 16.

6. The fourth century was a watershed in Christian history. In 314 Constantine became the first emperor to espouse Christianity; in 392 Theodosius I decreed all non-Christian worship to be illegal; in 416 Theodosius II ordered that there be no non-Christian soldiers in the Roman army. As a result of this alliance of church with society, state and army, the nature of the church changed from a voluntarist, persecuted, deviant minority to a coerced, persecuting, conformist majority (A. von Harnack, *The Expansion of Christianity in the First Three Centuries* [London: Williams and Norgate, 1904], II, pp. 108ff.; Hans Lietzmann, *A History of the Early Church* [London: Lutterworth Press, 1961], IV, p. 97. The nature of Christian ethics also changed, with pacifism and the radical sharing of wealth being confined to the priestly caste, and the rest of Christian society adopting 'realistic' compromises in areas of wealth, warfare and abortion (Hornus, *It is Not Lawful*, ch. 5; Julio de Santa Ana, *Good News to the Poor: The Challenge of the Poor in the History of the Church* [Geneva: World Council of Churches, 1977], ch. 6; Robin Gill, *Theology and Social Structure* [London: Mowbray, 1977], pp. 36–41, 47–49).

7. John Eppstein, *The Catholic Tradition of the Law of Nations*

Notes

(London: Catholic Association for International Peace, 1935), pp. 57–61; Frederick H. Russell, *The Just War in the Middle Ages* (Cambridge: Cambridge University Press, 1975), ch. 1.

8. F. H. Russell, *Just War*, p. 18; Roland H. Bainton, *Christian Attitudes Toward War and Peace* (Nashville, Tenn.: Abingdon Press, 1960), pp. 90–91.

9. *The Church and the Atom* (London: Press and Publications Board of the Church Assembly, 1948); J. T. Johnson, *Ideology, Reason, and the Limitations of War* (Princeton, N.J.: Princeton University Press, 1975), pp. 10, 131; W.M. Abbott (ed.), *The Documents of Vatican II* (London: Geoffrey Chapman, 1966), pp. 290–294.

10. For examples from the Second World War, see Bishop George Bell of Chichester, *The Church and Humanity* (London: Longmans Green, 1946), pp. 129–141 (House of Lords speech of 9 Feb. 1944); John C. Ford, 'The Morality of Obliteration Bombing', *Theological Studies 5* (1944), 261–309. For current examples, see John R. W. Stott, 'Calling for Peacemakers in a Nuclear Age', *Christianity Today*, 8 Feb. and 7 March 1980 (also published in *Crusade*, Nov. 1980); Walter Stein (ed.), *Nuclear Weapons and the Christian Conscience* (London: Merlin Press, 1961, 1981); Roger Ruston, *Nuclear Deterrence – Right or Wrong?* (Abbots Langley, Herts.: Catholic Information Service, 1981). The more typical Christian response is that of just war ethicist Paul Ramsey, who in 1942 was urging the American warrior not 'to blubber over his gunpowder' but to 'get on with the shooting' (R. H. Bainton, *Christian Attitudes*, p. 220).

11. G. H. C. Macgregor, *The New Testament Basis of Pacifism* (London: Fellowship of Reconciliation, 1953), pp. 32, 37; Martin Hengel, *Was Jesus a Revolutionist?*, trans. by William Klassen (Philadelphia, Pa.: Fortress Press, 1971), pp. 27–28; *idem, Victory Over Violence*, trans. by David E. Green (London: SPCK Press, 1975); John H. Yoder, *The Original Revolution* (Scottdale, Pa.: Herald Press, 1971), chs. 1–2.

12. Advocates of Christian participation in war may cite texts countering this point, especially Luke 22:36–38, where Jesus tells his disciples to 'buy a sword', and Matthew 10:34, 'I have not come to bring peace, but a sword.' But neither of these texts can be used to support war.

John Ferguson cites both William Barclay and George Caird in support of a metaphorical interpretation of Luke 22:36: it is 'a vivid eastern way of telling the disciples that their lives are at stake' (Barclay), in Ferguson, *The Politics of Love: The New Testament and Nonviolent Revolution* (Cambridge: James Clarke, n.d.), p. 33; so also Macgregor, *New Testament Basis*, pp. 22–24. Both Ferguson (pp. 30–31) and Macgregor (p. 20) rightly argue that the sword of Matthew 10:34 symbolizes division, as its Lukan parallel (12:51) clearly indicates; it has nothing to do with military fighting and war. For an index

Notes

to the replies of eight pacifist writers to the military use of 24 such New Testament texts see Willard M. Swartley, *Slavery, Sabbath, War and Women: Case Issues in Biblical Interpretation* (Scottdale, Pa.: Herald Press, 1983), App. 2.

13. Yoder, *Original Revolution*, pp. 47–48; Paul Minear, *Commands of Christ* (Edinburgh: Saint Andrew Press, 1972), pp. 70–71; Martin Luther King, *Strength to Love* (London: Hodder and Stoughton, 1963), pp. 34–41.

14. Paul Ramsey, *Basic Christian Ethics* (New York, N.Y.: Charles Scribner, 1951), p. 167.

15. Victor Paul Furnish, *The Love Command in the New Testament* (Nashville/New York: Abingdon Press, 1972), p. 47. In Luke 19:27 the term denotes enemies of God. See also W. Foerster, *TDNT* II, pp. 813–814. Note also William Klassen's discussion of the larger biblical use and meaning of the word *enemy* in 'Love Your Enemy: A Study of New Testament Teaching on Coping with an Enemy' in *Biblical Realism Confronts the Nations*, ed. by Paul Peachey (Scottdale, Pa.: Herald Press [Fellowship Publications, 1963]), pp. 158–159.

16. Although the Samaritans were also considered to be Israel's enemies, as in the parable of the Good Samaritan (Luke 10:30–37), the phrase 'hate your enemy' finds a parallel in the attitude of the Essene community of Qumran toward the Romans. The Covenanters were enjoined 'to love the sons of light' but 'to hate all the sons of darkness', which, as O. J. F. Seitz says, referred predominantly to the Romans (the Kittim). See O. J. F. Seitz, 'Love Your Enemies', *New Test. Stud.* 16 (1969–70), 50–51.

17. The history and resultant conflict of these offences is ably presented by S. G. F. Brandon, *Jesus and the Zealots* (Manchester: University Press, 1967), ch. 3. See also Hengel, *Victory*, ch. 5. For a shorter and more popular presentation of the offences see Donald B. Kraybill, *The Upside-Down Kingdom* (Scottdale, Pa.: Herald Press, 1978), ch. 2. While Brandon seeks to identify Jesus with the Zealot cause, Jesus' call to love the enemy shows clearly his divergence from the Zealot response toward the Romans. For the structure and method of Roman government in Palestine, see Richard J. Cassidy, *Jesus, Politics, and Society: A Study of Luke's Gospel* (Maryknoll, N.Y.: Orbis Press, 1978), App. 1; pp. 87–97.

18. Josephus, *Wars of the Jews*, II, ix, 4, in *Complete Works*, trans. by William Whiston (London: Pickering and Inglis, 1960), p. 479.

19. Josephus, *Antiquities of the Jews*, XVII, x, 5, 10, in *Complete Works*, pp. 371–372.

20. Hengel, *Victory*, p. 56.

21. *Ibid.*, chs. 6–7.

22. Although Morton Smith has argued that the Zealot party as such did not originate until AD 66 ('Zealots and Sicarii, Their Origins and Relation', *Harvard Theological Review* 64 [1971], 2–19), we

follow the more common view that the Zealot movement – perhaps though not a party as such – had its genesis in Judas the Galilean's revolt in AD 6 (Hengel, *Victory*, pp. 29–30; Oscar Cullmann, *Jesus and the Revolutionaries*, trans. by Gareth Putnam [New York: Harper & Row, 1970], pp. 73–82).

23. Hengel, *Jesus*, p. 26. This command, however, is not unique to Jesus. William Klassen cites numerous pre-Christian parallels ('The Novel Element in the Love Commandment of Jesus' in *The New Way of Jesus*, ed. by William Klassen [Newton, Ks.: Faith and Life Press, 1980], pp. 106–110). See also his survey of the history of research on the love command ('Love Your Enemy', pp. 155–157). Krister Stendahl observes that Jewish parallels to Jesus' teaching on non-retaliation, especially in Qumran literature, are generally motivated by storing up the wrath for God's final judgment. But Jesus' command to love seeks the welfare and friendship of the enemy; it *reflects the attitude of God* ('Hate, Non-retaliation, and Love', *Harvard Theological Review* 55 [1962], 343–355).

24. Joachim Jeremias, *The Sermon on the Mount* (Philadelphia: Fortress Press, 1963), pp. 34–35. See also A. M. Hunter's exposition under the title, *Design for Life* (London: SCM Press, rev. ed., 1965).

25. Cited by Hengel, *Victory*, p. 75.

26. This has been argued well by Luise Schottroff in 'Non-Violence and the Love of One's Enemies', trans. by Reginald H. and Ilse Fuller in *Essays on the Love Commandment* (Philadelphia: Fortress Press, 1978), pp. 9–28.

It has also been suggested that Matthew 5:39 should be translated 'Do not resist by evil means', taking the third inflection (*tō ponerō*) as an instrument of means rather than a predicate object (John Ferguson, *Politics*, pp. 4–5). This translation, however, is questionable, for it breaks the literary parallelism between this statement of principle and the four following illustrations which show specific responses to people. These four examples of non-resistance are effective expressions of the radical nature of Jesus' teaching; they make our mouth fall open, exclaiming, 'We should do even that?' They 'attack . . . our natural tendency to put self-protection first'. See Robert C. Tannehill's excellent literary study of these and related teachings of Jesus (*The Sword of His Mouth* [Philadelphia: Fortress Press, 1975], p. 71).

27. John Piper has ably documented the fundamental unity between Jesus' command to 'love the enemy' and this 'fixed rule . . . in the [early] Christian paraenetic tradition' ('*Love Your Enemies*': *Jesus' Love Command in the Synoptic Gospels and in the Early Christian Paraenesis* [Cambridge: Cambridge University Press, 1979], pp. 17, 171–174).

28. Ronald J. Sider, *Christ and Violence* (Scottdale, Pa.: Herald Press, 1979), p. 26.

29. Kraybill, *Kingdom*, pp. 41–64; Yoder, *Original Revolution*,

pp. 18–20; *idem, The Politics of Jesus* (Grand Rapids: Eerdmans, 1972), pp. 30–34; Dale Brown, *The Christian Revolutionary* (Grand Rapids: Eerdmans, 1971), pp. 102–113.

John P. Meier says that Jesus' tempters in three episodes (Matthew 4:8–10; 16:21–23; 27:29–43) 'are enemies of the cross because they think of sonship in terms of glory without suffering' (*The Vision of Matthew* [New York/Ramsey/Toronto: Paulist Press, 1979], p. 61). Millard Burrows comments similarly: 'The temptation to adopt Satanic means to gain God's ends, to seak peace by making war, to use force to accomplish what can never be accomplished by anything but persuasion and love is always with us. But Jesus saw that while the way of political power and compulsion might seem shorter, it was Satan's way, not God's' (*Jesus in the First Three Gospels* [Nashville, Tenn.: Abingdon, 1977], p. 43).

30.   The Greek of Mark 8:33 and Matthew 16:23 reads '*Hypage opisō mou Satana*'. The better manuscripts do not include *opisō mou* in Matthew 4:10, but the meaning of the phrase is essentially the same, as we have translated it.

31.   Two perspectives much at home in biblical thought are essential to grasp adequately the link between Jesus' atonement and our discipleship. These are 'corporate personality' and 'representative man'. See H. Wheeler Robinson, *Corporate Personality in Ancient Israel* (Philadelphia: Fortress Press, 1964) and Vincent Taylor, *The Atonement in New Testament Teaching* (London: Epworth Press, 1945), pp. 176, 179, 197–199.

32.   A vast amount of scholarly literature has addressed the meaning and significance of the NT teaching on the principalities and powers. A most helpful study, reporting the thought and literature on both sides of the issue, specifically whether Romans 13:1 belongs to this thought complex, is Clinton D. Morrison's book, *The Powers That Be: Earthly Rulers and Demonic in Romans 13:1–7*, SBT 29 (London: SCM Press, 1960). Important also are Karl Barth, *Against the Stream* (London: SCM Press, 1954), pp. 15–50, and Oscar Cullmann, *The State in the New Testament* (New York: Scribner, 1956), pp. 95–116; H. Berkhof, *Christ and the Powers*, trans, by John H. Yoder (Scottdale, Pa.: Herald Press, 1962, 1977); G. B. Caird, *Principalities and Powers: A Study in Pauline Theology* (Oxford: Clarendon Press, 1956); and Yoder, *Politics*, ch. 8. For John Stott's critical evaluation of this interpretation, see his *God's New Society: The Message of Ephesians* (Leicester: Inter-Varsity Press, 1979), pp. 267–275. Cf. also Wesley Carr, *Angels and Principalities: the Background, Meaning and Development of the Pauline Phrase hai Archai kai hai Exousiai*, SNTMS 42 (Cambridge: Cambridge University Press, 1981). Carr's exegesis is often forced and his arguments unconvincing (see esp. pp. 38, 40, 43, 52, 60–66, 96–98).

The Church Fathers also emphasized Christ's and the believer's

Notes

freedom from the powers. See Gustav Aulén, *Christus Victor* (New York: Macmillan, 1961), pp. 16–60.

33.   For discussions of this enmity between Jews and Gentiles, see Markus Barth, *Ephesians*, Vol. I (Garden City, N.Y.: Doubleday, 1974), p. 297; see also 'Gentiles', *Encyclopaedia Judaica*, Vol. 7 (Jerusalem: Keter Publishing House, 1971), pp. 411–412: 'Jewish antipathy [was] . . . motivated by their [Gentile] idolatry, moral laxity, and other such faults' (col. 411).

34.   Recent scholarship has shown the centrality of reconciliation in Pauline theology. Markus Barth and Krister Stendahl have argued that Paul's doctrine of justification arose from the uniting of Jew and Gentile in Christ (Barth, 'Jews and Gentiles: The Social Character of Justification in Paul', *Journal of Ecumenical Studies 5*, 2 [Spring, 1968], 241ff.; Stendahl, *Paul Among Jews and Gentiles* [Philadelphia, Pa.: Fortress Press, 1976]). John H. Yoder has also advanced this position, *Politics*, pp. 226–229. Ralph P. Martin has recently devoted an extensive monograph to the subject, stressing both the personal and social aspects of reconciliation (*Reconciliation: A Study of Paul's Theology* [Atlanta: John Knox Press, 1981], esp. pp. 166–198). Peter Stuhlmacher has proposed that reconciliation is the nerve centre of New Testament theology, the hermeneutical key to New Testament interpretation (*Vom Verstehen des Neuen Testaments: Eine Hermeneutik* [Göttingen: Vandenhoeck & Ruprecht, 1979], pp. 224–247).

35.   Marlin E. Miller, 'The Gospel of Peace', in *Mission and the Peace Witness*, ed. by Robert L. Ramseyer (Scottdale, Pa.: Herald Press, 1979), p. 16.

36.   Sider, *Christ*, p. 33.

37.   Ernst Lohmeyer, *Lord of the Temple: A Study of the Relation Between Cult and Gospel*, trans. by Steward Todd (Edinburgh/London: Oliver and Boyd, 1962), pp. 40–51; Eduard Schweizer, *The Good News According to Mark*, trans. by D. H. Madwig (Richmond, Va.: John Knox Press, 1970), pp. 14, 233–241; Lloyd Gaston, *No Stone on Another: Studies in the Significance of the Fall of Jerusalem in the Synoptic Gospels*, NovT.Supp. 23 (Leiden: E. J. Brill, 1970), pp. 474–475; and William W. Watty, 'Jesus and the Temple – Cleansing or Cursing?' *ExpT* 93, 8 (May, 1982), 235–239.

38.   In this alternative exegesis the antecedent of the masculine *pantas* (all) is *Boas* (the oxen). The *te . . . kai* phrase then explains what all is meant: both the sheep and the oxen. Quite likely the people selling these animals also left the temple court accompanying their capital investment, since v. 16 indicates that Jesus spoke only to those selling the doves. Since Jesus could not drive the doves out with a whip (a comic scene, had he tried!) he commanded the sellers to remove them. This confirms the alternative exegesis, for if the sellers had been the object of the whip, those who sold the doves would have been

driven out with the other merchants. For a detailed exegetical study supporting this interpretation of this text see the article by Jean Lasserre in *Cahiers de la Reconciliation* (October, 1967), trans. by John H. Yoder, 'A Tenacious Misinterpretation: John 2:15', *Occasional Papers No. 1* (Elkhart, Ind.: Institute of Mennonite Studies, 1981, and available from the London Mennonite Centre, 14 Shepherds Hill, Highgate, London N6 5AQ). For similar exegetical emphasis see Macgregor, *Pacifism*, pp. 17–18 and Ferguson, *Politics*, pp. 28–30.

39. William R. Farmer, *Jesus and the Gospel: Tradition, Scripture, and Canon* (Philadelphia: Fortress Press, 1982), pp. 206–221.

40. In his commentary on Revelation, Vernard Eller develops this textual emphasis (*The Most Revealing Book of the Bible: Making Sense Out of the Book of Revelation* [Grand Rapids, Mich.: Eerdmans, 1947], pp. 43–71). G. B. Caird's excellent commentary on Revelation supports also this interpretation of non-violence as the way of the Lamb and his followers, even in Revelation (*The Revelation of St. John the Divine* [London: Adam & Charles Black, 1966], pp. 74–77, 244–246).

41. This practice, known as *herem* in the literature on ancient warfare, is difficult for us to understand. The act, which appears in part culticly based (all is sacrificed to Yahweh), is no more helpful to just war Christians than it is to pacifist Christians.

42. Even though Israel rejected Yahweh as king, Samuel, whose prophetic word had been spurned, called the people to follow the Lord to avoid their punishment of death (1 Samuel 12:19–25). The kingship reality had now become part of Israel's history and two crucial developments emerged; God raised up prophets who possessed the charisma of the former judge-saviours (*sôphet*) to exercise power over the kings and, because the kings fell short of the divine standard, the hope for a perfect future king, anointed one (*mashiach*/Messiah) arose (Isaiah 11:1–5). Jesus' fulfilment of the Messianic hope transformed the concept of kingship. See Paul Hanson's helpful treatment of this topic (*The Diversity of Scripture: A Theological Interpretation* [Philadelphia, Pa.: Fortress Press, 1982], pp. 23–33, 67–78).

43. Yoder, *Original Revolution*, p. 106.

44. See especially Richard J. Cassidy's treatment of this subject (*Jesus, Politics, and Society: A Study of Luke's Gospel* [Maryknoll, N.Y.: Orbis Books, 1978], pp. 50–76, and esp. 78–79). Cassidy rightly points out that even Luke's Gospel, which is usually said to emphasize Pilate's innocence, nevertheless shows Pilate to be responsible: see Luke 23:24, 28, 47, 52.

45. Mark 13:9, 11, parr.; Acts 4:1–4; 5:17–41; 7:1 – 8:3; 12:1–5; the recognition that both 1 Peter and Revelation were written to encourage Christians suffering at the hands of political rulers; and the many texts reflecting Paul's conflict with the authorities: Acts 16:20–24; Romans 8:35f.; 1 Corinthians 4:9, 12; 15:30f.; 2 Corinthians 1:8f.;

4:3–11; 6:4f., 9; 7:5; 11:23ff.; Philippians 1:30; 1 Thessalonians 2:2 (*cf.* Hebrews 10:32f.) (Morrison, *Powers*, p. 13, n. 1).

46.   Hans Conzelmann has argued that Luke-Acts contains a pro-Roman redaction (*The Theology of St. Luke*, trans. by Geoffrey Buswell [New York: Harper & Row, 1960], pp. 138–148). For an evaluation of the opposing theses of Cassidy and Conzelmann see Willard M. Swartley, 'Politics and Peace (*Eirēnē*) in Luke's Gospel', in *Political Issues in Luke-Acts*, ed. by Richard J. Cassidy and Philip Scharper (Maryknoll, N.Y.: Orbis Books, 1983), ch. 2.

47.   Yoder, *Politics*, pp. 193–214; Cassidy, *Jesus, Politics*, pp. 55–61; Donald D. Kaufman, *What Belongs to Caesar?* (Scottdale, Pa.: Herald Press, 1969), pp. 35–54.

48.   Significantly, Jesus did not himself have the idolatrous coin with Caesar's image on it, and he apparently did not pay the tax (*cf.* Luke 23:2). The tax paid in Matthew 17:24–27 was the temple tax (Exodus 30:13) and thus cannot support the claim that Jesus paid tax to Rome. The image on the denarius, the required tax coin, was idolatrous: the obverse side of the tax denarius showed 'a bust of Tiberius . . . adorned with the laurel wreath, the sign of his divinity'. The legend read TI(BERIUS) CAESAR DIVI AUG(USTI) F(ILIUS) AUGUSTUS, meaning 'Emperor Tiberius August Son of the August God'. On the other side was the title PONTIF(EX) MAXIM(US), meaning high priest, with Tiberius' mother, Julia Augusta, sitting on the throne of the gods. The coin was the official and universal sign of the idolatrous divinization and worship of the Emperor. For further discussion of this issue see Willard Swartley, 'A Study on the Payment of War Taxes', *Sojourners* 8 (Feb., 1979), 18–20, and a larger unpublished paper, 'The Christian and the Payment of Taxes Used for War', 1981 (available from the London Mennonite Centre, 14 Shepherds Hill, Highgate, London, N6 5AQ).

49.   Yoder, *Politics*, pp. 173–175, and C. E. B. Cranfield, *A Commentary on Romans 12–13, SJTOP* 12 (London/Edinburgh: Oliver and Boyd, 1965), pp. 69–71; *idem, A Critical and Exegetical Commentary on the Epistle to Romans, ICC*, Vol. II (Edinburgh: T. & T. Clark, 1979), pp. 660–663.

50.   This results in books whose titles betray their individualistic bias (*e.g.,* Sir Fred Catherwood's *The Christian in Industrial Society*) or the typical response to political issues within the church: it's an individual matter, we speak as citizens, not as the church!

51.   Yoder, *Politics*, pp. 123–130.

52.   Sider, *Christ*, p. 95.

53.   Myron Augsburger, 'Beating Swords Into Plowshares', *Christianity Today* 20 (Nov. 21, 1975), 196.

54.   Myron Augsburger, 'Facing the Problem', in *Perfect Love and War*, ed. by Paul Hostetler (Nappanee, Ind.: Evangel Press, 1974), p. 15.

Notes

55. Augsburger, 'Beating Swords', 197.

56. See the various essays in *Mission and the Peace Witness*, especially Robert L. Ramseyer's, 'Mennonite Mission and the Christian Peace Witness', pp. 114–134; also Samuel Escobar and John Driver, *Christian Mission and Social Justice* (Scottdale, Pa.: Herald Press, 1978).

57. Suetonius, *The Lives of the Twelve Caesars*, Book V, XXV, *The Loeb Classical Library*, vol. 148 (Latin Series), trans. by J. C. Rolfe (Cambridge: Harvard University Press, 1959), p. 53. In this text Chrestus is a variant form of Christus; this reference suggests that the Jewish political threat arose from disputes between Jews and Jewish Christians over the Messianic significance of Jesus.

58. For the historical reconstruction of the events lying behind Romans 12–13, especially the tax issue, see J. Friedrich, W. Pöhlmann and P. Stuhlmacher, 'Zur historischen Situation und Intention von Rom 13.1–7', *Zeitschrift für Theologie und Kirche* 73 (1967), 131–166, and Swartley, 'Taxes Used for War'. The primary source is *The Annals of Tacitus*, Book XIII, *The Loeb Classical Library*, vol. 153 (Latin Series), trans. by John Jackson (Cambridge, Mass.: Harvard University Press, 1956), p. 89.

59. The same emphases appear in 1 Peter. In 3:8–17 the dominant contrast is between evil (*kakos*), recurring seven times (vv. 8(2), 10, 11, 12, 13, 17), and good (*agathos*), recurring six times (vv. 10, 11, 13, 16(2), 17). In 2:14–15, 18–25 similar contrasts occur. Again, following love (3:10), seeking peace (3:11) and maintaining a good conscience (3:16) are correlative ethical directives. See also 1 Thessalonians 5:15.

The divine basis for the authority of government in Romans 13 is complemented by the phrase, human creation (*anthrōpine ktisei*) in 1 Peter 2:13. Note also that in 1 Timothy 2:1 kings stand in grammatical apposition to *all men*; they are no more and no less.

60. In fact, the violent end of the continuum extends still further, to global lethal violence (cosmocide) in which both the people and the environment are destroyed. Adherents to the just war draw their line of acceptable intervention short of their unacceptable extreme of 'indiscriminate' and 'disproportionate' killing (*e.g.* Oliver O'Donovan, *In Pursuit of a Christian View on War* [Bramcote, Notts: Grove Books, 1977]). In our view, Christians should regard *all* killing to be an unacceptable extreme.

61. For the testimony of a former Lockheed missile engineer who left his job for Christian reasons, see Robert C. Aldridge, 'The Courage to Start', in Christopher Grannis, Arthur Laffin and Elin Schade, *The Risk of the Cross: Christian Discipleship in the Nuclear Age* (New York: Seabury Press, 1981), pp. 46–50.

62. Chris Sugden, *A Different Dream: Non-violence as Practical Politics* (Bramcote, Notts: Grove Books, 1976); Richard K. Taylor,

Blockade; A Guide to Non-Violent Intervention (Maryknoll, N.Y.: Orbis Books, 1977); Peter D. Bishop, *A Technique for Loving: Non-Violence in Indian and Christian Traditions* (London: SCM Press, 1981). For the inspiring story of how a French congregation during the Second World War through non-violent resistance saved the lives of over two thousand Jews, see Philip Hallie, *Lest Innocent Blood Be Shed* (New York: Harper and Row and London: Michael Joseph, 1979).

63.   1 Timothy 2:1–2. Jim Wallis, 'The Work of Prayer', *Sojourners* 8 (Mar. 1979), 3–5; Henri Nouwen, 'Letting Go of All Things', *Sojourners* 8 (Mar. 1979), 5–6.

64.   For such a miracle in our time, see Sarah Corson, 'Welcoming the Enemy: A Missionary Fights Violence with Love', *Sojourners* 12 (April 1983), 29–31. See also David Jackson, *Dial 911: Peaceful Christians and Urban Violence* (Scottdale, Pa.: Herald Press, 1981) and John H. Yoder, ' "What Would You Do If . . . .?" An Exercise in Christian Ethics', *Journal of Religious Ethics* 2, 2(1974), 81–105.

65.   Two special problems that arise are use of force in the discipline of children and in the restraint of a thief or rapist. For the former, the good of the child and love for the child require the clear expression of parental authority; the discipline (which rarely may include spanking, in our judgment) must be guided not by anger and revenge but by genuine love and concern for the child's well-being (Ephesians 6:1–4). In the latter case, diversionary tactics and the *word*-weapon of reprimand should be our foremost responses. While force as an expression of care to whom it is applied may be used so long as no permanent physical harm is done, it must be remembered that force evokes more force. For stories of non-violent resistance in such situations see Elizabeth Hershberger Bauman, *Coals of Fire* (Scottdale, Pa.: Herald Press, 1954); Cornelia Lehn, *Peace Be With You* (Newton, Kan.: Faith and Life Press, 1980); and A. Ruth Fry, *Victories Without Violence* (London: Dennis Dobson, 1957).

66.   Hornus, *It Is Not Lawful*, pp. 158, 163, 243.

67.   This happened in 1981 to Superior Court Judge William Bontrager in Elkhart, Indiana, USA, reported in *Newsweek*, Dec. 2, 1981, 1259–1260.

68.   Nationwide Initiative in Evangelism, *Prospects for the Eighties: from a Census of the Churches in 1979* (London: The Bible Society, 1980), p. 15.

69.   *Hansard*, House of Lords, 420, no. 28, col. 325 (11 May 1981).

70.   *Statement on the Defence Estimates, 1981* (London: HMSO, 1981), pp. 64, 66.

71.   Letter of 28 September 1981 from Michael Randle, Co-ordinator of the Alternative Defence Commission, to Alan Kreider.

72.   For both a theological basis for such action and samples of issues on which this might be done see John H. Yoder, *The Christian*

Notes

Witness to the State (Newton, Kan.: Faith and Life Press, 1964), esp. pp. 71–73.

73. Jacques Ellul, *Violence: Reflections from a Christian Perspective* (London: SCM Press, 1970), pp. 93–108.

74. A powerful description of the dilemma of our age has come from the pen of Jonathan Schell, *The Fate of the Earth* (New York: A. Knopf, 1982). Analysing war from secular and historical perspectives, Schell argues that the only hope for humanity's future depends upon learning to live amicably with the enemy, a point approaching the teaching of Jesus. See also Donald B. Kraybill, *Facing Nuclear War* (Scottdale, Pa.: Herald Press, 1982).

Response to Willard Swartley and Alan Kreider · Arthur F. Holmes

1. Roland Bainton, *Christian Attitudes Toward War and Peace* (Abingdon Press, 1960), p. 66.

2. *Idem*, pp. 71–72.

3. See Oscar Cullmann, *The Early Church* (Westminster Press, 1956), and *The State in the New Testament* (Scribner, 1956), ch. III and Excursus on recent discussion of Romans 13:1.

Response to Sir Frederick Catherwood · Alan Kreider

1. Alternative Defence Commission, *Defence without the Bomb* (London, Taylor & Francis, 1983).

2. *Strategic Survey 1981–1982* (London, International Institute for Strategic Studies, 1982), 1.

3. *The Effects of Nuclear War* (Washington, D.C., U.S. Congress Office of Technology Assessment, 1979), 81–94.

4. Herbert Butterfield, *Human Nature and the Dominion of Fear*, Christian CND Pamphlet No. 3 (London, 1964), 4.

4. The case for all-out pacifism · Robert E. D. Clark

1. J. Ellul, *Violence*, 1970.

2. P. Thompson, *Bound for Broadmoor*, 1972.

3. M. Middlebrook, *The Battle of Hamburg*, 1980.

4. Gordon Wilson, Letter to *The Times*, 1 May 1982.

5. Albert Post, *Popular Freethought in America 1825–1850*, Columbia UP PhD Thesis No. 497.

6. H. S. Levy, *Chinese Footbinding*, 1966.

7. Nikolai Tolstoy, *Victims of Yalta*, 1977, chs. 7–8.

8. For a photograph of three such cages at Nürnberg see Alan Eyre, *The Protesters*, 1975.

5. The case against all-out pacifism · John Peck

1. Deuteronomy 32:8, NIV.

2. Acts 17:26.

3. *E.g.* in the intercessions of Ezra 9, Nehemiah 9 and Daniel 9.

Notes

4. Genesis 10:1 – 12:2; 17:20. The development of Israel's national sovereignty, however, was atypical. The divine attitude to kingship is ambiguous; but once it was established it continued to exist by divine appointment and will (Deuteronomy 17:14f.; 1 Samuel 8).

5. Hosea 3:4; Jeremiah 16:13, *etc.*; Jeremiah 7.

6. Acts 21:39; 22:3; Romans 9:1–3; Philippians 3:5.

7. Revelation 21:22–24.

8. Matthew 25:31ff.; 28:19. In general see Acts 17:26.

9. Galatians 3:28 and Colossians 3:11 – 4:1 are sometimes cited in this kind of debate, '. . . for you are all one in Christ Jesus'. Paul's teaching elsewhere about the obligations of each of the human groupings mentioned (*e.g.* in Ephesians 5 and 6) shows that the statement is not meant to be absolute, and, as the context indicates, is about the kind of people God is prepared to accept. When Paul is talking about how Christians should behave, he assumes always that such groupings determine people's role-play. So husbands must be good husbands, wives must be good wives, Gentiles must be good Gentiles, and Jews, good Jews (Romans 9:3f.; *cf.* Acts 16:3).

10. The history of Israel up to the present day exemplifies the significance of these three factors: ponder Genesis 12:1–3; 15:12ff.; Exodus 3:17, and Deuteronomy as a whole.

11. John 11:48.

12. John 7:32ff.; 18:3; Matthew 17:24ff. (The moneychangers whose tables Christ overturned in the Temple court dealt in the Temple shekel.)

13. Romans 13:3f.; 1 Peter 2:14.

14. Romans 13:1–6; 1 Peter 2:13–17.

15. Matthew 5:41.

16. Matthew 22:21.

17. Luke 3:14f. It is interesting to find this only in the Gospel addressed to 'Your Excellency'.

18. John 19:11.

19. 1 Timothy 2:2.

20. I am aware of the interpretation of Romans 13:1ff., connected with scholars such as Brunner and Cullmann, which regards the 'powers' as demonic. Space forbids detailed discussion, but the fact that the powers are authorized by God to 'bear the sword' surely means that it cannot affect the force of the argument here.

21. *E.g.* Isaiah 2:4.

22. *E.g.* the prohibition of David, as a 'man of blood', from building the Temple (1 Chronicles 22:8f.). Some of the constraints upon the Israelites in war must have been quite as frightening to them as the abandonment of nuclear weapons would be to us. Consider Joshua 5:2 at the beginning of an invasion!

23. Genesis 15:13–16.

24. 2 Chronicles 14:9ff.

Notes

25. 2 Samuel 10:1–14.
26. Joshua 10:6ff.
27. Psalms 20:7; 147:10.
28. Deuteronomy 17:16.
29. 2 Kings 18 and 19. Hezekiah paid the agreed penalty, but Sennacherib continued the attack after accepting it.
30. Jeremiah 27, *etc.*
31. Matthew 5:17ff.
32. *E.g.* quotations from the Decalogue in Matthew 5–7, Ephesians 6:2 and elsewhere.
33. *E.g.* Romans 12:20; 1 Corinthians 9:9; 2 Corinthians 8:15.
34. Matthew 26:52. The disciples had misunderstood Jesus in Luke 22:36ff., as is shown by Jesus' dismissive reply in v.38.
35. Matthew 26:53.
36. John 18:36.
37. The reasons for this pacifism are complex. The military obligation to partake in pagan ceremonies of worship was a powerful consideration. As time went on, there are some indications that Christians were only putting into action what many were beginning to feel – that maybe the Empire was no longer worth fighting for. In understanding the actual ethical understanding of the time, however, the most subtle and powerful influence was the prevailing Gnostic atmosphere of thought which tended to devalue all material and human concerns. It operated elsewhere, too; for instance in the exaltation of celibacy and virginity over marriage. Such a *Zeitgeist* was as penetrating into Christian and general thought as evolutionary attitudes are today.
38. This phenomenon would explain why so often the Bible can attribute two or more causes for the same event without any sense of conflict or contradiction. David's census is attributed to motivations from both God and Satan (2 Samuel 24:1; 1 Chronicles 21:1). Jesus puts a poultice on a man's eyes, but he is also doing a miracle of power (John 9:6; *cf.* v.32). The same thing happens with Hezekiah (2 Kings 20:7ff.). Judges 1–2 lists five reasons why the Promised Land was not completely subdued; Deuteronomy adds a sixth (Deuteronomy 7:22).
39. Matthew 18:21–22.
40. Matthew 5:25.
41. Matthew 5:22, NIV.
42. Matthew 5:26.
43. See Luke 12:14. Jesus' disclaimer here shows his recognition of a principle of governmental power, namely, that to bear it you have to be 'made' by somebody further up in the hierarchy. He was Lord in the kingdom of God, and would not defy its own principles.
44. See the reasoning in Deuteronomy 25:3; *cf.* 2 Corinthians 11:24.
45. Deuteronomy 24:5.
46. Matthew 19:12.

Notes

6. The just war revisited · Jerram Barrs

1. John H. Yoder (trans. and ed.), *The Schleitheim Confession* (Scottdale, Pa.: Herald Press, 1977), pp. 13–15.

2. This has been the view of traditional Christian pacifism; cf. *The Schleitheim Confession*; also Myron S. Augsburger and Herman A. Hoyt in *War: Four Christian Views*, edited by Robert G. Clouse (Downers Grove, Ill.: InterVarsity Press, 1981), pp. 50–86.

3. A. Kreider, 'Enemy Loving and Peace Making: Old and New Testament' (tape available from the London Mennonite Centre).

4. Ronald J. Sider and Richard K. Taylor, *Nuclear Holocaust and Christian Hope: A Book for Christian Peacemakers* (Downers Grove, Ill.: InterVarsity Press, 1982).

5. P. London, *The Modes and Morals of Psychotherapy* (New York: Holt, Reinhart and Winston, 1964), pp. 169ff.

6. Lenin first made this statement. It was repeated by Leonid Brezhnev as a guiding principle for all Communists in *Pravda* (November 25, 1970) and quoted by Magstadt, 'Marx, Moral Responsibility and the Cambodian Revolution', *National Review* (July 24, 1981): 83.

7. 'Cambodia: An Experiment in Genocide', *Time* (July 31, 1978).

8. John Calvin, *Institutes of the Christian Religion*, Library of Christian Classics (Philadelphia: Westminster Press, 1980), pp. iv, xx, 1–10.

9. C. S. Lewis, 'The Humanitarian Theory of Punishment', in *God in the Dock: Essays on Theology and Ethics*, edited by Walter Hooper (Grand Rapids, Mich.: Eerdmans, 1970), pp. 287–300.

10. George F. Will, 'Religion and Nuclear Arms', *Newsweek* (December 21, 1981).

11. Vladimir Bukovsky, 'The Peace Movement and the Soviet Union', *Commentary* (May 1982): 25. The following paragraph in the text is a view of Vietnamese refugees who have fled to the West. We shall of course never have accurate data of this type given us by the present government. However, the United Nations estimates that at least 350,000 Vietnamese have been lost at sea while attempting to escape. Numerous newspaper and periodical articles have also referred to killing within Vietnam on a huge scale.

12. Bukovsky, *op. cit.*, p. 108.

13. *Ibid.*, p. 41.

7. The just war: a sympathetic critique · Neil Summerton

1. A review of this tradition is to be found in M. E. Howard, *War and the Liberal Conscience* (Temple Smith, 1978).

2. Carl von Clausewitz, *On War*, trans. Col. J. J. Graham (Kegan Paul, Trench, Trubner, 1908), vol. i, p. 23, and vol. iii, p. 121 (Clausewitz's italics). See also M. E. Howard, *War in European History* (Oxford University Press, 1976).

Notes

3. Scriptural quotations are from the Revised Standard Version unless otherwise indicated.

4. This thought was taken up by Luther and subsequent theologians. Luther contrasted Christ's 'proper work' (salvation) with God's 'strange work' (judgment). There is no similar contrast to be found in the text cited, though there are promises of deliverance for the repentant (*e.g.* Isaiah 29:14, 17–24). See A. R. Vidler, *Christ's Strange Work* (SCM Press, 1963).

5. See the Bishop of London, 'The Morality of Nuclear Deterrence', a lecture given at St Lawrence Jewry, 3 November 1982, for a position very close to that described in this paragraph, even if he finally draws back from the full implications of the line of argument.

6. Admiral Sir Terence Lewin in oral evidence to the House of Commons Defence Committee, 27 October 1982 (reported in *The Times*, 28 October 1982, p. 2).

7. See R. J. Cassidy, *Jesus, Politics and Society: A Study of Luke's Gospel* (Orbis, New York, 1978), pp. 50–62.

8. On war in the Old Testament, see Millard C. Lind, *Yahweh is a warrior: The Theology of Warfare in Ancient Israel* (Herald Press, Scottdale, Penn., 1980). In his opening chapter Lind reviews earlier works such as G. von Rad, *Der heilige Krieg im alten Israel* (Zwingli-Verlag, Zurich, 1951).

9. Frederick Schwally (*Der heilige Krieg im alten Israel*, Dieterichische Verlagsbuchhandlung, Theoder Weicher, Leipzig, 1901) claimed that all ancient peoples thought of their gods as participating in their battles, thus requiring their warriors to fight all the harder, whereas Yahweh's participation was seen in Israelite thought as rendering it unnecessary for Israel's warriors to fight (see Lind, *op.cit.*, p. 24).

10. Abraham's second line of advocacy to God before Sodom and Gomorrah relied on a feature already noted: that God's loving kindness and mercy required that judgment should be a last resort. The quality of his case was demonstrated in the promise that if there were only ten righteous in the city the whole would be spared (Genesis 18:32).

11. See pp. 48f., above.

12. On the just war, see Frederick H. Mitchell, *The Just War in the Middle Ages* (Cambridge University Press, 1975); Joan D. Tooke, *The Just War in Aquinas and Grotius* (SPCK, 1965); S. D. Bailey, *Prohibitions and Restraints in War* (Oxford University Press, 1972); Roland H. Bainton, *Christian Attitudes toward War and Peace: A Historical Survey and Critical Re-evaluation* (Hodder & Stoughton, 1960), pp. 33–44, 85–135. Arthur F. Holmes summarized the basic elements of the concept earlier; see pp. 27ff., above.

13. See, *e.g.*, G. E. M. Anscombe, 'War and Murder' and R. A. Markus, 'Conscience and Deterrence' in *Nuclear Weapons and Christian Conscience*, ed. Walter Stein (Merlin Press, 1961); Arthur F. Holmes, 'The Just War' in *War: Four Christian Views*, ed. Robert G.

Notes

Clouse (InterVarsity Press, Downers Grove, 1981); and Oliver O'Donovan, *In Pursuit of a Christian View of War* (Grove Books, Bramcote, 1977).

14. See, *e.g.*, Arthur F. Holmes: '. . . while Scripture is the final (that is, decisive) authority in matters of faith and practice, it is neither the only nor an exhaustive source of knowledge about moral matters. Scripture (for example, Rom. 1–3) makes plain that general revelation attests to our moral responsibilities, and the apostle Paul indicates that some kinds of acts are "contrary to nature". Many Christian writers, including some of the Reformers, identify the Old Testament Decalogue with a natural law written into the created order and the nature of man' (*War: Four Christian Views*, pp. 121–122).

15. See p. 177, above.

16. Clausewitz, *On War*, vol. i, p.2.

17. See, *e.g.*, Malcolm Heath, 'In defence of wrongdoing', *Third Way*, Vol. 5, No. 9, September 1982, pp. 8–10.

18. E. Miall, *The Politics of Christianity* (London, 1863), pp. 151, 153.

19. Jean-Michel Hornus, *It is not lawful for me to fight. Early Christian attitudes toward war, violence, and the state.* Revised edition, trans. Alan Kreider and Oliver Coburn (Herald Press, Scottdale, Penn., 1980), especially pp. 160–168. See also Bainton, *op.cit.*, pp. 44–48.

20. Contrast the views of the Fathers on the benefits derived from the existence of the Empire as set out in chapter 1 of Hornus, *op.cit.*, and the teaching and canons of the church on military service analysed in chapter 5 of the work.

21. See, *e.g.*, Hermon A. Hoyt, 'Nonresistance' in *War: Four Christian Views*, pp. 29–57; and E. R. Sandeen, *The Roots of Fundamentalism: British and American Millenarianism, 1800–1930* (University of Chicago Press, 1970), for the wider theological background.

22. I have not been able to find a single adjective which is an entirely satisfactory designation of this position. Here, I am using 'apocalyptic' in a rather technical theological sense, with the books of Daniel and Revelation in mind, where, at least at some points, the ruler is seen as going beyond his legitimate sphere, and making demands which are illegitimate and even demonic in their opposition to the divine purpose. That seems to me to be the essence of the thoroughgoing Christian pacifist position.

23. Augustine, *Contra Faustum*, xxii.

About the contributors

Mr Jerram Barrs is one of the staff of L'Abri Fellowship based in Greatham, Liss, Hants, England. He is an author and lecturer on a variety of topics.

Sir Frederick Catherwood is a British member of the European Parliament and was previously in business and for five years Director of the National Economic Development Council. He has written several books on Christian attitudes to business and citizenship.

Dr R. E. D. Clark has retired from lecturing in chemistry. He is a prolific writer on 'science and faith' questions, and has recently published *Does the Bible teach Pacifism?* (Marshall, Morgan and Scott, 1983), which had earlier (1976) been published by the Fellowship of Reconciliation, an interdenominatal Christian pacifist organization.

Dr Arthur F. Holmes is Head of Department and Professor of Philosophy at Wheaton College, Illinois, USA.

Dr Alan Kreider is Director of the London Mennonite Centre.

About the contributors

The Rev. John Peck is the Head of Staff at College House, Earl Soham, Woodbridge, Suffolk, England and a lecturer and writer on various themes relating to the development of a Christian mind.

Dr Neil Summerton was Joint Convenor of the Shaftesbury Project Study Group on War and Peace. His PhD was in military history. He is an elder at Cholmeley Evangelical Church, London.

Professor Willard M. Swartley is Professor of New Testament at the Associated Mennonite Biblical Seminaries and Director of the Institute of Mennonite Studies, both at Elkhart, Indiana, USA.

Series editor **Dr Oliver R. Barclay** was, until his retirement, General Secretary of the Universities and Colleges Christian Fellowship, and is author of several IVP books on current issues.

Index of biblical references

All verse-groupings are indexed separately. References in **bold type** *are to whole chapters rather than individual verses.*

245

Index of biblical references

Psalms *(cont.)*
89:19–37 *143*
94; 96; 97; 100   *159*
103:6–8 *20*
106:15 *102*
110 *148*
118:8–9 *155*
118:10 *156*
119 *154*
120:6–7 *19*
136:10–22 *49*
137:9 *109*
144:1 *147*
146:7–9 *144*
147:10 *239n.*
149:6–9 *147*

Proverbs
8:15–16 *144*
17:15 *144*
25:21–22 *108*
31:8–9 *144*

Isaiah
2:1–4 *28, 48*
2:3–4 *19*
2:4 *238n.*
2:7–10 *49*
3:1–3, 25–26 *49*
7:1–14 *49*
9:1–7 *28*
9:5–7 *168*
9:6–7 *19*
10:5–7 *49*
10:5–19 *198*
11 *148*
11:1–5 *233n.*
11:1–9 *28, 48*
13 – 27 *167*
13:3–5 *49*
14:26 *167*
28:21 *170*
29:14, 17–24 *241n.*
31:1–3 *49*
32:1 *48*
32:15–18 *169*
32:16–17 *48*
37 *49*
42:1 *45*
45 *88*
45:1–5 *198*
48:18 *171*
48:18–19 *169*
52:7 *45*
52:7–9 *48*
52:13 – 53:12 *47*
61:2 *45*

Jeremiah
2:34 *177*
7 *238n.*
7:6 *177*
16:13 *238n.*
19:4 *177*
21:4–6 *49*
21:4–14 *38*
25:9 *88*
27 *239n.*
27:6 *88*
28:8 *166*
31:31–34 *197, 199*
38:4 *104*
44:25 *102*
46 – 52 *167*
48:10 *175*

Ezekiel
20:25–26 *102*
25 – 32 *167*
34:23–29 *48*
38 – 39 *167*

Daniel
3:17–18 *99*
9 *237n.*

Hosea
3:4 *238n.*
10:13–14 *38*
10:13–15 *49*
12:13 *48*
13:10–11 *49*

Joel
3:11–16 *60*

Amos
1:3–15 *30*
1:11 *19*
8 *60*

Micah
3:5–12 *166*
4:3–4 *168*
6:8 *19, 153, 162*

Nahum
2:13 *49*

Habakkuk
1 – 2 *198*
1:6 – 2:17 *174*

Zephaniah
1:14–18 *60*
1:18 *38*

Index of biblical references

2 Timothy
2:3 *52*
2:3–4 *150*
2:17–18 *151*

Titus
3:1 *50f., 88*

Philemon
1–25 *202*

Hebrews
10:32–33 *234n.*
11:1 – 12:5 *52*
11:7 *177*
11:14–16 *171*
11:31 *177f.*
12:5–11 *182*
13:8 *147*

James
1:25 *154*

1 Peter
2 *14, 163, 192, 195, 215*
2:12–15 *20*
2:12–17 *194*
2:13 *235n.*
2:13–14 *88*
2:13–15 *20*
2:13–17 *50, 238n.*
2:14 *69, 178, 238n.*
2:14–15 *235n.*
2:16–17 *88*
2:17 *51*
2:18–25 *235n.*
2:20–21 *52*
2:21–25 *14*
3:8–17 *235n.*
3:9 *43*
3:9–17 *194*
3:9–18 *192*
3:10–13 *235n.*
3:14–18 *52*
3:22 *44, 51*
4:12–16 *52*
4:12–19 *194*

1 Peter *(cont.)*
5:10 *52*

2 Peter
2:5, 7–8 *177*
3:8–13 *60*

1 John
4:17–18 *188*

Revelation
1:5, 16 *47*
2 – 3 *53*
2:7, 11, 17, 26 *47*
2:27 *87, 148*
3:5, 12, 21 *47*
5:9 *176*
5:9–10 *47*
6:12–17 *167*
6:16–17 *148*
11:15–18 *148*
11:17–18 *101*
12:10ff. *53*
12:11 *47*
13 *50, 152*
13:7, 9–10 *192*
13:10 *40*
15:2 *47*
15:3–4 *148*
17:14 *47, 53*
18 *60*
18:24 *91*
19 *60*
19:11–16 *26, 47*
19:11–21 *62, 148*
19:17–21 *167*
21 *60*
21:7 *47*
21:22–24 *238n.*
22:15 *107*

APOCRYPHAL BOOKS

Ecclesiasticus
36:2–3, 7 *41*

General index

Many topics indexed are in fact pervasive throughout the book. In general they have been indexed where they are key concepts in the argument. Bible characters are indexed when they appear as subjects, but not when they appear as authors. The notes are indexed only for biblical references. The Index of biblical references should be used in conjunction with this index; e.g. when looking for information on the Sermon on the Mount, references to Matthew 5 – 7 should also be consulted.

252

General index

General index

General index

Sider, Ronald 43, 45
sin 169 and *passim*
single eye, the 136f.
slavery 23f., 97, 132, 135f., 197
social gospel 23
Sodom and Gomorrah 146, 177, 207
soldiers, Roman 24f., 39, 50, 63, 110, 123, 128
Solidarity (Poland) 76, 160
Solzhenitsyn, Alexander 115
sovereignty neither nationhood nor government 121
Soviet Union 72ff., 76ff.
sphere sovereignty 128ff.
SS20 missile 77f.
Stalin, Josef 106, 115
State, the
  biblical attitudes to S. 47ff., 147ff.
  Christian duty to S. 123ff.
  Christian relationship to S. 12, 14, 23ff., 55, 57ff., 125, 129ff., 143ff.
  Christian response to S. 54ff.
  Christians holding office in and serving the S. 15, 26, 55ff., 89ff., 96f., 123ff., 138, 171, 211ff. and *passim*
  corruption in the S. 20, 141, 163
  duty of S. 68ff., 144f.
  obedience to S. 14, 20ff., 35, 51, 88f., 122, 152
  S. as punisher of evil-doers 15, 19, 123
  S. as resister of evil 19, 24, 85ff., 207ff. and *passim*
  S. instituted by God 123ff., 144, 148
  use of just force by S. 20, 24, 26, 122f., 178

taxes 123ff.
Temple, cleansing of the 45ff.
ten Boom, Corrie 152
territory 118ff.
Tertullian 25, 102, 109, 111
Testaments, Old and New
  false antithesis 208ff.
  implication of continuity for just war theory 27ff.
  NT adopts OT language 119

relation of Old and New 21ff., 127ff., 150, 156, 175f. and *passim*
Thirty Years' War 164
Trident missiles 77, 83
turning the other cheek 128, 162

unilateral disarmament 16, 32, 116, 158

Vatican II Council 34
vengeance *See* revenge
victory the Lord's alone 155
Vietnam 159
violence 12, 22, 44, 61ff.
'vocational interpretation' of Bible teaching 196–199

War
  alternatives 179 and *passim*
  an absolute ethic? 101, 103, 132, 139
  apparent contradiction in biblical attitude 192
  biblical attitudes to 47–51:
    OT 18ff., 25, 35, 47ff., 101ff., 126ff., 166ff.; NT 105ff., 175ff. *passim*
  defensive 92
  defined 118, 185
  glorification of 16, 33f., 100f., 125f.
warfare
  absolute limits to 97ff., 131, 180, 185
  a choice against mission 53ff.
  church's changing attitudes to 39
  regulating 180f., 183f.
  results in breakdown of order 186
  Westminster Confession 25
wheat and tares, parable of 164
witchcraft, persecution 112
world government an end to war 118
World War II 70, 94, 98, 106
wrath of God 15, 51 and *passim*

Yahweh as King and Warrior 47–50
Yalta Agreement (1945) 106
Yoder, John H. 53

Zealots 41f., 64
'zero option' 78